I0210319

Verse by Verse Commentary on

EZRA, NEHEMIAH, & ESTHER

Enduring Word Commentary Series
By David Guzik

The grass withers, the flower fades,
but the word of our God stands forever.
Isaiah 40:8

Commentary on Ezra, Nehemiah, & Esther

Copyright ©2024 by David Guzik

Printed in the United States of America
or in the United Kingdom

ISBN: 978-1-939466-88-4

Enduring Word
5662 Calle Real #184
Goleta, CA 93117

Email: ewm@enduringword.com

Website: www.enduringword.com

All rights reserved. No portion of this book may be reproduced in any form (except for quotations in reviews) without the written permission of the publisher.

Scripture references, unless noted, are from the New King James Version of the Bible, copyright ©1979, 1980, 1982, Thomas Nelson, Inc., Publisher.

Contents

Ezra 1 – Cyrus Allows the Exiles to Return

A. The decree of Cyrus the Persian.

1. (1) God stirs Cyrus to make a decree.

Now in the first year of Cyrus king of Persia, that the word of the LORD by the mouth of Jeremiah might be fulfilled, the LORD stirred up the spirit of Cyrus king of Persia, so that he made a proclamation throughout all his kingdom, and also *put it* in writing, saying,

a. **Now in the first year of Cyrus king of Persia**: God gave the Persian king a sense of urgency about this, and the relief from exile was granted in the very **first year** of his reign as **the LORD stirred up** his **spirit**.

i. Cyrus made a decree giving the Jewish exiles in his empire the right to return to Jerusalem and rebuild the temple in 538 B.C. (Ezra 1:1-4 and Ezra 5:13-17). "The greater part of this book, though it bears the name of Ezra, tells of the pioneers who came back from exile to Jerusalem a whole lifetime before him. We shall not meet Ezra till chapter 7." (Kidner)

ii. It is quite possible that the prophet Daniel was instrumental in this stirring up of Cyrus. He may have showed the king the prophecies of Jeremiah 25:8-13 and Jeremiah 29:10-14, which refer to the punishment of Babylon and the end of Israel's exile. And if he showed Cyrus such prophecies, he almost certainly would have included Isaiah 44:28-45:5, which mentions Cyrus by name some 150 years before he was born.

iii. "Josephus accounts for his partiality to the Jews from this circumstance; that he was shown the places in Isaiah the prophet where he is mentioned by name, and his exploits and conquests foretold." (Clarke)

iv. "We know that Persian kings paid close heed to prophecies: Cambyses to Egyptian oracles, Darius and Xerxes to Greek oracles (*Herodotus* 8.133; 9.42, 151)." (Yamauchi)

v. "The difference between 'sacred' and 'profane' history is not that one is under His direct control, and the other is not. What was true of Cyrus and his policy is as true of England. Would that politicians and all men recognised the fact as clearly as this historian did!" (Maclaren)

b. **And also put it in writing**: This writing was also recorded in 2 Chronicles 36:22-23 but existed in contemporary documents that have been discovered by archaeologists.

i. "Cyrus's policy of cooperating with local religions and of encouraging the return of exiles has received explicit archaeological confirmation from the inscriptions of the king himself (cf. especially the famous 'Cyrus Cylinder')." (Payne)

2. (2-4) The decree Cyrus made.

Thus says Cyrus king of Persia:

All the kingdoms of the earth the LORD God of heaven has given me. And He has commanded me to build Him a house at Jerusalem which *is* in Judah. Who *is* among you of all His people? May his God be with him, and let him go up to Jerusalem which *is* in Judah, and build the house of the LORD God of Israel (He *is* God), which *is* in Jerusalem. And whoever is left in any place where he dwells, let the men of his place help him with silver and gold, with goods and livestock, besides the freewill offerings for the house of God which *is* in Jerusalem.

a. **All the kingdoms of the earth the LORD God of heaven has given me**: This remarkable recognition of God's hand upon his life may be connected with the extraordinary prophecies regarding Cyrus in Isaiah 44:28-45:4.

i. Yet it was also according to the general policy of the Persians. "A notable feature of the Persian empire was its integration of a great diversity of peoples into a single administrative system, while maintaining at the same time a tradition of respect for their local customs and beliefs... they were encouraged to seek the king's welfare by observing the proper forms of their own religions." (Kidner)

ii. "The so-called Cyrus Cylinder, from which the following is an extract, gives his own account of this: 'I returned to these sacred cities..., the sanctuaries of which have been in ruins for a long time, the images which (used) to live therein and established for them permanent sanctuaries. I (also) gathered all their (former) inhabitants and returned (to them) their habitations... May all the gods whom I have resettled in their sacred cities ask daily Bel and Nebo for a long life for me...; to Marduk, my lord, may they say this: 'Cyrus, the king who worships you, and Cambyses, his son...'" (Kidner)

b. **He has commanded me to build Him a house at Jerusalem**: The command of Cyrus not only allowed the return of the exiled people, but also a rebuilding of the destroyed temple.

i. "'To build him a house' is a deliberate echo of the central promise of the Davidic covenant (*cf.* 1 Chronicles 17:11-12; 22:10; 28:6; 2 Chronicles 6:9-10). Cyrus of course is thinking only of the house in *Jerusalem*, but in the Chronicler's thought this phrase is inevitably connected with both houses of the Davidic covenant, the dynasty as well as the temple." (Selman)

c. **Who is among you of all His people? May his God be with him, and let him go up to Jerusalem**: The Books of 1 and 2 Chronicles end with this wonderful and remarkable encouragement to return and rebuild Jerusalem. This was the necessary and helpful encouragement to the first readers of Chronicles, letting them see their connection with God's broader plan of the ages.

i. Sadly, only a small percentage decided to return from exile, but those who did needed the encouragement of knowing they were making a valuable contribution to God's work. In passages such as Isaiah 10:22, God promised that a remnant would return from exile – and *only* a remnant.

ii. "After the deportations only the poor of the land – the vine-growers and farmers – were left (2 Kings 25:12; Jeremiah 39:10; 40:7; 52:16). They occupied the vacant lands (Jeremiah 6:12). A few refugees who fled to different areas drifted back (Jeremiah 40:11-12). For the next fifty years those left behind eked out a precarious existence under the Babylonian yoke (Lamentations 5:2-5), subjected to ill treatment and forced labor (Lamentations 5:11-13)." (Yamauchi)

d. **Besides the freewill offerings for the house of God which is in Jerusalem**: This introduces a central theme for the Book of Ezra – the rebuilding of the temple. Beginning with the decree of Cyrus, the intention was not merely to return and reoccupy Jerusalem but also to rebuild the temple.

i. "Thus we see from the first that the idea which characterized the restoration is religious. The exiles return as a Church. The goal of their pilgrimage is a holy site. The one work they are to aim at achieving is to further the worship of their God." (Adeney)

B. The response of the people to the invitation to go back to Jerusalem.

1. (5-6) Those returning to Jerusalem are encouraged.

Then the heads of the fathers' *houses* **of Judah and Benjamin, and the priests and the Levites, with all whose spirits God had moved, arose to go up and build the house of the LORD which** *is* **in Jerusalem. And all those who** *were* **around them encouraged them with articles of silver and gold, with goods and livestock, and with precious things, besides all** *that* **was willingly offered.**

a. **With all whose spirits God had moved**: Though the returning exiles were a minority, they were a spirit-stirred minority. They were dedicated to the difficult and discouraging task of returning to a ruined city and once there to **build the house of the LORD which is in Jerusalem**.

i. It was essential that God *move* the spirits of these returning exiles because they faced many difficulties.

- The journey itself was long, dangerous, and expensive.
- They returned to a city in ruins with no proper homes, roads, or city institutions.
- They didn't have all the material resources they needed.
- They didn't all return to Jerusalem but spread out over the province of Judea.
- They had many enemies.
- Their land was actually the possession of another empire.

ii. "*The chief of the fathers of Judah and Benjamin*; and with them some of the other tribes, as appears from 1 Chronicles 9:3; but these only are named, because they were most considerable for number and quality." (Poole)

b. **Arose to go up and build the house of the LORD**: So, a good number of the descendants of those exiled some two generations before decided to return to their ancestral land. These went; substantially more stayed behind in the land of their exile.

c. **And all those who were around them encouraged them**: This encouragement was more than verbal; it was a material encouragement of financial and practical backing for the work. We can imagine that many of those who decided to stay in their lands of exile still were happy that others were going to **build the house of the LORD** and wanted to support that work.

i. "An important difference between the deportations by the Babylonians and by the Assyrians is that the Babylonians did not replace the deportees with pagan newcomers. Thus Judah, though devastated, was not contaminated with polytheism to the same degree as Israel." (Yamauchi)

ii. Yamauchi mentions a cave inscription from this period, found at Khirbet Beit Lei, five miles east of Lachish. The inscription reads, "I am Yahweh thy God: I will accept the cities of Judah and will redeem Jerusalem." It has been suggested that this may reflect the mind of a returning exile, expressing his trust in God's faithfulness to restore despite the desolation of Jerusalem.

2. (7-11) The return of the articles of the house of the LORD.

King Cyrus also brought out the articles of the house of the LORD, which Nebuchadnezzar had taken from Jerusalem and put in the temple of his gods; and Cyrus king of Persia brought them out by the hand of Mithredath the treasurer, and counted them out to Sheshbazzar the prince of Judah. This *is* the number of them: thirty gold platters, one thousand silver platters, twenty-nine knives, thirty gold basins, four hundred and ten silver basins of a similar *kind, and* one thousand other articles. All the articles of gold and silver *were* five thousand four hundred. All *these* Sheshbazzar took with the captives who were brought from Babylon to Jerusalem.

a. **King Cyrus also brought out the articles of the house of the LORD**: When Jerusalem was conquered, the remaining treasures of the temple were taken to Babylon (2 Chronicles 36:18). Now, after conquering the Babylonians, Cyrus adopted a much more generous policy towards their subject peoples, including the Jewish people.

i. "*Objection*. These are said to have been *cut in pieces*, 2 Kings 24:13; how then are they here returned? *Answer*. That Hebrew word used 2 Kings 24:13, signifies not so properly *to cut in pieces* as to *cut off*, as from the use of the word, Deuteronomy 25:12; 2 Samuel 4:12; 2 Kings 18:16; Jeremiah 9:26. And these vessels, when they were taken away from the temple, might very well be said to be cut off from it, because they had for so long been so constantly, and as it were inseparably, united to it, and kept in it." (Poole)

b. **Sheshbazzar the prince of Judah**: This man was an important leader of this first part of the resettlement of Judah. Some believe that he was a partner to Zerubbabel (Ezra 2:2, 3:2), and others believe that these were simply two names for the same person.

i. "There is a view that Sheshbazzar was a second name for Zerubbabel, used in all transactions with the ruling power.... Alternatively Sheshbazzar and Zerubbabel may have been, respectively, the official and unofficial leaders of the enterprise. Neither view is without its difficulties." (Kidner)

ii. "This was probably the Chaldean name of him who was originally called Zerubbabel: the former signifies *joy in affliction*; the latter, *a stranger in Babylon*. The latter may be designed to refer to his captive state; the former to the prospect of release." (Clarke)

c. **This is the number of them**: The careful reckoning of the returned articles shows how valued they were and how carefully they were treated.

i. What is conspicuously *missing* from the list is any mention of the more significant articles of the temple – the altar of incense, the table of showbread, the brazen altar, the golden lampstand, and especially the ark of the covenant. These articles were presumably lost to history at the destruction of the temple by the Babylonians.

ii. "The businesslike transfer of articles, 'counted out' from one custodian to another, may have been outwardly undramatic, but it was momentous. The closing words of the chapter, *from Babylonia to Jerusalem*, mark one of the turning points of history." (Kidner)

iii. "We might have expected some kind of production of the enthusiasm of the returning exiles, some account of how they were sent on their journey, something which we should have felt worthier of the occasion than a list of bowls and nine-and-twenty knives.... The list here indicates the pride and joy with which the long hidden and often desecrated vessels were received." (Maclaren)

iv. "Had they not been things of great price and use, they would not have been numbered.... Men use not to count how many pebbles they have in their yard, or piles of grass in their field, as they do how many pence in their purse or sheep in their fold." (Trapp)

v. "They show that the generosity of Cyrus in restoring so great a hoard was genuine and considerable. It might have been urged that after the treasures had been lying for two generations in a heathen temple the original owners had lost all claim upon them. It might have been said that they had been contaminated by this long residence among the abominations of Babylonian idolatry. The restoration of them swept away all such ideas." (Adeney)

Ezra 2 – List of the Returning Exiles

A. Those returning from exile.

1. (1-2) Those immediately associated with Zerubbabel.

Now these *are* the people of the province who came back from the captivity, of those who had been carried away, whom Nebuchadnezzar the king of Babylon had carried away to Babylon, and who returned to Jerusalem and Judah, everyone to his *own* city.

***Those* who came with Zerubbabel *were* Jeshua, Nehemiah, Seraiah, Reelaiah, Mordecai, Bilshan, Mispar, Bigvai, Rehum, *and* Baanah. The number of the men of the people of Israel:**

a. **Now these are the people of the province who came back from the captivity**: Here begins the list of the families and individuals who made the return to Judah and Jerusalem now that it was a province of the Persian Empire.

i. "The returning exiles were described as 'children of the province' (Ezra 2:1) – *i.e.*, of the Persian province of Judea – and their leader bore the title of a Persian governor (*Tirshatha*, Ezra 2:63). Zerubbabel was no new Moses." (Adeney)

ii. The word **province** is *medina*. "That Medina, a city in Arabia, holdeth this Medina in hard subjection; making her children pay for the very heads they wear; and so grievously affecting them, that they have cause enough to take up anew Jeremiah's elegy over their doleful captivity." (Trapp)

b. **Those who came with Zerubbabel**: Here are eleven names mentioned, yet the list probably should contain twelve names (comparing with Nehemiah 7:7 and noting the twelve sacrificial bulls of Ezra 8:35).

i. "There are eleven names here, but Nehemiah's copy of the list preserves one more, that of Nahamani (Nehemiah 7:7), which has evidently dropped out of this verse in the course of copying. The choice of twelve, like that of the twelve apostles, was a tacit declaration that the community they led was no mere rump or fragment but the embodiment of *the people of Israel*." (Kidner)

ii. **Nehemiah…Mordecai**: "Not that famous Nehemiah nor that renowned Mordecai so much spoken of in the Book of Esther, but others of the same name." (Trapp)

c. **Zerubbabel**: Zerubbabel was the appointed governor over the province of Judah. He was also a descendent of the last reigning Judean king.

i. "He was the lineal descendant of the royal house, the heir to the throne of David. This is a most significant fact. It shows that the exiles had retained some latent national character to the return, although, as we have already observed, the main object of it was religious." (Adeney)

ii. He is probably the same person mentioned in Ezra 1:8 as Sheshbazzar. Ezra 5:16 says that Sheshbazzar laid the foundation of the temple; Ezra 3:8 seems to attribute that work to Zerubbabel. This strengthens the idea that they were in fact the same person.

d. **Jeshua**: Haggai 2:1-5 and several other passages among the post-exilic prophets mention this notable co-worker with Zerubbabel.

i. "*Jeshua* the High Priest (Zechariah 3:1), whose name (in Greek, 'Jesus') is spelt Joshua in Haggai and Zechariah, was Zerubbabel's fellow-leader." (Kidner)

2. (3-35) A list of the families returning to Judah and Jerusalem.

The people of Parosh, two thousand one hundred and seventy-two; the people of Shephatiah, three hundred and seventy-two; the people of Arah, seven hundred and seventy-five; the people of Pahath-Moab, of the people of Jeshua *and* Joab, two thousand eight hundred and twelve; the people of Elam, one thousand two hundred and fifty-four; the people of Zattu, nine hundred and forty-five; the people of Zaccai, seven hundred and sixty; the people of Bani, six hundred and forty-two; the people of Bebai, six hundred and twenty-three; the people of Azgad, one thousand two hundred and twenty-two; the people of Adonikam, six hundred and sixty-six; the people of Bigvai, two thousand and fifty-six; the people of Adin, four hundred and fifty-four; the people of Ater of Hezekiah, ninety-eight; the people of Bezai, three hundred and twenty-three; the people of Jorah, one hundred and twelve; the people of Hashum, two hundred and twenty-three; the people of Gibbar, ninety-five; the people of Bethlehem, one hundred and twenty-three; the men of Netophah, fifty-six; the men of Anathoth, one hundred and twenty-eight; the people of Azmaveth, forty-two; the people of Kirjath Arim,

Chephirah, and Beeroth, seven hundred and forty-three; the people of Ramah and Geba, six hundred and twenty-one; the men of Michmas, one hundred and twenty-two; the men of Bethel and Ai, two hundred and twenty-three; the people of Nebo, fifty-two; the people of Magbish, one hundred and fifty-six; the people of the other Elam, one thousand two hundred and fifty-four; the people of Harim, three hundred and twenty; the people of Lod, Hadid, and Ono, seven hundred and twenty-five; the people of Jericho, three hundred and forty-five; the people of Senaah, three thousand six hundred and thirty.

a. **The people of**: This list names the heads of families, with the numbers of the men in those families. It means that the total number of people would be more, because the **people** listed here do not include the women and children – only the heads of families.

i. "The thousands of homecomers are not lumped together, but (in characteristic biblical fashion) related to those local and family circles which humanise a society and orientate an individual. Such is God's way, who 'setteth the solitary in families' (Psalm 68:6)." (Kidner)

b. **The people of Arah, seven hundred and seventy-five**: This differs from the record at Nehemiah 7:10, and points to the often difficult correlation of numbers between the two passages. It seems that perhaps copyist error is the fault, but others have suggested alternative solutions.

i. "In Nehemiah 7:10, they were only six hundred and fifty-two. It seems seven hundred and seventy-five marched out of Babylon, or gave in their names that they would go; but some of them died, others changed their minds, others were hindered by sickness, or other casualties, happening to themselves or their near relations; and so there came only six hundred and fifty-two to Jerusalem.... And the like is to be said in the like differences; which it suffices to hint once for all." (Poole)

ii. "There are many difficulties in this table of names; but as we have no less than *three* copies of it, *that* contained here from Ezra 2:1-67, a *second* in Nehemiah 7:6-69, and a *third* in 1 Esdras 5:7-43, on a careful examination they will be found to correct each other." (Clarke)

c. **Parosh...Shephatiah...Arah**: These names reflect the variety of influences that came in and among the children of Israel during the exile. Many of the names are connected to Biblical ideas, and others have connections to their exilic culture.

i. "The practice of giving Babylonian or Persian names to Jews in captivity (Esther 2:7; Daniel 1:7) is richly illustrated by the archives of Murashu." (Yamauchi)

ii. The names themselves give a personal flavor.

- **Parosh** means *flea.*
- **Shephatiah** means *Yahweh has judged.*
- **Arah** means *wild ox.*
- **Zaccai** means either *pure* or is a shortened form of *Zechariah.*
- **Bani** is a shortened form of *Benaiah*, meaning *Yahweh has built.*
- **Bebai** means *pupil of the eye.*
- **Azgad** means *Gad is strong.*
- **Adonikam** means *my Lord has arisen.*
- **Adin** means *voluptuous.*
- **Ater** means *lefty.*
- **Bezai** is a shortened form of *Bezaleel* and means *in the shadow of God.*
- **Jorah** means *autumn rain.*
- **Hashum** means *broad nose.*
- **Gibbar** means *strong man.*

3. (36-57) A list of the priests, Levites, and temple workers returning from exile.

The priests: the sons of Jedaiah, of the house of Jeshua, nine hundred and seventy-three; the sons of Immer, one thousand and fifty-two; the sons of Pashhur, one thousand two hundred and forty-seven; the sons of Harim, one thousand and seventeen.

The Levites: the sons of Jeshua and Kadmiel, of the sons of Hodaviah, seventy-four.

The singers: the sons of Asaph, one hundred and twenty-eight.

The sons of the gatekeepers: the sons of Shallum, the sons of Ater, the sons of Talmon, the sons of Akkub, the sons of Hatita, and the sons of Shobai, one hundred and thirty-nine *in* all.

The Nethinim: the sons of Ziha, the sons of Hasupha, the sons of Tabbaoth, the sons of Keros, the sons of Siaha, the sons of Padon, the sons of Lebanah, the sons of Hagabah, the sons of Akkub, the sons of Hagab, the sons of Shalmai, the sons of Hanan, the sons of Giddel, the sons of Gahar, the sons of Reaiah, the sons of Rezin, the sons of Nekoda, the sons of Gazzam, the sons of Uzza, the sons of Paseah, the sons of Besai, the sons of Asnah, the sons of Meunim, the sons of Nephusim,

the sons of Bakbuk, the sons of Hakupha, the sons of Harhur, the sons of Bazluth, the sons of Mehida, the sons of Harsha, the sons of Barkos, the sons of Sisera, the sons of Tamah, the sons of Neziah, and the sons of Hatipha.

The sons of Solomon's servants: the sons of Sotai, the sons of Sophereth, the sons of Peruda, the sons of Jaala, the sons of Darkon, the sons of Giddel, the sons of Shephatiah, the sons of Hattil, the sons of Pochereth of Zebaim, and the sons of Ami.

a. **Jedaiah...Immer...Pashhur...Harim**: These families represent only four of the twenty-four divisions of the priesthood established by King David in 1 Chronicles 24:3. Most of the priests stayed behind in Babylon.

b. **The sons of Hanan**: "'Hanan' ('[God] is gracious') is derived from the verb *hanan* ('to be gracious'), and its derivatives are the components of numerous names borne by fifty-one persons in the Old Testament. These include Baalhanan, Elhanan, Hananel, Hanani, Hananiah, Hannah, Hanun, Henadad, Jehohanan, and Tehinnah. 'Johanan' ('Yahweh is gracious') has given us the name John. The woman's name Hannah gives us Anna, Ann, Nan, and Nancy." (Yamauchi)

i. **Bakbuk** means "bottle," referring to an earthenware container with a neck and a bulging body. Mr. **Bakbuk** may have earned his nickname by his big belly, or because his constant chatter sounded like the bubbling sound of water poured out from a bottle.

c. **The Levites**: The total number of Levites was actually less than the number of priests that returned. This means that a remarkably small percentage of the Levites returned from Babylon.

i. "An examination of this list is remarkable principally from the small number of Levites who returned. Nearly ten times as many priests as Levites went back to the land. This, of course, was an inversion of the original order." (Morgan)

ii. Some speculate that the Levites were particularly invested in worship at the high places, scattered on the hills all around pre-exilic Israel and Judah. The purifying fires of exile effectively burned out this idolatrous impulse, and therefore few Levites wanted to return to the Promised Land.

4. (58) Two special groups who came back from exile.

All the Nethinim and the children of Solomon's servants were three hundred and ninety-two.

a. **All the Nethinim**: These seem to be the descendants of the Gibeonites

(Joshua 9), who were made special servants of the Levites and the priests at the temple.

i. "These were those Gibeonites that, having saved their lives by a lie, were made drawers of water to the temple as a punishment.... Their employment was to minister to the Levites." (Trapp)

ii. "It seems likely that the more menial tasks fell to these men; and the presence of some foreign-looking names in the list may indicate that some of these groups came into Israel from David's conquests, whether as immigrants or perhaps as prisoners of war." (Kidner)

b. **The children of Solomon's servants**: Most believe that these were those employed by Solomon who came from other people groups. They came into Israel as foreign proselytes.

i. "These also were strangers, that had been employed by Solomon, and becoming proselytes, were incorporated into the commonwealth of Israel. God is no respecter of persons." (Trapp)

5. (59-63) Those among the priests with uncertain genealogies who returned from exile.

And these *were* the ones who came up from Tel Melah, Tel Harsha, Cherub, Addan, and Immer; but they could not identify their father's house or their genealogy, whether they *were* of Israel: the sons of Delaiah, the sons of Tobiah, and the sons of Nekoda, six hundred and fifty-two; and of the sons of the priests: the sons of Habaiah, the sons of Koz, and the sons of Barzillai, who took a wife of the daughters of Barzillai the Gileadite, and was called by their name. These sought their listing *among* those who were registered by genealogy, but they were not found; therefore they *were excluded* from the priesthood as defiled. And the governor said to them that they should not eat of the most holy things till a priest could consult with the Urim and Thummim.

a. **These sought their listing among those who were registered by genealogy, but they were not found**: This shows an admirable respect for God's law concerning the priesthood of Israel. These were those who had some claim to a priestly lineage but could not prove their **genealogy**. They were therefore **excluded from the priesthood as defiled**.

i. "So shall all be at the last day that are not written among the living in Jerusalem, that are not registered in the Lamb's book of life." (Trapp)

ii. "*Barzillai* was a name that carried considerable weight; its bearer had been a staunch supporter of David, and a man of wealth (2 Samuel 19:32). It may be that in adopting this family's name (and becoming its heir?) the ancestor of these claimants had laid himself open to the charge that he had renounced his own birthright, the priesthood." (Kidner)

b. **They should not eat of the most holy things till a priest could consult with the Urim and Thummim**: Those with questionable genealogies were not permanently excluded; each case required more time spent in research and seeking God.

i. "The Urim and Thummim, together with the Ark and the Shekinah, are named by the rabbis among the precious things that were never recovered." (Adeney)

6. (64-67) The summary of the returning exiles.

The whole assembly together *was* forty-two thousand three hundred *and* sixty, besides their male and female servants, of whom *there were* seven thousand three hundred and thirty-seven; and they had two hundred men and women singers. Their horses *were* seven hundred and thirty-six, their mules two hundred and forty-five, their camels four hundred and thirty-five, and *their* donkeys six thousand seven hundred and twenty.

a. **The whole assembly together**: The size of this entire group is here stated to be about 50,000. However, this was only the first wave of repatriation to Israel from the Babylonian captivity and includes only the heads of families. The approximate total of the returned exiles was probably somewhere between 100,000 and 150,000. This was only a small percentage of those who had been exiled and their descendants; the great majority stayed behind in Babylon.

i. As a whole, Israelites had some reason to feel comfortable in Babylon. The Murashu tablets were discovered in 1873 and are records from Murashu and his sons, wealthy bankers and brokers of the late period of exile, who seemed to loan out almost anything for a price. "Among their customers are listed about sixty Jewish names from the time of Artaxerxes I, and forty from the time of Darius II. These appear as contracting parties, agents, witnesses, collectors of taxes, and royal officials. There seems to have been no social or commercial barriers between the Jews and the Babylonians. Their prosperous situation may explain why some chose to remain in Mesopotamia." (Yamauchi)

ii. Indeed, Josephus wrote, "many remained in Babylon, being unwilling to leave their possessions." (Antiquities XI, 8)

iii. One should not think that there was no spiritual life among the Jewish exiles; Ezekiel (who went into exile after 597 or 586 B.C.) describes what we might call a "home Bible study" at his home with the elders of Judah (Ezekiel 8:1). "Deprived of the temple, the exiles laid great stress on the observation of the Sabbath, on the laws of purity, and on prayer and fasting. It has often been suggested that the development of synagogues began in Mesopotamia during the Exile." (Yamauchi) Indeed, "In the Talmud it is said that only the chaff returned, while the wheat remained behind." (Adeney)

iv. When the exiles came back to Judah, they found a much smaller state than their forefathers had before the Babylonians conquered Judah. One estimate cited in Yamauchi says that the post-exilic province of Judah was about 25 miles from north to south and about 32 miles from east to west. The total area was about 800 square miles, about one-third of which was uncultivable desert.

v. "Depending on one's estimate of the numbers deported and the number of returning exiles, we have widely varying estimates for the population of postexilic Judah: 20,000 to 50,000 by W.F. Albright, 60,000 by H. Kreissig, 50,000 to 80,000 by J. de Fraine, 85,000 by R. Kittel, 100,000 by S. Mowinckel, 150,000 by J. Weinberg, and 235,000 by A. Schultz. An estimate of 150,000 is more probably correct than Albright's estimate." (Yamauchi)

vi. "The figure of 42,360 appears as the total also in Nehemiah 7:66 and 1 Esdras 5:41, yet the individual items add up to three different totals, as follows: Ezra, 29,818; Nehemiah, 31,089; 1 Esdras, 30,143. There have been attempts to explain the missing thousands: as members of the northern tribes, or as women, or as adolescents. But the narrative is silent on such points." (Kidner)

b. **Their horses...their mules...their camels...their donkeys**: This group did not return with much, but they also did not return with nothing.

i. "They went into captivity, stripped of everything; they now return from it, abounding in the most substantial riches.... Thus we find that God, in the midst of judgment, remembered mercy, and gave them favour in the land of their captivity." (Clarke)

B. The returned exiles make their home in the Promised Land.

1. (68-69) The offerings made for the rebuilding of the temple.

Some **of the heads of the fathers'** *houses,* **when they came to the house of the Lord which** *is* **in Jerusalem, offered freely for the house of God, to erect it in its place: According to their ability, they gave to the treasury for the work sixty-one thousand gold drachmas, five thousand minas of silver, and one hundred priestly garments.**

a. **Offered freely for the house of God**: Because of the prominence of those who made this offering (**the heads of the fathers' houses**) and the priority in this record, we see how important it was for the leaders and the people to sacrificially give to the work of rebuilding the temple.

b. **According to their ability**: These people gave generously, as generously as they could **according to their ability**. This showed how highly valued the house of God was in their eyes.

i. Kidner notes, "The phrase, *according to their ability*, does credit to these donors, and Paul may have had it in mind in his charge to the Corinthians to give in proportion to their gains (1 Corinthians 16:2)." Yet Paul also noted those who gave even *beyond* their ability (2 Corinthians 8:3).

2. (70) The restoration of a substantial Israeli presence in the Promised Land.

So the priests and the Levites, *some* of the people, the singers, the gatekeepers, and the Nethinim, dwelt in their cities, and all Israel in their cities.

a. **The priests and the Levites...dwelt in their cities**: This shows that Jerusalem was once again populated, even though it was a humble beginning.

i. "There would soon be daily sacrifices to offer, many worshippers to attend to, and much work to supervise." (Kidner)

ii. "Later Nehemiah would be compelled to move people by lot to reinforce the population of Jerusalem, as the capital city had suffered the severest loss of life at the time of the Babylonian attacks." (Yamauchi)

b. **Dwelt in their cities, and all Israel in their cities**: After two generations in exile, there was again a substantial presence of Jewish people in the land that was promised to Abraham, Isaac, and Jacob. This was a wonderful fulfillment of God's promise to bring Israel back from exile.

i. "For during their abode in Babylon Judaea lay utterly waste and uninhabited. The land kept her Sabbaths, resting from tillage, and God, by a wonderful providence, kept the room empty till the return of the natives." (Trapp)

ii. "Almost the whole community of Babylonian exiles who stayed when Babylon was destroyed came to this country then years ago – and their number was nearly thrice the number of those who returned to Zion in the days of Ezra and Nehemiah." (David Ben-Gurion, cited in Yamauchi describing the modern emigration of Jews from Iraq to Israel)

Ezra 3 – A Foundation for the New Temple

A. The restoration of regular worship in Jerusalem.

1. (1) Beginning in the **seventh month**.

And when the seventh month had come, and the children of Israel *were* in the cities, the people gathered together as one man to Jerusalem.

> a. **When the seventh month had come**: This was an important month on the spiritual calendar of Israel. In the **seventh month** they celebrated the Day of Atonement, the Feast of Trumpets, and the Feast of Tabernacles.

> b. **The people gathered together as one man to Jerusalem**: This was an encouraging sign of obedience among the returned exiles. In a time of small resources and great work to be done, they took the time and money to observe the command to gather in Jerusalem for the major feasts.

2. (2-3) The altar is rebuilt on its ancient foundation.

Then Jeshua the son of Jozadak and his brethren the priests, and Zerubbabel the son of Shealtiel and his brethren, arose and built the altar of the God of Israel, to offer burnt offerings on it, as *it is* written in the Law of Moses the man of God. Though fear *had come* upon them because of the people of those countries, they set the altar on its bases; and they offered burnt offerings on it to the LORD, *both* the morning and evening burnt offerings.

> a. **Jeshua...and Zerubbabel**: These were the two main leaders in this rebuilding project, beginning their work with building the altar that stood outside the temple on the temple mount in Jerusalem. Out of the rubble of the destroyed temple and its courts, an altar now stood ready to receive sacrifices both on behalf of the people as a whole and individuals who brought their offerings.

>> i. It is significant that they **built the altar** in *Jerusalem*, on the same ground where it had once stood. They might have reasoned that the altar (and conceivably also the temple) could go anywhere, because

22

Yahweh was God of the entire earth. Yet in the Jewish mind, there was only *one* place where the altar and the temple could stand: on God's holy hill (Psalm 2:6, 99:9), in His holy land (Zechariah 2:12).

ii. **Jeshua** "was the grandson of Seraiah the high priest, who was put to death by Nebuchadnezzar, 2 Kings 25:18, 21. This Jeshua or Joshua was the first high priest after the captivity." (Clarke)

b. **Arose and built the altar of the God of Israel**: Long before they could rebuild the temple, they wisely started with building the **altar** for **burnt offerings** and other sacrifices.

i. They **built the altar** first because it was something they could do relatively quickly and easily. We begin a great work by doing first *what we can*.

ii. They **built the altar** first because they understood its *spiritual significance*. Fundamentally, the altar was where sin was dealt with and where the common man met with God (the temple was only for the priests to enter). They started with the **altar** because it was a *wise spiritual priority*, showing they understood their need to have atonement from sin and perform acts of dedication to God.

iii. They **built the altar** first because it was an act of *obedience* to do so. They needed to resume the **burnt offerings** for the atonement of sin, and the **morning and evening burnt offerings** because all this was **written in the Law of Moses the man of God**.

iv. "This is the first thing that must be done before our temple-building or other undertakings can be crowned with success.... The new start that God Himself was giving would have been invalidated without the altar, which meant forgiveness for the past, and renewed consecration for the future." (Meyer)

v. "Thus, we see, the full establishment of religious services precedes the building of the temple. A weighty truth is enshrined in this apparently incongruous fact. The worship itself is felt to be more important than the house in which it is to be celebrated." (Adeney)

vi. "There cannot be a temple without an altar, but there may be an altar without a temple. God meets men at the place of sacrifice, even though there be no house for His name." (Maclaren)

c. **Though fear had come upon them because of the people of those countries**: When they **built the altar** to the LORD on the temple mount in Jerusalem, they probably destroyed a crude altar that had been built on that spot by the scattered remnant who inhabited the area during the two generations of exile. In building this altar they formally announced their presence and proclaimed their intention to rebuild the temple.

> i. Morgan suggests they also were afraid of the spiritual threat from the **people of those countries**: "They were conscious of how, in the neglect of the altar of God in the past, they had become contaminated by the idolatrous practices of surrounding peoples, and in order to prevent a repetition of such failure, they immediately set up the true altar."

> ii. "The ruined Jerusalem was better guarded by that altar than if its fallen walls had been rebuilt." (Maclaren)

d. **They set the altar on its bases**: This means that they found the old foundations for the previous altar and built the new one upon the exact place as the old, which dated back to David's altar on the threshing floor of Araunah (2 Samuel 24:16-19).

> i. "The altar was set *in its place, i.e.* its traditional and proper place." (Kidner) "Rebuilt it on the *same spot* on which it had formerly stood." (Clarke)

> ii. "There is something very pathetic in the picture of the assembled people groping amid the ruins on the Temple hill, to find 'the bases,' the half-obliterated outlines, of the foundations of the old altar of burnt offerings." (Maclaren)

> iii. The centrality of the altar, set upon its ancient foundations, was essential for them – as it is for us. We have an altar (Hebrews 13:10, the cross of Jesus Christ, set upon its ancient foundations. The altar was to them what the cross is to Christians under the new covenant.

3. (4-6) The feast is observed, and regular sacrifice is resumed.

They also kept the Feast of Tabernacles, as *it is* written, and *offered* the daily burnt offerings in the number required by ordinance for each day. Afterwards *they offered* the regular burnt offering, and *those* for New Moons and for all the appointed feasts of the Lord that were consecrated, and *those* of everyone who willingly offered a freewill offering to the Lord. From the first day of the seventh month they began to offer burnt offerings to the Lord, although the foundation of the temple of the Lord had not been laid.

a. **They also kept the Feast of Tabernacles**: This great, joyful feast (one of the three major feasts of Israel) celebrated God's faithfulness to Israel during the wilderness journey from Egypt to the Promised Land.

> i. During this feast the families of Israel were commanded to camp out in temporary shelters, meant to remind them of how their forefathers lived during the exodus. In this context – when in returning to

destroyed cities, they were forced to live this way until they could properly rebuild – the **Feast of Tabernacles** held a special meaning for these returned Jews to Judah.

b. **They offered the regular burnt offering...all the appointed feasts of the LORD...freewill offering to the LORD**: This describes the regular resumption of sacrifice at the altar, and all this was done before **the foundation of the temple** had been laid.

i. "During their long stay in Babylon, the Jews were not able to offer any sacrifices, as this could only be done in Jerusalem. Instead they were surrounded by a myriad of pagan temples. About fifty temples are mentioned in Babylonian texts together with 180 open-air shrines for Ishtar, three hundred daises for the Igigi gods, and twelve hundred daises for the Anunnaki gods." (Yamauchi)

ii. "The new moon marked the first day of the month and was a holy day (Numbers 28:11-15)." (Yamauchi)

4. (7) Preparations for rebuilding the temple.

They also gave money to the masons and the carpenters, and food, drink, and oil to the people of Sidon and Tyre to bring cedar logs from Lebanon to the sea, to Joppa, according to the permission which they had from Cyrus king of Persia.

a. **They also gave money to the masons and the carpenters**: Once the work of restoration began at the altar of sacrifice, they followed through by assembling and hiring the workers they needed to build the temple.

b. **Cedar logs from Lebanon**: The cedar trees of Lebanon were legendary for their excellent timber. This meant that they wanted to use the best materials they could in construction and the same materials that Solomon used in building the first temple (1 Kings 5:6), though they had far fewer resources than Solomon.

c. **According to the permission which they had from Cyrus king of Persia**: This **permission** was not only the legal allowance to build the temple, but it also included financial support from the royal treasury (**permission** can also be translated *grant*).

i. "Since permission to buy materials would hardly need specifying, it is reasonable to take the work to include provision as well as permission, as with our own word 'grant'." (Kidner)

ii. This shows that they used Gentile money to purchase the supplies (from Gentile Lebanon) to build the second temple. Solomon's temple used Gentile supplies and laborers; God directed the building of the second temple to likewise be built with Gentile cooperation.

B. Work begins on the temple.

1. (8-9) Those present and overseeing the laying of the foundation of the temple.

Now in the second month of the second year of their coming to the house of God at Jerusalem, Zerubbabel the son of Shealtiel, Jeshua the son of Jozadak, and the rest of their brethren the priests and the Levites, and all those who had come out of the captivity to Jerusalem, began *work* **and appointed the Levites from twenty years old and above to oversee the work of the house of the LORD. Then Jeshua** *with* **his sons and brothers, Kadmiel** *with* **his sons, and the sons of Judah, arose as one to oversee those working on the house of God: the sons of Henadad** *with* **their sons and their brethren the Levites.**

> a. **In the second month of the second year of their coming to the house of God at Jerusalem**: The work seemed to begin as soon as it could, allowing for the logistical preparations described in Ezra 3:7. Significantly, the site was called **the house of God at Jerusalem** *before* the temple was built and while the former temple was still a ruin.

> > i. "This would hardly have escaped their notice – the second was the month in which Solomon's Temple had been started (1 Kings 6:1)." (Kidner)

> b. **Appointed the Levites from twenty years old and above to oversee the work**: The Law of Moses commanded that the Levites begin their service at thirty years of age (Numbers 4:1-3, 4:34-48). David changed the starting point for Levitical service to twenty years of age (1 Chronicles 23:24). Under the leadership of Zerubbabel and Jeshua, they adopted David's revised practice.

2. (10-11) The foundation stone is set as the people praise the LORD.

When the builders laid the foundation of the temple of the LORD, the priests stood in their apparel with trumpets, and the Levites, the sons of Asaph, with cymbals, to praise the LORD, according to the ordinance of David king of Israel. And they sang responsively, praising and giving thanks to the LORD:

"For *He is* **good,
For His mercy** *endures* **forever toward Israel."**

Then all the people shouted with a great shout, when they praised the LORD, because the foundation of the house of the LORD was laid.

> a. **When the builders laid the foundation of the temple of the LORD:** This was a memorable scene. The priests were dressed in their ceremonial

apparel, the musicians were ready to **praise the** LORD with instruments and song, and they **sang responsively** in an arranged presentation.

i. In general, the description matches the massive and elaborate dedication ceremony for Solomon's temple (2 Chronicles 5:13), except this was held in far humbler circumstances.

b. **For He is good, for His mercy endures forever toward Israel!** This is almost an exact quotation of a line from Psalm 136:1. All 26 verses of that psalm end with the phrase, *for His mercy endures forever*. In Zerubbabel's day, they added two appropriate words: **toward Israel**. They understood that God's never-ending mercy (*hesed*) was for *them*. It wasn't a theoretical love, grace, and mercy. It was given to specific people, those who in covenant with God received it by faith. The believer should be able to say, *for His mercy endures forever toward me*.

i. The wonderful phrase **His mercy endures forever** appears more than 40 times in the Bible. God's constant mercy is a precious truth in which believers take rest, and find boldness in their life and service to God.

c. **They praised the** LORD**, because the foundation of the house of the** LORD **was laid**: It was an appropriately joyful occasion. Since the destruction of the temple under the Babylonian conquest, there had been no proper place for sacrifice and worship for the people of Israel. Another important step was made in the long and difficult process of the restoration of biblical worship and service to God.

i. "This time there is no ark, no visible glory, indeed no Temple; only some beginnings, and small beginnings at that. But God is enthroned on the praises of Israel, and these could be as glorious as Solomon's." (Kidner)

3. (12-13) The mixed reaction among the people.

But many of the priests and Levites and heads of the fathers' *houses,* **old men who had seen the first temple, wept with a loud voice when the foundation of this temple was laid before their eyes. Yet many shouted aloud for joy, so that the people could not discern the noise of the shout of joy from the noise of the weeping of the people, for the people shouted with a loud shout, and the sound was heard afar off.**

a. **Old men who had seen the first temple, wept with a loud voice when the foundation of this temple was laid before their eyes**: The older men knew that this temple would never match up to the glory of the first. After all, King Solomon spent the modern equivalent of five to eight billion dollars on building the first temple. They also had memories of the horrible end of the first temple, and these combined with the joy of the restoration to make profoundly mixed feelings in the **old men**.

i. This was much more than a nostalgic longing for the "good old days." Some of the old men present saw the temple first built by Solomon, and it is likely that some of them stood in the same spot as 50 years before, when they saw the temple on fire with Babylonian soldiers laughing, celebrating, looting, raping, murdering. The memory would be painful to relive.

ii. "Possibly some of them had stood on this very spot half a century before, in an agony of despair, while they saw the cruel flames licking the ancient stones and blazing up among the cedar beams, and all the fine gold dimmed with black clouds of smoke." (Adeney)

iii. They could weep when they thought of all this temple didn't have:

- $5 to $8 billion invested in the building.
- The ark of the covenant.
- The mercy seat.
- The pot of manna and Aaron's rod that budded.
- The Urim and Thummim.
- The cloud of glory, the shekinah of God.
- The fire from heaven to consume the sacrifice on the altar.

iv. Despite all this temple didn't have, it was nevertheless glorious. It was a fulfillment of God's promise, and a beginning of a great restoration of God's work.

v. There was a danger in their weeping. "The backward look which discounts present activity is always a peril. Regrets over the past which paralyse work in the present are always wrong. Moreover all such regrets, as in this case, are in danger of blinding the eyes to the true value and significance of the present." (Morgan)

vi. The prophets warned against despising this temple for its humble beginnings (Haggai 2:1-9, Zechariah 4:8-10).

b. **Yet many shouted aloud for joy**: The younger, who had no remembrance of the prior temple, felt nothing but joy in seeing this important step in the restoration of the temple and its worship.

c. **So that the people could not discern the noise of the shout of joy from the noise of the weeping of the people**: This profound scene showed the extent of the mixed feelings among the people.

i. "The sight must have been very affecting: a whole people, one part *crying* aloud with *sorrow*; the other shouting aloud for *joy*; and on the same occasion too, in which both sides felt an equal interest!" (Clarke)

Ezra 4 – The Samaritan Attempts to Stop the Work

"From this point onwards right to the end of Nehemiah there is conflict. Nothing that is attempted for God will now go unchallenged, and scarcely a tactic be unexplored by the opposition." (Derek Kidner)

A. The offer of a dangerous alliance.

1. (1-2) Adversaries try to join the work of building the temple.

Now when the adversaries of Judah and Benjamin heard that the descendants of the captivity were building the temple of the LORD God of Israel, they came to Zerubbabel and the heads of the fathers' *houses,* and said to them, "Let us build with you, for we seek your God as you *do;* and we have sacrificed to Him since the days of Esarhaddon king of Assyria, who brought us here."

a. **Now when the adversaries**: There were people who did live in Judea during the time when most of the Jewish population of Judah was exiled to Babylon. This included a remnant descended from the lowest and poorest of the land who were left behind in the exile (Jeremiah 39:10), combined with the few who had drifted into the largely desolate area. These people were not happy that **Judah and Benjamin** had come back to Judea and therefore they were their **adversaries**.

i. Those who drifted into Judea were related to the *Samaritans*, those brought into the lands of the former kingdom of Israel after its fall to the Assyrians (733 B.C.), who intermarried with those left behind after the exile. In the two generations of exile after the fall of the kingdom of Judah, they had also expanded somewhat into the lands of Judah.

ii. The Samaritans continued as a people into New Testament times. Because the Samaritans had some historical connection to the people of Israel, their faith was a combination of regulations and rituals from the Law of Moses and various superstitions. Most Jews in Jesus' time *despised* the Samaritans, often more than the Gentiles because they were (religiously speaking) "half-breeds" who were thought to have an eclectic, mongrel faith. This context is essential in understanding the parable of the good Samaritan in Luke 10:25-37.

iii. 2 Kings 17:33 tells the attitude of the Samaritans: *They feared the* LORD, *yet served their own gods; according to the rituals of the nations from among whom they were carried away.*

b. **Heard that the descendants of the captivity were building the temple of the LORD God of Israel**: The noise from the dedication ceremony at the end of Ezra 3 got the attention of these scattered peoples, alerting them that the returning Jews were serious about re-establishing a permanent presence in Judea.

c. **Let us build with you, for we seek your God as you do**: They wanted to become partners in the building work, yet they were still **adversaries**. They wanted to partner in the work either to ruin it or to influence it to their benefit.

i. "Their subsequent conduct was so bitterly ill-natured that we are driven to think that they must have had some selfish aims from the first." (Adeney)

ii. "The proposal to unite in building the Temple was a political move; for, in old-world ideas, co-operation in Temple-building was incorporation in national unity. The calculation, no doubt, was that if the returning exiles could be united with the much more numerous Samaritans, they would soon be absorbed in them." (Maclaren)

iii. They did this on the claim that **we seek your God as you do**. They probably said this with all sincerity; they genuinely believed that they sought the same God in the same way. Yet they also added, **"and we have sacrificed to Him since the days of Esarhaddon king of Assyria."** This means they sacrificed without either a temple or a priesthood, which was obviously against the commandment of God. This completely contradicted their claim, **"we seek your God as you do."**

iv. To the Samaritans, Yahweh was one of many powerful gods. Their idolatry represented a serious danger because Israel was exiled for idolatry. This was a dangerous partnership for the returned exiles.

v. "There may seem to be great loss and needless sacrifice in dispensing with the help of Rehum and Shimshai; but if once we accepted their help, we should discover to our cost that they were adversaries still, and that their only desire was to retard our efforts." (Meyer)

2. (3) Zerubbabel rightly refuses their offer.

But Zerubbabel and Jeshua and the rest of the heads of the fathers' *houses* **of Israel said to them, "You may do nothing with us to build a house for our God; but we alone will build to the LORD God of Israel, as King Cyrus the king of Persia has commanded us."**

a. **Zerubbabel and Jeshua and the rest of the heads of the fathers' houses of Israel said to them**: Importantly, their response was unified. All the returned exiles were agreed upon this answer to the Samaritans.

b. **You may do nothing with us to build a house for our God**: With one voice, they refused the help offered by the Samaritans. They did this knowing they had the permission (even the **command**) of **King Cyrus**, and despite lacking both human and financial resources.

> i. It was an important step of faith to refuse a partnership that might have seemed helpful. We can imagine that there were a few pragmatists among them who said, "We need any help we can get. We can guard ourselves against ungodly influences they may bring." In weak or early circumstances of a building work there is often a serious temptation to take *any* help and to ignore the dangers of unwise and ungodly partnerships.

> ii. "The Samaritans did not worship Jehovah as the Jews, but along with their own gods (2 Kings 17:25-41). To divide His dominion with others was to dethrone Him altogether. It therefore became an act of faithfulness to Jehovah to reject the entangling alliance." (Maclaren)

> iii. "If they had taken an active share and labour and sacrifice of the construction of the temple, they could not have been excluded afterwards from taking part in the temple worship." (Adeney)

> iv. "Men of faith have often fallen into this blunder, and have associated with themselves those not sharing their faith, and therefore in the deepest sense opposed to their enterprises. These leaders were not deceived. They detected the peril." (Morgan)

> v. "Such inclusion of the unyielded is, moreover, a wrong done to them, as it gives them a false sense of security." (Morgan)

B. The broad outline of Samaritan resistance to the work in Jerusalem.

1. (4-5) The resistance under the reign of Cyrus [539-530 B.C.].

Then the people of the land tried to discourage the people of Judah. They troubled them in building, and hired counselors against them to frustrate their purpose all the days of Cyrus king of Persia, even until the reign of Darius king of Persia.

a. **Then the people of the land tried to discourage the people of Judah**: This response to the refusal of partnership revealed their evil intent. If they could not attack the work through a subversive partnership, they would then attack the work by discouraging the workers, troubling the builders, and lobbying against them in the court of King Cyrus.

i. "'To discourage' is literally 'to weaken the hands,' a Hebrew idiom (cf. Jeremiah 38:4)." (Yamauchi)

b. **All the days of Cyrus king of Persia, even until the reign of Darius king of Persia**: This section (Ezra 4:4-23) is a broad overview of Samaritan resistance to the work of rebuilding the temple and the city of Jerusalem, extending into the days of Nehemiah. It is a section in itself, somewhat interrupting the flow of the text in chapter 4.

i. By taking out this section and simply reading Ezra 4:3 followed by Ezra 4:24, we see that the work of building the *temple* was interrupted for several years during the reigns of **Cyrus king of Persia, even until the reign of Darius king of Persia**.

ii. There are two other kings described in this chapter: *Ahasuerus* (Xerxes, who reigned between 485 and 465 B.C.) and Artaxerxes I (who reigned between 464 and 424 B.C.). Even after the temple was finished under Zerubbabel, the Samaritans continued to oppose the work of rebuilding the *city* of Jerusalem, and this ongoing resistance is briefly chronicled in this section of Ezra 4:4-23.

2. (6) The resistance under the reign of Ahasuerus [485-465 B.C.].

In the reign of Ahasuerus, in the beginning of his reign, they wrote an accusation against the inhabitants of Judah and Jerusalem.

a. **In the reign of Ahasuerus...they wrote an accusation**: The Samaritan adversaries against the people of Judah sought to stop the work in this way through influencing the king against the builders.

b. **In the beginning of his reign**: This showed a true enterprising spirit among the adversaries of God's people. They were wrong, but they were energetic and enterprising in the work they did.

i. "*Ahasuerus*, familiar to us from the book of Esther.... The mention of him here marks simply the passage of time, which had still not cooled the enemy's antagonism. But evidently nothing came of this attempt." (Kidner)

3. (7-16) The resistance under the reign of Artaxerxes I [464-424 B.C.].

In the days of Artaxerxes also, Bishlam, Mithredath, Tabel, and the rest of their companions wrote to Artaxerxes king of Persia; and the letter *was* written in Aramaic script, and translated into the Aramaic language. Rehum the commander and Shimshai the scribe wrote a

letter against Jerusalem to King Artaxerxes in this fashion:

From Rehum the commander, Shimshai the scribe, and the rest of their companions—*representatives* of the Dinaites, the Apharsathchites, the Tarpelites, the people of Persia and Erech and Babylon and Shushan, the Dehavites, the Elamites, and the rest of the nations whom the great and noble Osnapper took captive and settled in the cities of Samaria and the remainder beyond the River—and so forth.

(This *is* a copy of the letter that they sent him)

To King Artaxerxes from your servants, the men *of the region* beyond the River, and so forth:

Let it be known to the king that the Jews who came up from you have come to us at Jerusalem, and are building the rebellious and evil city, and are finishing *its* walls and repairing the foundations. Let it now be known to the king that, if this city is built and the walls completed, they will not pay tax, tribute, or custom, and the king's treasury will be diminished. Now because we receive support from the palace, it was not proper for us to see the king's dishonor; therefore we have sent and informed the king, that search may be made in the book of the records of your fathers. And you will find in the book of the records and know that this city *is* a rebellious city, harmful to kings and provinces, and that they have incited sedition within the city in former times, for which cause this city was destroyed.

We inform the king that if this city is rebuilt and its walls are completed, the result will be that you will have no dominion beyond the River.

a. **And translated into the Aramaic language**: Starting at Ezra 4:8 and continuing all the way until Ezra 6:18, everything is written in Aramaic (instead of Hebrew); Ezra 7:12-26 is also in Aramaic.

i. "The letter was probably dictated in Persian to a scribe, who translated it into Aramaic and wrote it down in Aramaic script." (Yamauchi)

b. **And are building the rebellious and evil city, and are finishing its walls and repairing the foundations**: This indicates that the work they complained against was not the work of rebuilding the temple, because that work was already completed. This was resistance to the work of rebuilding the city and its walls.

i. We know that the temple was completed sooner rather than later for several reasons. One is that the same Zerubbabel who started the work also saw it finished (Zechariah 4:9). Another is that some of the same people who saw the glory of Solomon's temple also lived long enough to see Zerubbabel's temple finished (Haggai 2:3).

ii. "It should hardly need emphasising that the *walls* and *foundations* are those of the *city*, not the Temple; but the two operations are often confused. By the reign of Artaxerxes the new Temple had been standing for half a century." (Kidner)

c. **They will not pay tax, tribute, or custom**: This was a lie and a false accusation. They recalled the prior sins of Jerusalem (**the rebellious and evil city**) and attributed them to these chastened, returned exiles.

d. **It was not proper for us to see the king's dishonor**: They skillfully shaped their words to claim they were supporting and protecting the king.

i. **Now because we receive support from the palace**: "More literally: *Now because at all times we are salted with the salt of the palace*; i.e., We live on the king's bounty, and must be faithful to our benefactor." (Clarke)

ii. Spurgeon took the hypocritical words of Jerusalem's enemies and applied them to the believer. His idea that the believer has received support from God's bounty, and was therefore obligated to prevent the LORD's dishonor, and to honor the LORD himself.

e. **This city is a rebellious city, harmful to kings and provinces**: Cleverly calling attention to Jerusalem's sinful past, the Samaritans argued that allowing the building work to continue would make it so that the king of Persia would **have no dominion beyond the River**.

i. Their attack by letter was a skillful combination of truth and lies. It was true that Jerusalem had a sinful past; yet with these returned exiles, it truly was the past and not the present. However, that truth was completely irrelevant because of the great lie – the lie that the Jews and the builders of Jerusalem had a rebellious intent.

ii. In a similar pattern, our adversaries – Satan and his angels, the enemies of our soul – often attack us with a combination of truth and lies. They tell us of our great sin (an accusation that is often true), but they lie about the greater work of Jesus. Since Satan also accuses us before God (Revelation 12:10), he brings his accusing report against us before the Great King.

4. (17-23) The king commands that the work stops until further notice.

The king sent an answer:

To Rehum the commander, *to* Shimshai the scribe, *to* the rest of their companions who dwell in Samaria, and *to* the remainder beyond the River:

Peace, and so forth.

The letter which you sent to us has been clearly read before me. And I gave the command, and a search has been made, and it was found that this city in former times has revolted against kings, and rebellion and sedition have been fostered in it. There have also been mighty kings over Jerusalem, who have ruled over all *the region* beyond the River; and tax, tribute, and custom were paid to them. Now give the command to make these men cease, that this city may not be built until the command is given by me.

Take heed now that you do not fail to do this. Why should damage increase to the hurt of the kings?

Now when the copy of King Artaxerxes' letter *was* read before Rehum, Shimshai the scribe, and their companions, they went up in haste to Jerusalem against the Jews, and by force of arms made them cease.

a. **It was found that this city in former times has revolted against kings, and rebellion and sedition have been fostered in it**: The Samaritan letter to stop the work was a combination of truth and lies, and here the Persian king focused on the *truth* in the letter – the sinful and tragic past of Jerusalem.

b. **There have also been mighty kings over Jerusalem**: Artaxerxes I also noted that in times past there were in fact powerful kings of Judah, who had the power to **tax** and impose **tribute** on their neighbors. In his mind, it meant that Judah had the potential to return to this powerful past.

i. **Who have ruled over all the region beyond the River**: "That is, the Euphrates. Both David and Solomon carried their conquests beyond this river. See 2 Samuel 8:3 and following, and 1 Kings 4:21, where it is said, *Solomon reigned over all the kingdoms from the river* (Euphrates) *unto the land of the Philistines; and unto the borders of Egypt.*" (Clarke)

c. **Now give the command to make these men cease**: The letter from the Samaritan adversaries was successful. Artaxerxes, king of Persia, perhaps the most powerful man in the world at that time, commanded that the work be stopped.

d. **By force of arms made them cease**: The adversaries made the most of the decree of Artaxerxes and used it to make the work stop immediately.

5. (24) The previous work of rebuilding the temple in the days of Darius is again considered.

Thus the work of the house of God which *is* at Jerusalem ceased, and it was discontinued until the second year of the reign of Darius king of Persia.

a. **Thus the work of the house of God which is at Jerusalem ceased**: Through the kinds of tactics of the Samaritans mentioned in the broad survey of Ezra 4:4-23, these adversaries succeeded in stopping the building work for some 15 years.

> i. "The word '*Then*' ['Thus'] would at first point us to the verse immediately before this; but it only makes sense if it is picking up the thread of verse 5 which was dropped for the long parenthesis (6-23). The time is again that of Zerubbabel." (Kidner)

b. **Until the second year of the reign of Darius**: This shows us that the work did not stop forever. By their subversive partnership, and with the lies they told the authorities, their adversaries attacked them, and seemed to succeed with their second tactic, they could not succeed forever against God and His people. Their only victory was to *delay* the work, not to *defeat* it.

Ezra 5 – The Construction of the Temple Is Resumed

A. God helps His people.

1. (1-2) God helps by sending prophets to get the work started again.

Then the prophet Haggai and Zechariah the son of Iddo, prophets, prophesied to the Jews who *were* in Judah and Jerusalem, in the name of the God of Israel, *who was* over them. So Zerubbabel the son of Shealtiel and Jeshua the son of Jozadak rose up and began to build the house of God which *is* in Jerusalem; and the prophets of God *were* with them, helping them.

a. **Then the prophet Haggai**: The words of the prophet Haggai to the community of returned exiles are found in the Old Testament book that bears his name. The heart of his prophecy is communicated in Haggai 1:2-10.

i. "The two prophets who now proclaimed their message in Jerusalem appeared at a time of deep depression. They were not borne on the crest of a wave or a religious revival, as its spokesmen to give it utterance." (Adeney)

ii. In Haggai 1:2-10 we see that the prophet rebuked the people for their attitude towards the building of the temple. They said, "*The time has not come, the time that the LORD's house should be built*" (Haggai 1:2). In saying this, the people made their excuse sound spiritual. They couldn't speak against the *idea* of building the temple, so they spoke against its *timing*. "It isn't God's timing to rebuild the temple."

iii. Therefore, the prophet rebuked them with pointed words: "*Is it time for you yourselves to dwell in your paneled houses, and this temple to lie in ruins?*" (Haggai 1:4) The problem was simply wrongly ordered priorities. They were content to let the cause of the LORD suffer at the expense of their comfort. Instead, they should have felt no rest until the work of God was as prosperous as their personal lives, and been as willing to sacrifice for the work of God as they were for their personal comfort and luxury.

iv. Then God spoke to the people through the prophet: "*Consider your ways! Go up to the mountains and bring wood and build the temple, that I may take pleasure in it and be glorified*" (Haggai 1:7-8). God called them to *work*. Sometimes God's cause needs *work*, work that is supported by prayer, not work that is neglected because of pretended "spiritual" service. The people had allowed a delay beyond their control to become a delay of their own choosing.

b. **And Zechariah the son of Iddo**: Some of Zechariah's prophecy is also recorded for us in the Book of Zechariah. Haggai's prophecy was a more direct encouragement to get busy on the work of building the temple; Zechariah's prophecy was mostly directed to the spiritual condition of the returned exiles.

i. The name **Zechariah** means "The LORD Remembers," and is a fitting name for a prophet of restoration. This prophet was called to encourage and mobilize God's people to accomplish a task that they began, yet lost momentum in completing. He encouraged them indirectly by telling them about God's care for them and by keeping the presence of the Messiah very much in their minds. He worked with others, notably Haggai, Zerubbabel, and Ezra. He warned them of the consequences of neglecting God's work and he emphasized that God wants to do a work through His people.

ii. If all we had was Haggai's prophecy, we might conclude that all God was really only interested in the temple. Zechariah gives the rest of the story, and shows how God is interested in lives, not only buildings.

c. **And the prophets of God were with them, helping them**: The work of these prophets was effective, and helped the people properly re-order their priorities and resume the building work on the temple (**rose up and began to build the house of God**). This verse also indicates that their work went beyond the directly prophetic, and that they took a hand in helping with the practical work of building.

i. Darius came to the throne in a time of conflict and struggle. Therefore the Jews in Jerusalem started their work "without receiving any permission from him, and they did this when he was far too busy fighting for his throne to attend to the troubles of a small, distant city." (Adeney)

2. (3-5) God helps by protecting the work and allowing it to continue.

At the same time Tattenai the governor of *the region* beyond the River and Shethar-Boznai and their companions came to them and spoke thus to them: "Who has commanded you to build this temple and finish this wall?" Then, accordingly, we told them the names of the men who were constructing this building. But the eye of their God was upon the elders of the Jews, so that they could not make them cease till a report could go to Darius. Then a written answer was returned concerning this *matter*.

a. **Tattenai the governor of the region beyond the River**: This was the man appointed by the king of Persia to govern the province that included Judea. He and his **companions** wanted to know why the work of building both the **temple** and the **wall** had resumed.

i. "There is a mention of *Tattenai's* name (probably) and office (certainly) in a Babylonian record dated 502 B.C. which speaks of 'Ta-at[-tan-ni] governor of Ebernari' (*i.e.*, of *Beyond the River*)." (Kidner)

ii. "Like every spiritual advance, from Abraham's to the missionary expansion in Acts, this venture began with a word from the Lord. And, in common with the rest, it was quickly tested and threatened." (Kidner)

iii. Tattenai seems much more reasonable than the Samaritans who opposed the work some 15 years previous to this. This shows us that not all who oppose God's work do it out of premeditated evil; some do it out of custom and a sense of duty.

b. **Then, accordingly, we told them the names of the men**: This was recorded by Ezra to demonstrate that there was no hint of rebellion among the returned Jews. In no way were they trying to rebel against the authority of the Persian king.

c. **But the eye of their God was upon the elders of the Jews, so that they could not make them cease**: God's blessing was upon them, so that the work – resumed under a response to the prophets of God – did not have to stop almost as soon as it started. The work continued, and this blessing was a confirmation of God's hand on His prophets.

i. "We are not to suppose for a moment that this was something new. That eye had always been upon them, but through the teaching of the prophets, and their rousing call, their consciousness of relationship to God had again been renewed." (Morgan)

ii. "The *eye of their God* upon them was better than fortune, and the integrity of the leaders evidently showed through well enough to make any immediate action other than a report seem called for." (Kidner)

d. **Till a report could go to Darius**: This was good for two reasons. First, the nature of bureaucracy and the slow postal system meant that the work could continue for some time. Second, they could pray and trust that God would guide King Darius to a favorable decision.

i. "That he should accede to such a request rather than exercise his immediate authority one way or the other, was in itself somewhat remarkable." (Morgan)

B. The letter to King Darius.

1. (6) The address of the letter.

This is a copy of the letter that Tattenai sent:

The governor of *the region* beyond the River, and Shethar-Boznai, and his companions, the Persians who *were in the region* beyond the River, to Darius the king.

a. **A copy of the letter that Tattenai sent**: As a good administrator, Tattenai not only sent a letter to Darius, he also preserved **a copy** that made its way into Ezra's record.

2. (7-17) The message of the letter.

(They sent a letter to him, in which was written thus.)

To Darius the king:

All peace.

Let it be known to the king that we went into the province of Judea, to the temple of the great God, which is being built with heavy stones, and timber is being laid in the walls; and this work goes on diligently and prospers in their hands.

Then we asked those elders, *and* spoke thus to them: "Who commanded you to build this temple and to finish these walls?" We also asked them their names to inform you, that we might write the names of the men who *were* chief among them.

And thus they returned us an answer, saying: "We are the servants of the God of heaven and earth, and we are rebuilding the temple that was built many years ago, which a great king of Israel built and completed. But because our fathers provoked the God of heaven to wrath, He gave them into the hand of Nebuchadnezzar king of Babylon, the Chaldean, *who* destroyed this temple and carried the people away to Babylon. However, in the first year of Cyrus king of Babylon, King Cyrus issued a decree to build this house of God. Also, the gold and silver articles of the house of God, which Nebuchadnezzar had taken from the temple

that *was* in Jerusalem and carried into the temple of Babylon—those King Cyrus took from the temple of Babylon, and they were given to one named Sheshbazzar, whom he had made governor. And he said to him, 'Take these articles; go, carry them to the temple *site* that *is* in Jerusalem, and let the house of God be rebuilt on its former site.' Then the same Sheshbazzar came *and* laid the foundation of the house of God which *is* in Jerusalem; but from that time even until now it has been under construction, and it is not finished."

Now therefore, if *it seems* good to the king, let a search be made in the king's treasure house, which *is* there in Babylon, whether it is *so* that a decree was issued by King Cyrus to build this house of God at Jerusalem, and let the king send us his pleasure concerning this *matter*.

a. **Let it be known to the king**: In this letter, Tattenai seems to fairly recount the situation from his perspective. Without prejudice or malice, he explained the matter to King Darius.

i. "He seems to have been a mild and judicious man; and to have acted with great prudence and caution, and without any kind of *prejudice*. The manner in which he represented this to the king is a full proof of this disposition." (Clarke)

b. **Which is being built with heavy stones**: The **heavy stones** perhaps aroused suspicion in Tattenai; they made him wonder if the Jews were building a temple or a fortress.

i. **Timber is being laid in the walls**: "Courses of timber at intervals, between those of stone or brick, were quite a common constructional feature over a long period in the ancient Near East, and may have originated as a means of strengthening buildings against earthquakes." (Kidner)

c. **Sheshbazzar came and laid the foundation**: This leads many to believe that Sheshbazzar is actually another name for Zerubbabel and that Tattenai used this name because it would be more likely to appear in the searchable records.

i. There are other ideas about the identity of Sheshbazzar. "Sheshbazzar may have been viewed as the official Persian 'governor' whereas Zerubbabel served as the popular leader. This may be why the Jews mentioned Sheshbazzar here when speaking to the Persian authorities." (Yamauchi)

d. **Let a search be made...whether it is so that a decree was issued by King Cyrus to build this house of God at Jerusalem**: Respectfully, Tattenai asked King Darius to research the matter, to determine if the rebuilding of the temple and Jerusalem was royally sanctioned.

i. "Tattenai, who was now opposing them as they resumed the work, either did not believe that such a decree had ever been promulgated, or considered that it could not be found." (Morgan)

Ezra 6 – The Second Temple Is Completed

A. Darius responds to the request of the governor, Tattenai.

1. (1-2) A diligent search for the decree of Cyrus.

Then King Darius issued a decree, and a search was made in the archives, where the treasures were stored in Babylon. And at Achmetha, in the palace that *is* in the province of Media, a scroll was found, and in it a record *was* written thus:

> a. **Then King Darius issued a decree, and a search was made**: This was the response to the respectful request made by Tattenai described in the last part of Ezra 5.

> b. **At Achmetha...a scroll was found**: This indicates that there must have been some diligence required in the search. This in itself was an evidence of God's hand in the matter; otherwise, they might have easily given up the search.

>> i. "It is easy to realize how easily this might not have been found. If such a document was not in the proper libraries, what more natural than to abandon the search? But under the Divine compulsion that search was prosecuted until the decree was found." (Morgan)

>> ii. This request was initiated in Judea, referred to Babylon, and the answer was found in records from the remote city of **Achmetha**. All this gave the builders lots of time to continue their work because they did not stop during the inquiry process (Ezra 5:5).

>> iii. "Diodorus (2.32.4) declared that the Persians had 'royal parchments' recording their history. Persian officials wrote on scrolls of papyrus and leather, as discoveries made in Egypt show." (Yamauchi)

>> iv. "In 'The Decrees of Cyrus' (p. 89), de Vaux observes that 'now we know that it was the custom of the Persian sovereigns to winter in Babylon and depart in the summer to Susa or Ecbatana [Achmetha],.. and we also know that Cyrus left Babylon in the spring of 538 B.C....

A forger operating in Palestine without the information which we possess could hardly have been so accurate." (Yamauchi)

2. (3-5) The text of the record found: Cyrus' decree.

In the first year of King Cyrus, King Cyrus issued a decree *concerning* the house of God at Jerusalem: "Let the house be rebuilt, the place where they offered sacrifices; and let the foundations of it be firmly laid, its height sixty cubits *and* its width sixty cubits, *with* three rows of heavy stones and one row of new timber. Let the expenses be paid from the king's treasury. Also let the gold and silver articles of the house of God, which Nebuchadnezzar took from the temple which *is* in Jerusalem and brought to Babylon, be restored and taken back to the temple which *is* in Jerusalem, *each* to its place; and deposit *them* in the house of God"—

a. **King Cyrus issued a decree**: This is the decree originally recorded in Ezra 1, giving the Jewish people who wanted to return to Jerusalem and Judea the right to return, to repopulate Judea, and to rebuild Jerusalem.

b. **Let the house be rebuilt.... Let the expenses be paid from the king's treasury**: Not only did Cyrus give *permission* for the temple to be rebuilt, he commanded the *funding* of the work from the royal **treasury**.

i. **Heavy stones**: "The *great stones* which had excited suspicion were now found to be expressly authorised – for the term is the same as for the 'huge stones' of Ezra 5:8 – literally, stones for rolling, too massive to be transported by other means." (Kidner)

ii. **Heavy stones and one row of new timber**: This construction technique seems to have been a precaution against earthquakes. "Kenyon has identified as the only visible remains of Zerubbabel's building a straight joint of stones with heavy bosses [reinforced connections] about 108 feet north of the southeast corner of the temple platform, which Dunand confirmed as similar to Persian masonry found in Phoenicia." (Yamauchi)

iii. There is some question about the *size* of the temple as mentioned here because these dimensions are greater than even Solomon's temple. The best answer is that Cyrus gave the *limits* of what they could build, instead of the actual dimensions of the new structure. "He did not command them to make it so large, for he left the ordering of the proportions of the building to their skill and choice; but he restrained them that they should make it no larger, lest they should hereafter make use of it to other purposes against himself." (Poole)

c. **Let the gold and silver articles of the house of God...be restored and taken back to the temple which is in Jerusalem**: Furthermore, Cyrus ordered that the spoils taken from the **house of God** *some two generations before* now be returned to the Jerusalem temple.

> i. It was a remarkable example of God's providence that so many of these **gold and silver articles of the house of God** still existed intact and that King Cyrus commanded them to be returned.

3. (6-12) The reply of Darius to Tattenai.

Now *therefore*, Tattenai, governor of *the region* beyond the River, and Shethar-Boznai, and your companions the Persians who *are* beyond the River, keep yourselves far from there. Let the work of this house of God alone; let the governor of the Jews and the elders of the Jews build this house of God on its site.

Moreover I issue a decree *as to* what you shall do for the elders of these Jews, for the building of this house of God: Let the cost be paid at the king's expense from taxes *on the region* beyond the River; this is to be given immediately to these men, so that they are not hindered. And whatever they need; young bulls, rams, and lambs for the burnt offerings of the God of heaven, wheat, salt, wine, and oil, according to the request of the priests who *are* in Jerusalem—let it be given them day by day without fail, that they may offer sacrifices of sweet aroma to the God of heaven, and pray for the life of the king and his sons.

Also I issue a decree that whoever alters this edict, let a timber be pulled from his house and erected, and let him be hanged on it; and let his house be made a refuse heap because of this. And may the God who causes His name to dwell there destroy any king or people who put their hand to alter it, or to destroy this house of God which is in Jerusalem. I Darius issue a decree; let it be done diligently.

> a. **Let the work of this house of God alone**: Based on the search and recovery of the relevant document from King Cyrus, Darius made the appropriate command to **Tattenai, governor of the region beyond the River**. Darius commanded him to allow the work on the temple and the city of Jerusalem to continue without interruption.

> b. **Build the house of God on its site**: Darius recognized what the **elders of the Jews** recognized, that it was essential to build the temple upon its old foundations.

> c. **Let the cost be paid at the king's expense**: Based on the prior decree from Cyrus, King Darius did more than *allow* the work to continue. He commanded that it be *funded* by local **taxes on the region beyond the River**. Darius did what is common for politicians to do; he put the burden for funding this work on the province itself, not on his own treasury.

i. And it was funded in an impressive manner: **whatever they need** and **let it be given to them day by day without fail** means that this was a substantial grant.

ii. In this, we see the wonderful hand of God at work against the objections raised by Tattenai and Shethar-Bozenai as recorded in Ezra 5:3. The end result of these objections was to *further* the work of God instead of hindering it. This is an example of God working all things together for good for His people (Romans 8:28). On this point, Kidner quotes a line from a William Cowper poem: *The clouds which ye so much dread, Are big with mercy.*

d. **And pray for the life of the king and his sons**: This explains part of the motivation of King Darius. Not only did he base his decision on the precedent of King Cyrus, but he also wanted the prayers of the Jewish people for **the king and his sons**.

e. **Let him be hanged on it...let his house be made a refuse heap...destroy any king or people who put their hand to alter it**: Finally, Darius was careful to make the decree *strong*, with severe punishments for those who violated both the letter and the spirit of the decree.

i. According to Adam Clarke, there is some debate as to if this punishment involved flogging a man at his own house, hanging him to death at his house, or impaling him at his house as an early form of crucifixion.

ii. Darius was the type of man to see such brutal executions through to completion. "According to Herodotus (3.159) Darius I impaled three thousand Babylonians when he took Babylon, an act that Darius himself recorded in the Beshitun Inscription." (Yamauchi)

f. **Let it be done diligently**: At the end of it all, the king of the mightiest empire on the earth commanded that the temple be finished by the returned exiles and funded by the empire.

i. This might seem absolutely unique, but there is good evidence that Persian monarchs had similar concern for the conquered temples in other regions of their empire. "In 1973 French archaeologists discovered at Xanthos in Lycia in southwestern Turkey a cult foundation charter – written in Greek, Lycian, and Aramaic – dated to 358 B.C., a period when the area was controlled by a Persian satrap, that provided some striking parallels with the decree of Cyrus." (Yamauchi)

ii. "One can easily imagine with what surprise Tattenai received the answer of Darius, characterized by clearness and determination. The man who would have hindered and stayed the progress of the building,

was compelled not only to not hinder, but to help with great gifts."
(Morgan)

iii. "If certain matters can only be settled by reference to great men,
kings or men of affairs, make the application;' and then betake yourself
to prayer, believing that as He inclined the heart of Darius, in the
instance before us, so He can do as He will among the armies of
heaven, and the inhabitants of earth." (Meyer)

iv. This is a powerful illustration of the principle from Proverbs: *The
king's heart is in the hand of the LORD, like the rivers of water; He turns it
wherever He wishes.* (Proverbs 21:1)

B. The temple is finished and dedicated.

1. (13-15) The temple is completed.

**Then Tattenai, governor of *the region* beyond the River, Shethar-Boznai,
and their companions diligently did according to what King Darius had
sent. So the elders of the Jews built, and they prospered through the
prophesying of Haggai the prophet and Zechariah the son of Iddo. And
they built and finished *it,* according to the commandment of the God of
Israel, and according to the command of Cyrus, Darius, and Artaxerxes
king of Persia. Now the temple was finished on the third day of the
month of Adar, which was in the sixth year of the reign of King Darius.**

a. **Diligently did according to what King Darius had sent**: They were
diligent in supporting and funding the work of rebuilding the temple and
were diligent in punishing anyone who opposed it.

i. "The political motives for this forthrightness may have been many,
including a desire to show respect for the policies of Cyrus and to
promote stability in a part of the empire which was important for
communications with Egypt, at a time when widespread unrest had
only recently been quelled." (Kidner)

b. **They prospered through the prophesying of Haggai the prophet and
Zechariah**: The words and personal ministry of these post-exilic prophets
were an important component in the success of the work. The work and
the workers were genuinely strengthened by the word of God through
these prophets.

i. The initial ministry of these prophets is mentioned in Ezra 5:1-2.
First, the prophets had to encourage the people of God to resume
the work after a significant period of inactivity. Then, they had to
encourage them to keep working when God had opened the doors
for the work to be done. Even with the open doors, the work was still

difficult and needed prophetic encouragement. God's blessing on the work did not make the work *easy* to do.

ii. "Work on the temple made little progress because of opposition and the preoccupation of returnees with their own homes (Haggai 1:2-3). Because they had placed their own interests first, God sent them famine as a judgment (Haggai 1:5-6, 10-11). Spurred by the preaching of Haggai and Zechariah, and under the leadership of Zerubbabel and Joshua, a new effort was begun (Haggai 1:12-15)." (Yamauchi)

c. **The temple was finished on the third day of the month of Adar, which was in the sixth year**: This means that it took four years from resuming the construction to finishing the temple. It was such a big job that, even with everyone doing the work **diligently**, it was not quickly completed.

i. "The mention of Artaxerxes, who belongs to the next century, takes us forward to the restoration of the city walls by Nehemiah, which this king authorised. His name, as the third royal patron of Israel's rehabilitation, is added here to complete the picture, whether by the author or by an early scribe." (Kidner)

2. (16-18) The dedication ceremony of the second temple.

Then the children of Israel, the priests and the Levites and the rest of the descendants of the captivity, celebrated the dedication of this house of God with joy. And they offered sacrifices at the dedication of this house of God, one hundred bulls, two hundred rams, four hundred lambs, and as a sin offering for all Israel twelve male goats, according to the number of the tribes of Israel. They assigned the priests to their divisions and the Levites to their divisions, over the service of God in Jerusalem, as it is written in the Book of Moses.

a. **Celebrated the dedication of this house of God with joy**: There was a previous celebration, many years before, at the founding of this second temple (Ezra 3). This was the celebration for the finishing of a functioning temple.

i. "The word for *dedication* (*hanukka*) was later to become the name of a festival in memory of the Temple's re-consecration in 165 B.C. after its profanation by Antiochus Epiphanes (*cf.* John 10:22f.)." (Kidner)

b. **And they offered sacrifices**: Compared to the dedication of Solomon's temple (1 Kings 8:62-66), this was a meager celebration. Solomon sacrificed some 142,000 animals at the dedication of his temple; here at the dedication of the second temple they only sacrificed a total of 712 animals.

i. However, given the relative wealth of Israel in the days of the first temple as compared to the second temple, the smaller gift recorded in

Ezra may have been more beautiful to God, because it came at greater cost in a time of limited resources.

ii. **As a sin offering for all Israel twelve male goats**: "It was a confession of failure but also faith. There was still atonement and still the covenant with the whole people – for this was the implication of the *twelve* sacrifices." (Kidner)

iii. The fact that sacrifice was made for the *twelve tribes* shows that regathered Israel had the real sense that they were the collective product of all twelve tribes, and there were not ten or any other number of "lost" tribes.

c. **They assigned the priests to their divisions...as it is written in the Book of Moses**: They took care to resume the proper priestly service as commanded by the **Book of Moses** and the previous pattern of David.

i. Yet, *all* was not the same as in the previous service in the days of Solomon's temple. "The general plan of the second temple resembled the first. But the [Most Holy Place] was left empty as the ark of the covenant had been lost through the Babylonian conquest.... [The Holy Place] was furnished with a table for showbread, the incense altar, and one menorah instead of Solomon's ten." (Yamauchi)

3. (19-22) The first Passover celebrated in the second temple.

And the descendants of the captivity kept the Passover on the fourteenth *day* of the first month. For the priests and the Levites had purified themselves; all of them *were ritually* clean. And they slaughtered the Passover *lambs* for all the descendants of the captivity, for their brethren the priests, and for themselves. Then the children of Israel who had returned from the captivity ate together with all who had separated themselves from the filth of the nations of the land in order to seek the LORD God of Israel. And they kept the Feast of Unleavened Bread seven days with joy; for the LORD made them joyful, and turned the heart of the king of Assyria toward them, to strengthen their hands in the work of the house of God, the God of Israel.

a. **The descendants of the captivity kept the Passover on the fourteenth day of the first month**: This shows that they were careful to keep the Passover on the proper day, according to the command of Moses. In keeping Passover they remembered the central act of redemption of the Old Testament, the deliverance of God's people from Egypt.

b. **They slaughtered the Passover lambs for all the descendants of the captivity**: In this, we see that the people themselves did not sacrifice the **Passover lambs**; rather, the priests did this for them. It seems that there was no absolute custom for this; sometimes the people sacrificed the Passover lambs under the supervision of the priests and sometimes the priests did it for the people.

c. **With all who had separated themselves from the filth of the nations of the land**: Connected with the remembrance of the deliverance of Passover was the **Feast of Unleavened Bread**, which marked the purity of God's delivered people.

> i. **The children of Israel who had returned from the captivity ate together with all who had separated themselves from the filth of the nations of the land in order to seek the LORD God of Israel**: "This is a crucial verse for correcting the impression one might gain from Ezra 4:1-3 of a bitterly exclusive party.... in reality we find that only the self-excluded were unwelcome. The convert found an open door, as Rahab and Ruth had done." (Kidner)

> ii. **Filth of the nations**: This is a strong statement, "But it was only too true that both the Canaanite and the Babylonian habits of life were disgustingly immoral." (Adeney)

d. **The LORD made them joyful**: In the context of obedience and purity, they did not lose their joy. The purity of God's delivered people was *joyful* in its character (instead of dour). It also led them **to strengthen their hands in the work of the house of God**.

> i. "Do not be afraid of joy; when God makes you joyful, do not think it necessary to restrain your songs or smiles." (Meyer)

> ii. "So ends the first stage, a generation long, of Israel's rehabilitation. It had opened when the Lord 'stirred up the spirit of Cyrus' (Ezra 1:1), and it concluded with His turning the heart of one of that king's most powerful successors." (Kidner)

> iii. **The heart of the king of Assyria**: "He had 'turned the heart of the king of Assyria' – a title for Darius that speaks for the authenticity of the narrative, for it represents an old form of speech for the ruler of the districts that had once belonged to the king of Assyria." (Adeney)

Ezra 7 – Ezra's Return from Babylon

"At Jerusalem, Malachi may well have prophesied shortly before the coming of Ezra, giving us, if so, a sharp taste of the mood and temper of the times which occupy our chapters 7-10." (Derek Kidner)

A. An overview of Ezra's return.

1. (1-5) The genealogy of Ezra the Scribe.

Now after these things, in the reign of Artaxerxes king of Persia, Ezra the son of Seraiah, the son of Azariah, the son of Hilkiah, the son of Shallum, the son of Zadok, the son of Ahitub, the son of Amariah, the son of Azariah, the son of Meraioth, the son of Zerahiah, the son of Uzzi, the son of Bukki, the son of Abishua, the son of Phinehas, the son of Eleazar, the son of Aaron the chief priest—

a. **Now after these things**: Some 60 largely uneventful years passed between Ezra 6 and Ezra 7. The ruler of Persia at the end of that period was **Artaxerxes**, who is also known to history as Artaxerxes Longimanus, the successor to Xerxes, the king who married Esther. The events of the book of Esther took place between Ezra 6 and 7.

i. "There can be no reasonable doubt that his reference is to the son and successor of Xerxes – known by the Greeks as 'Macrocheir,' and by the Romans as 'Longimanus' – Artaxerxes 'of the long hand,' for this Artaxerxes alone enjoyed a sufficiently extended reign to include both the commencement of Ezra's public work and the later scenes in the life of Nehemiah which the chronicler associates with the same king." (Adeney)

ii. "If this was Artaxerxes I as the traditional view maintains, which we believe is correct, Ezra arrived in Palestine in 458 (457).... The traditional view assumes a gap of almost sixty years between the events of chapter 6 and chapter 7." (Yamauchi)

b. **Son of Seraiah, the son of Azariah...the son of Zadok... the son of Aaron the chief priest**: This list is not all-inclusive (there are some generations left out). Nevertheless, it shows that Ezra was a descendant both of **Aaron** and also of **Seraiah**, who was the last High Priest before the captivity.

i. **The son of Zadok**: "'Zadok' was a priest under David whom Solomon appointed chief priest in place of Abiathar, who supported the rebel Adonijah (1 Kings 1:7-8; 2:35). Ezekiel regarded the Zadokites as free from idolatry (Ezekiel 44:15-16). Zadokites held the office of high priest till 171 B.C. The Sadducees were named after Zadok, and the Qumran community looked for the restoration of the Zadokite priesthood." (Yamauchi)

2. (6) Ezra, a skilled scribe.

This Ezra came up from Babylon; and he *was* a skilled scribe in the Law of Moses, which the LORD God of Israel had given. The king granted him all his request, according to the hand of the LORD his God upon him.

a. **This Ezra came up from Babylon**: Ezra was one of the *later* Jews who returned from the captivity to Judea and Jerusalem. Though there was a first great return (described in Ezra 1-2), there were also many others who returned in the years following.

i. "His name stands very high in Jewish tradition, where he came to be regarded as a second Moses, and indeed it was he, more than any other man, who stamped Israel with its lasting character as the people of a book." (Kidner)

b. **A skilled scribe in the Law of Moses**: To many modern readers, a **scribe** sounds like a glorified secretary or someone who simply writes. That is not the idea of this description of Ezra. For the Jewish culture of that day, **a skilled scribe** was an *expert* in the Law of Moses, someone who was like a highly trained lawyer in the word of God.

i. "In his case it is emphasised by the word *skilled*, or literally 'rapid' (*cf.* Psalm 45:1) – suggesting a quickness of grasp and ease of movement amid this complex material which was the fruit of the devoted study described in Ezra 7:10." (Kidner)

ii. Scribes were important and influential, and one might say that they had three main duties: to *preserve* the word of God, to *teach* the word of God, and to *administer* the word of God (in the sense of interpreting and applying it).

iii. By the time of Jesus there were many scribes and they were respected as experts of the law of God among most of the Jews of that time. However, they had degenerated greatly from the ideal originally established by Ezra, so much so that they were active opponents of Jesus and His ministry, and were the targets of His rebukes (Matthew 7:29; Matthew 23).

iv. "As messengers of the will of God, they took the place of the prophets, with this difference: instead of receiving new revelations, they explained and applied the old. Of this new order, Ezra was at once the founder and type." (Morgan)

v. Critical theories in fashion since the Enlightenment popularized the idea that Ezra, or others in his day, actually first compiled the Pentateuch (or more) from various written and oral traditions they gathered. Yet this verse alone (**which the LORD God of Israel had given**) shows this is wrong. As Derek Kidner observed, "Incidentally the present verse shares none of the doubts of some modern criticism over the antiquity (*Moses*) or the authority (*the Lord*) of the law, nor does it see Ezra as a reviser or compiler. He is concerned with it as something *given*."

c. **The king granted him all his request**: The favor of God toward Jerusalem and the Jewish people is again evident. The great generosity of the king was because **the hand of the LORD his God** was **upon him.**

3. (7-10) Ezra's arrival at Jerusalem and his mission.

Some **of the children of Israel, the priests, the Levites, the singers, the gatekeepers, and the Nethinim came up to Jerusalem in the seventh year of King Artaxerxes. And Ezra came to Jerusalem in the fifth month, which *was* in the seventh year of the king. On the first *day* of the first month he began *his* journey from Babylon, and on the first *day* of the fifth month he came to Jerusalem, according to the good hand of his God upon him. For Ezra had prepared his heart to seek the Law of the LORD, and to do *it*, and to teach statutes and ordinances in Israel.**

a. **And Ezra came to Jerusalem**: Ezra came to a city that had been repopulated by the Jewish people from their exile for about 60 years.

i. "Though the direct distance between Babylon and Jerusalem is about five hundred miles, the travelers would have had to traverse nine hundred miles, going northwest along the Euphrates River and then south." (Yamauchi)

ii. **Some of the children of Israel**: "And but some; for many chose rather to continue in the land of their captivity, though God by his prophets, and the king by his proclamation, had cried out, 'Ho, ho, come forth' [and so forth]. 'Deliver thyself, O Zion, that dwellest with the daughter of Babylon,' Zechariah 2:6-7." (Trapp)

b. **According to the good hand of his God upon him**: Ezra credited his successful journey (lasting four months) to God's **good hand** of blessing on him.

> i. "This little summary of the expedition gives no hint of the initial disappointment and delay, the fasting and prayer, and the dangers of such a journey, which will emerge in the full account." (Kidner)

c. **Ezra had prepared his heart to seek the Law of the LORD, and to do *it*, and to teach**: We see here a threefold intention in Ezra. He came to **seek**, to **do**, and to **teach** God's word.

> i. **Had prepared his heart**: "An instrument must be tuned ere it can be played upon; sour wines need good sweetening." (Trapp)

> ii. We may say that this threefold intention is essential in anyone who wants to make an impact on others with the word of God.

> - First, to **seek the Law of the LORD**. This means that the full impact of God's word is made by those who diligently **seek** after His word and fellowship with God in His word.

> - Second, **to do it**. This means that the full impact of God's word is made by those who are not only hearers of the word, but actual *doers* of the word. It has to be lived, not only known.

> - Third, **to teach**. This means that the full impact of God's word is made by those who actually **teach** it to others. What has been learned in the seeking and the doing must be put into effect through the *teaching* of God's word.

> iii. "Here is a fine character of a minister of God: He *prepares*, he fixes, purposes, and determines, *with his heart* – with all his powers and affections, to *seek the law of God*, and *to do it* himself, that he may be properly qualified to *teach* its *statutes* and *judgments* to Israel." (Clarke)

> iv. The Living Bible translates Ezra 7:10 as follows: *This was because Ezra had determined to study and obey the laws of the Lord and to become a Bible teacher, teaching those laws to the people of Israel.*

B. The letter of Artaxerxes.

1. (11-16) The king commissions helpers, a copy of the Law, and gifts for the temple to go with Ezra upon his return to Jerusalem.

This *is* a copy of the letter that King Artaxerxes gave Ezra the priest, the scribe, expert in the words of the commandments of the LORD, and of His statutes to Israel:

Artaxerxes, king of kings,

To Ezra the priest, a scribe of the Law of the God of heaven:

Perfect *peace,* and so forth.

I issue a decree that all those of the people of Israel and the priests and Levites in my realm, who volunteer to go up to Jerusalem, may go with you. And whereas you are being sent by the king and his seven counselors to inquire concerning Judah and Jerusalem, with regard to the Law of your God which *is* in your hand; and *whereas you are* to carry the silver and gold which the king and his counselors have freely offered to the God of Israel, whose dwelling *is* in Jerusalem; and *whereas* all the silver and gold that you may find in all the province of Babylon, along with the freewill offering of the people and the priests, *are to be* freely offered for the house of their God in Jerusalem—

> a. **Ezra the priest, the scribe, the expert in the words of the commandments of the LORD**: Ezra was indeed more than a glorified secretary or copyist. He was a well-trained **expert** in the word of God.

> b. **Whereas you are being sent by the king and his seven counselors to inquire concerning Judah and Jerusalem**: This tells us that not only did Ezra *go* to Jerusalem, he was actually **sent** by Artaxerxes to gather information for the **king and his seven counselors**.

> c. **Who volunteer to go up to Jerusalem**: With this, Artaxerxes hoped to encourage others to go with Ezra to increase the chance of his success and to strengthen the province of Judah.

> d. **You are to carry the silver and gold**: Artaxerxes also authorized the giving of many **silver and gold** gifts to the temple, **along with the freewill offering of the people and the priests**.

> > i. "*The vessels* may have been some which had been overlooked when the captured vessels were restored by Cyrus (Ezra 1:7ff), but it is just as likely that they were a goodwill gift, newly presented." (Kidner)

2. (17-22) Providing for the temple and sacrificial expenses.

Now therefore, be careful to buy with this money bulls, rams, and lambs, with their grain offerings and their drink offerings, and offer them on the altar of the house of your God in Jerusalem.

And whatever seems good to you and your brethren to do with the rest of the silver and the gold, do it according to the will of your God. Also the articles that are given to you for the service of the house of your God, deliver in full before the God of Jerusalem. And whatever more may be needed for the house of your God, which you may have occasion to provide, pay *for it* from the king's treasury.

And I, *even* I, Artaxerxes the king, issue a decree to all the treasurers who *are in the region* beyond the River, that whatever Ezra the priest, the scribe of the Law of the God of heaven, may require of you, let it be done diligently, up to one hundred talents of silver, one hundred kors of wheat, one hundred baths of wine, one hundred baths of oil, and salt without prescribed limit.

a. **Be careful to buy with this money**: Ezra carried with him government money that was meant to advance the interests of Artaxerxes. This money was to be spent on sacrificial animals and the promotion of temple worship at the rebuilt temple in Jerusalem.

b. **Whatever seems good to you**: Ezra was commanded to **be careful**, but also given latitude to make his own decisions about how to best spend the money he came with.

c. **Whatever more may be needed for the house of your God...pay for it from the king's treasury**: Artaxerxes was very generous to Ezra and the work in Jerusalem, allowing him to draw on **the king's treasury** for whatever he needed.

i. "A 'talent' in the Babylonian sexagesimal system was 60 minas, with a mina being 60 shekels. A talent weighed about 75 pounds. A hundred talents was an enormous sum, about 3¾ tons of silver. This amount, together with a talent of gold, was the tribute that Pharaoh Neco imposed on Judah (2 Kings 23:33)." (Yamauchi)

3. (23) The motive of Artaxerxes.

Whatever is commanded by the God of heaven, let it diligently be done for the house of the God of heaven. For why should there be wrath against the realm of the king and his sons?

a. **Whatever is commanded by the God of heaven, let it diligently be done**: In all this, we see that Artaxerxes went to great lengths to promote the operations of the temple in Jerusalem.

i. "Without shucking and hucking, without delays and consults." (Trapp)

b. **For why should there be wrath against the realm of the king and his sons?** This shows the *motive* of Artaxerxes. Like other monarchs of the Persian Empire, he wanted to placate the gods of the people and the territory that they had conquered. He believed it was a good and safe policy for his kingdom to do this.

4. (24-26) Ezra is given legal power to enforce God's Law.

Also we inform you that it shall not be lawful to impose tax, tribute, or custom *on* any of the priests, Levites, singers, gatekeepers, Nethinim, or servants of this house of God. And you, Ezra, according to your God-given wisdom, set magistrates and judges who may judge all the people who *are in the region* beyond the River, all such as know the laws of your God; and teach those who do not know *them.* Whoever will not observe the law of your God and the law of the king, let judgment be executed speedily on him, whether *it be* death, or banishment, or confiscation of goods, or imprisonment.

a. **It shall not be lawful to impose tax**: To promote the work of the temple in Jerusalem, Artaxerxes commanded that **priests** and other workers at the temple be given tax-exempt status.

i. "Darius had ordered a similar exemption for cult-servants of Apollo." (Kidner)

b. **Set magistrates and judges**: Artaxerxes gave Ezra significant authority in the civil administration of the province (**the region beyond the River**).

i. **According to your God-given wisdom**: "*The wisdom of thy God that is in thine hand*, i.e. which God hath put into thy heart, and which appears in the works of thy hand. Wisdom is sometimes ascribed to the hands, as Psalm 78:72." (Poole)

c. **Teach those who do not know**: Artaxerxes gave Ezra authority to teach this generation of returned exiles. Yet this pagan ruler also gave authority – great authority – to punish those who did **not observe the law of your God and the law of the king**. Religious leaders like Ezra have a serious responsibility to use such authority justly, in a way that glorifies God and benefits man.

i. "Later passages show that Ezra was primarily a priest and scholar rather than an administrator. Yet the assurance that God had called him and had opened the doors gave Ezra the courage and strength to undertake this great task." (Yamauchi)

5. (27-28) Ezra gives thanks.

Blessed *be* the L<small>ORD</small> God of our fathers, who has put *such a thing* as this in the king's heart, to beautify the house of the L<small>ORD</small> which *is* in Jerusalem, and has extended mercy to me before the king and his counselors, and before all the king's mighty princes.

So I was encouraged, as the hand of the LORD my God *was* upon me; and I gathered leading men of Israel to go up with me.

a. **Blessed be the LORD God of our fathers**: Ezra knew that such generous and broad support and authority could only be granted by God who **put such a thing as this in the king's heart**.

i. God had moved the heart of Darius (Ezra 6:1-12), and now God also moved the heart of Artaxerxes. The principle of Proverbs 21:1 was again demonstrated: *The king's heart is in the hand of the LORD, like the rivers of water; He turns it wherever He wishes.*

b. **So I was encouraged, as the hand of the LORD my God was upon me**: Ezra was certainly **encouraged**, not only by the king's support but more so because all this was clear evidence of God's support and blessing. Ezra found great encouragement in knowing that **the hand of the LORD** was **upon** him.

Ezra 8 – Ezra Comes to Jerusalem

A. The people who came with Ezra to Jerusalem.

1. (1-14) A list of the families.

These *are* the heads of their fathers' *houses,* and *this is* the genealogy of those who went up with me from Babylon, in the reign of King Artaxerxes: of the sons of Phinehas, Gershom; of the sons of Ithamar, Daniel; of the sons of David, Hattush; of the sons of Shecaniah, of the sons of Parosh, Zechariah; and registered with him *were* one hundred and fifty males; of the sons of Pahath-Moab, Eliehoenai the son of Zerahiah, and with him two hundred males; of the sons of Shechaniah, Ben-Jahaziel, and with him three hundred males; of the sons of Adin, Ebed the son of Jonathan, and with him fifty males; of the sons of Elam, Jeshaiah the son of Athaliah, and with him seventy males; of the sons of Shephatiah, Zebadiah the son of Michael, and with him eighty males; of the sons of Joab, Obadiah the son of Jehiel, and with him two hundred and eighteen males; of the sons of Shelomith, Ben-Josiphiah, and with him one hundred and sixty males; of the sons of Bebai, Zechariah the son of Bebai, and with him twenty-eight males; of the sons of Azgad, Johanan the son of Hakkatan, and with him one hundred and ten males; of the last sons of Adonikam, whose names *are* these—Eliphelet, Jeiel, and Shemaiah—and with them sixty males; also of the sons of Bigvai, Uthai and Zabbud, and with them seventy males.

a. **These are the heads of their father's houses**: This list includes those who **went up with** Ezra **from Babylon.** Here Ezra begins to re-tell the account that was summarized in Ezra 7:1-10.

i. "There was little at Jerusalem to attract a new expedition; for the glamour which had surrounded the first return, with a son of David at its head, had faded in grievous disappointments; and the second series of pilgrims had to carry with them the torch with which to rekindle the flames of devotion." (Adeney)

60

b. **Of the sons of Phinehas, Gerhsom...Ithamar, Daniel...David, Hattush**: These seem to be prominent members of the entourage, coming from prominent families.

> i. "The interest of this forbidding list of names and numbers lies in the fact that in every case but one these groups are joining, at long last, the descendants of the pioneers from Babylon eighty years before." (Kidner)

> ii. **Shechaniah**: "There were three of this name; the second is mentioned in Ezra 8:5, and the third Ezra 10:2. They were all different persons, as may be seen from their fathers' houses." (Clarke)

c. **And with him two hundred males...three hundred males**: Adding the counts of the male members of the group together, there was a total count of at least 1,496 men in the group. Adding an estimated number of women and children (Ezra 8:21), we can surmise that the total number of the party coming with Ezra in the days of **King Artaxerxes** was something between 6,000 and 7,000 people.

> i. "The whole company consisted of one thousand four hundred ninety and six males: a good addition to those that went up before with Zerubbabel; yet nothing so many as might have been, but that they wanted hearts." (Trapp)

2. (15) The lack of Levites in the group.

Now I gathered them by the river that flows to Ahava, and we camped there three days. And I looked among the people and the priests, and found none of the sons of Levi there.

a. **Now I gathered them by the river**: Ezra was definitely the leader of this group, and in more than a spiritual sense. He led the expedition.

b. **And found none of the sons of Levi there**: The Levites were different from the priests. The priests came from one family among the entire tribe of Levi (the descendants of Aaron). These were the essential workers for the system of temple worship that Ezra was to promote.

> i. Perhaps the Levites were too comfortable with their lives in Babylon to go back to Jerusalem. Perhaps they were not willing to go back to their ancestral temple duties that put them under the authority of the priests. Whatever the reason was, Ezra had the money and the authority he needed, but not the *men*.

> ii. "A rabbinic midrash on Psalm 137 relates the legend that there were Levites in the caravan but that they were not qualified to officiate because when Nebuchadnezzar had ordered them to sing for him the

songs of Zion, 'they refused and bit off the ends of their fingers, so that they could not play on the harps.'" (Yamauchi)

3. (16-20) Ezra addresses the problem of a lack of Levites.

Then I sent for Eliezer, Ariel, Shemaiah, Elnathan, Jarib, Elnathan, Nathan, Zechariah, and Meshullam, leaders; also for Joiarib and Elnathan, men of understanding. And I gave them a command for Iddo the chief man at the place Casiphia, and I told them what they should say to Iddo *and* his brethren the Nethinim at the place Casiphia—that they should bring us servants for the house of our God. Then, by the good hand of our God upon us, they brought us a man of understanding, of the sons of Mahli the son of Levi, the son of Israel, namely Sherebiah, with his sons and brothers, eighteen men; and Hashabiah, and with him Jeshaiah of the sons of Merari, his brothers and their sons, twenty men; also of the Nethinim, whom David and the leaders had appointed for the service of the Levites, two hundred and twenty Nethinim. All of them were designated by name.

> a. **I gave them a command...that they should bring us servants for the house of our God**: With this, Ezra sent back to Babylon for Levites to come and join the work in Jerusalem. He didn't accept the initial failure of the Levites to join the group, but kept appealing for help.

> > i. Ezra carefully planned the Levite recruitment effort. He specifically chose the recruiters – nine **leaders**, and two **men of understanding** to make the appeal as persuasive as possible. Then he carefully instructed the recruiters as to **what they should say** and directed them specifically as to whom to make the appeal (**Iddo and his brethren**). Indeed, **the good hand of our God** was **upon** the recruitment effort, but it was also upon the *planning* of it.

> > ii. "*Iddo the chief*, the head of the rest, either by ecclesiastical order or government, which the Persian kings allowed to the Jews; or by some grant or commission from the king." (Poole)

> b. **They brought us a man of understanding...namely Sherebiah**: This man responded to the call and led a delegation of Levites.

B. On the journey.

1. (21-23) A prayer of protection.

Then I proclaimed a fast there at the river of Ahava, that we might humble ourselves before our God, to seek from Him the right way for us and our little ones and all our possessions. For I was ashamed to request of the king an escort of soldiers and horsemen to help us against

the enemy on the road, because we had spoken to the king, saying, "The hand of our God *is* upon all those for good who seek Him, but His power and His wrath *are* against all those who forsake Him." So we fasted and entreated our God for this, and He answered our prayer.

a. **I proclaimed a fast...that we might humble ourselves before our God**: Ezra understood the spiritual power of fasting as a demonstration of single-minded devotion to God and His cause. Therefore, he called **a fast**, and saw that **He answered our prayer**.

i. As with any spiritual discipline or duty, it is possible to fast without the right heart or to trust it as an empty ritual apart from its true spiritual reality. Real fasting – fasting that is partnered with true repentance and isn't only about image – has great power before God (Matthew 17:21).

ii. **To seek from Him the right way**: "Literally 'a straight way' unimpeded by obstacles and dangers." (Yamauchi)

b. **For I was ashamed to request of the king an escort**: Ezra had previously expressed great confidence in the hand of God upon him and his expedition. He did not want to contradict these prior words with later actions, in asking the king for **an escort of soldiers and horsemen**.

i. They needed protection because the danger was real. There was a constant threat of robbers and bandits, especially because they were transporting so many valuables. Yet because of their dependence on God (expressed through prayer and fasting), God protected them.

ii. "The voluntary gifts of the king were welcome. They were expressions of the king's sense of the greatness of his God. These Ezra accepted with gratitude. It would have been quite another matter if he had asked the king to help him do what he had declared God was able to do for him." (Morgan)

iii. "Thus we see that this good man had more anxiety for the glory of God than for his own personal safety." (Clarke)

iv. "There is an added interest in the fact that Nehemiah, in his day, would see the matter quite differently, accepting a military escort as part of God's bounty (Nehemiah 2:7-9)." (Kidner)

c. **So we fasted**: "They put their holy resolution into execution: purpose without practice is like Rachel, beautiful but barren." (Trapp)

2. (24-30) Distribution of articles to be offered among the tribal representatives.

And I separated twelve of the leaders of the priests—Sherebiah, Hashabiah, and ten of their brethren with them—and weighed out to

them the silver, the gold, and the articles, the offering for the house of our God which the king and his counselors and his princes, and all Israel *who were* present, had offered. I weighed into their hand six hundred and fifty talents of silver, silver articles *weighing* one hundred talents, one hundred talents of gold, twenty gold basins *worth* a thousand drachmas, and two vessels of fine polished bronze, precious as gold. And I said to them, "You *are* holy to the LORD; the articles *are* holy also; and the silver and the gold *are* a freewill offering to the LORD God of your fathers. Watch and keep *them* until you weigh *them* before the leaders of the priests and the Levites and heads of the fathers' *houses* of Israel in Jerusalem, *in* the chambers of the house of the LORD." So the priests and the Levites received the silver and the gold and the articles by weight, to bring *them* to Jerusalem to the house of our God.

a. **Weighed out to them**: Ezra divided the valuables among the **leaders of the priests**, making each of them responsible for their portion. They were responsible to **watch and keep them** until they arrived in Jerusalem and delivered everything to the **leaders of the priests and Levites**.

i. "These are enormous sums, worth millions of dollars." (Yamauchi) The king of Persia sent great treasure to support the ongoing work of the temple.

ii. "If the God of the Jews were no more than a name (he might have argued), the whole exercise was pointless; but if He existed, He would expect tangible courtesies from a king – and the scale of them should reflect the donor's power and majesty." (Kidner)

b. **So the priests and the Levites received the silver and the gold**: This took faith because holding this wealth made them targets for violence by robbers or bandits. They received this responsibility and stewardship.

3. (31-32) Summary of their departure, and arrival in Jerusalem.

Then we departed from the river of Ahava on the twelfth *day* of the first month, to go to Jerusalem. And the hand of our God was upon us, and He delivered us from the hand of the enemy and from ambush along the road. So we came to Jerusalem, and stayed there three days.

a. **And the hand of our God was upon us**: Ezra repeated what is now a familiar phrase. God's **hand** was indeed upon them to protect, guide, and bless.

i. "God never fails those who act in full dependence on Himself, and so in complete independence of all others." (Morgan)

b. **So we came to Jerusalem**: This ended the four-month journey from Babylon to Jerusalem. Ezra – together with the entire group – was now in the Promised Land which had been promised to their ancestors.

C. Arrival in Jerusalem.

1. (33-34) Precious articles offered to the LORD.

Now on the fourth day the silver and the gold and the articles were weighed in the house of our God by the hand of Meremoth the son of Uriah the priest, and with him *was* Eleazar the son of Phinehas; with them *were* the Levites, Jozabad the son of Jeshua and Noadiah the son of Binnui, with the number *and* weight of everything. All the weight was written down at that time.

a. **The silver and the gold and the articles were weighed**: The priests in Jerusalem expected a proper accounting for what had been sent from Babylon. We may say that this was more to *prove* the integrity of the men in Ezra's expedition than to disprove it.

b. **All the weight was written down at that time**: They did it all with a careful accounting, as is fitting for good stewardship of precious things.

i. "According to Babylonian tradition, almost every transaction, including sales and marriages, had to be recorded in writing. Ezra may have had to send back a signed certification of the delivery of the treasures." (Yamauchi)

2. (35) Sacrificial offerings made to the LORD.

The children of those who had been carried away captive, who had come from the captivity, offered burnt offerings to the God of Israel: twelve bulls for all Israel, ninety-six rams, seventy-seven lambs, and twelve male goats *as* a sin offering. All *this was* a burnt offering to the LORD.

a. **Offered burnt offerings**: These **burnt offerings** were to propitiate for general sin and to show dedication to the LORD. The entire animal was burnt as a sacrifice to God.

i. **Twelve bulls for all Israel**: "Though of *tribes* there were only *Judah* and *Benjamin*, yet they offered a bullock for *every tribe*, as if present. There can be little doubt that there were individuals there from all the twelve tribes, possibly some families of each." (Clarke)

ii. "The reason for offering *seventy-seven* lambs is not so obvious, whatever conjectures about the perfect number it may seem to invite." (Kidner)

b. **As a sin offering**: The **sin offering** was made mostly with the idea of purification, especially for specific acts of transgression. Taking the two sacrifices together (**burnt** and **sin** offerings), we can see that they dealt with both the problem of *sin* (addressing the general sin problem) and *sins* (addressing the problem of specific sins).

3. (36) The orders from Artaxerxes are related.

And they delivered the king's orders to the king's satraps and the governors *in the region* beyond the River. So they gave support to the people and the house of God.

a. **And they delivered the king's orders**: This would have particularly meant the commands that gave special authority to Ezra (Ezra 7:25).

i. **The king's orders**: "Presumably the documents that accredited Ezra as one who was authorised to administer the Jewish law among his fellow-countrymen in the various regions of the province." (Kidner)

b. **So they gave support to the people and the house of God**: This reminds us of the great *purpose* of Ezra's expedition. In the final two chapters, we will see Ezra administering strict correction as a reformer, although he did not come primarily as a disciplinarian. He came to **give support to the people and the house of God**, and only dealt with the problems of sin and compromise as necessary in the course of this greater goal.

Ezra 9 – Israel's Sin and Ezra's Confession

A. The problem is exposed.

1. (1-2) The leaders report to Ezra.

When these things were done, the leaders came to me, saying, "The people of Israel and the priests and the Levites have not separated themselves from the peoples of the lands, with respect to the abominations of the Canaanites, the Hittites, the Perizzites, the Jebusites, the Ammonites, the Moabites, the Egyptians, and the Amorites. For they have taken some of their daughters *as wives* for themselves and their sons, so that the holy seed is mixed with the peoples of *those* lands. Indeed, the hand of the leaders and rulers has been foremost in this trespass."

a. **The people of Israel and the priests and the Levites have not separated themselves from the peoples of the lands**: After his arrival and the proper accounting of all the gifts brought from Babylon, Ezra received discouraging news. The spiritual condition of the post-exile community was bad, and this was evident in their failure to separate from the pagan peoples who still populated the region.

i. "Feeble and isolated, the Jews were quite unable to resist the attacks of their jealous neighbours. Would it not be better to come to terms with them, and from enemies convert them into allies? Then the policy of exclusiveness involved commercial ruin; and men who knew how their brethren in Chaldea were enriching themselves by trade with the heathen were galled by a yoke which held them back from foreign intercourse." (Adeney)

b. **For they have taken some of their daughters as wives for themselves and their sons**: Their failure to separate resulted in intermarriage with the surrounding pagan communities.

i. It wasn't that this intermarriage was the *only* problem; but as these communities intermarried, there would be no areas left untouched by pagan associations – business, government, social life. To allow intermarriage with idolaters was to allow all these other areas of compromise.

c. **With respect to the abominations of the Canaanites, the Hittites, the Perizzites, the Jebusites, the Ammonites, the Moabites, the Egyptians, and the Amorites**: This shows that the problem was not primarily *ethnic*. The problem was they did not separate themselves from these **abominations**, specifically the idolatry of these people.

i. "All this testified abhorrence, not merely of the act of having taken strange wives, but their having also joined them in their *idolatrous* abominations." (Clarke)

ii. Due to this forsaking of Jewish identity and at least partial embrace of idolatry (or its toleration in the Jewish community), within a few generations there would cease to be *any* distinctive Jewish community in the Promised Land.

iii. Ezra 9:1-2 seems to recall passages from the Law of Moses against intermarriage with the surrounding Canaanite tribes – in particular, Exodus 34:11-16 and Deuteronomy 7:1-4. We may see this conviction of sin in the people and their leaders, and the way the conviction of sin was phrased, to indicate (spiritually speaking) that Ezra's ministry of teaching God's word was bearing fruit. The people heard the word, looked at their lives, and saw that the two did not match.

iv. "During the obscure period that followed the dedication of the temple – a period of which we have no historical remains – the rigorous exclusiveness which had marked the conduct of the returned exiles when they rudely rejected the proposal of their Gentile neighbours to assist them in rebuilding the temple was abandoned, and freedom of intercourse went so far as to permit intermarriage with the descendants of the Canaanites." (Adeney)

d. **Indeed, the hand of the leaders and rulers has been foremost in this trespass**: Worst of all, the **leaders** of the community were leaders (**foremost**) in this sin. They were leaders, but leading in the wrong direction.

i. "Leading aristocratic families were foremost in contracting the foreign alliances. It is such as they who would profit most, as it is such as they who would be most tempted to consider worldly motives and to forgo the austerity of their fathers." (Adeney)

2. (3) Ezra's complete astonishment.

So when I heard this thing, I tore my garment and my robe, and plucked out some of the hair of my head and beard, and sat down astonished.

a. **When I heard this thing**: Ezra had just finished a dangerous four-month journey from Babylon to Jerusalem. He had perhaps over-romanticized the spiritual commitment of the pioneers returned from exile and may have expected to find something completely different than the culture of compromise among the community of returned exiles.

b. **And sat down astonished**: Certainly, one of the reasons for his mourning (expressed in the tearing of his garment and the plucking of his beard) was Ezra's understanding that it was the same sins of idolatry and compromise which had caused the tribes of Israel to be exiled in the first place. He no doubt wondered how the people could endanger themselves like this again.

> i. **Astonished**: "Means 'to be appalled or stupefied'.... Rare is the soul who is so shocked at disobedience that he is appalled. (The English word originally meant 'to make pale.')." (Yamauchi)

> ii. Both Ezra and Nehemiah were confronted with the sin of pagan intermarriage. Nehemiah responded by plucking out the hair of the guilty (Nehemiah 13:25); Ezra responded by plucking out his own hair.

> iii. "It has been truly said that communion with the Lord dries many tears, but it starts many more." (Meyer)

4. (4) Ezra is joined by others who were also grieved by Israel's sin.

Then everyone who trembled at the words of the God of Israel assembled to me, because of the transgression of those who had been carried away captive, and I sat astonished until the evening sacrifice.

a. **Everyone who trembled at the words of the God of Israel assembled**: Others in the community were also horrified at the sin of their brethren. These people (who were marked by their respect for God's word) **assembled** together with Ezra.

b. **Because of the transgression of those who had been carried away captive**: This was an interesting title to give to those who had sinned. In a historical sense, they were among the captives who returned from Babylon (though many or most of them were actually born in Judea). Yet in a real spiritual sense, they were **carried away captive** by their sin of partnership with idolaters and idolatry.

> i. **Sat down astonished**: "Partly for grief and shame at the sin; and partly for fear of some great and dreadful judgment which he expected and feared for it." (Poole)

B. The prayer of Ezra.

1. (5-6) Ezra's sense of shame.

At the evening sacrifice I arose from my fasting; and having torn my garment and my robe, I fell on my knees and spread out my hands to the LORD my God. And I said: "O my God, I am too ashamed and humiliated to lift up my face to You, my God; for our iniquities have risen higher than *our* heads, and our guilt has grown up to the heavens.

a. **At the evening sacrifice I arose from my fasting**: Ezra knew there was a time to mourn and he did that for a long time. He also knew that there was a time to pray, and now he would begin his prayer.

> i. "The 'evening sacrifice' took place about three P.M. (cf. Exodus 12:6; Acts 3:1). The informants had probably visited Ezra in the morning, so that he must have sat in this position for many hours. The time of the evening sacrifice was also the appointed time for prayer and confession." (Yamauchi)

> ii. When Ezra prayed, he alone prayed – yet because he stood before an assembly of the people of God, there was a sense in which he led them in prayer. "The officiating minister is not merely to pray before the congregation, while the people kneel as silent auditors. His prayer is designed to guide and help their prayers, so that there may be 'common prayer' throughout the whole assembly." (Adeney)

b. **Fell on my knees and spread out my hands to the LORD my God**: Ezra was one of many in the Bible who prayed on his **knees**:

- Solomon prayed on his knees (1 Kings 8:54).
- The Psalmist called us to kneel before God (Psalm 95:6).
- Daniel prayed on his knees (Daniel 6:10).
- People presented themselves to Jesus in a kneeling posture (Matthew 17:14, Matthew 20:20, Mark 1:40).
- Stephen prayed on his knees (Acts 7:60).
- Peter prayed on his knees (Acts 9:40).
- Paul prayed on his knees (Acts 20:36, Ephesians 3:14).
- Some early Christians prayed on their knees (Acts 21:5).
- Most importantly, Jesus prayed on His knees (Luke 22:41).

> i. The Bible has enough prayer *not* on the knees to show us that it isn't required, but it also has enough prayer *on* the knees to show us that it is good.

> ii. Ezra also **spread out** his **hands to the LORD**. This was the most common posture of prayer in the Old Testament. Many modern people close their eyes, bow their heads, and fold their hands as they pray,

but the Old Testament tradition was to spread out the hands toward heaven in a gesture of surrender, openness, and ready reception. "With the palms open toward heaven, in a having, craving way, as beggars. This was the Jewish manner of praying, and it was very becoming." (Trapp)

c. **I am too ashamed and humiliated to lift up my face to You**: Though Ezra's hands were raised, his face was cast down in shame and humiliation before the LORD. He sensed that the sins of the people of Israel had weighed his head down so much that he could not lift his head (**our iniquities have risen higher than our heads**).

i. **Ashamed and humiliated**: According to Yamauchi, there is a difference between these two ancient Hebrew words. The first speaks of being **ashamed**; the second word speaks of the pain that accompanies shame.

ii. "God had been so often provoked, and had so often pardoned them and they had continued to transgress, that he was ashamed to go back again to the throne of grace to ask for mercy in their behalf. This is the genuine feeling of every reawakened *backslider*." (Clarke)

d. **Our iniquities have risen higher than our heads**: Significantly, Ezra prayed saying "**our iniquities**" instead of "*their* iniquities." Ezra had just arrived at this community and he had not shared any kind of life or conduct with them. Yet he knew that because they were bound together in the same covenant before God, *their* iniquities *were in fact* his.

2. (7-9) Ezra remembers God's past kindness to Israel in spite of their sins.

Since the days of our fathers to this day we *have been* very guilty, and for our iniquities we, our kings, *and* our priests have been delivered into the hand of the kings of the lands, to the sword, to captivity, to plunder, and to humiliation, as *it is* this day. And now for a little while grace has been *shown* from the LORD our God, to leave us a remnant to escape, and to give us a peg in His holy place, that our God may enlighten our eyes and give us a measure of revival in our bondage. For we *were* slaves. Yet our God did not forsake us in our bondage; but He extended mercy to us in the sight of the kings of Persia, to revive us, to repair the house of our God, to rebuild its ruins, and to give us a wall in Judah and Jerusalem.

a. **We have been very guilty**: Ezra recognized the generally sinful past of the tribes of Israel, and how their exile was a righteous work of God against His sinful people.

b. **And now for a little while grace has been shown**: Ezra reflected on the remarkable goodness of God in bringing a **remnant** of His people back from exile and allowing them to live in the Promised Land again.

c. **To give us a peg in His holy place**: The idea is that Israel once again had a safe position, a standing in God's favor and in His temple. In those days, houses didn't really have cupboards or storage closets as we think of them. Objects were stored on *pegs* set up all around the room. If something was on its peg, it was safe and secure, stored properly and ready for use at the appropriate time.

i. Only a few days before this, Ezra had seen the temple for the first time in his life. He was impressed that God had given His people **a peg in His holy place** once again and was therefore afraid that their casual disregard for this blessing would once again invite the righteous anger of God.

d. **And give us a measure of revival in our bondage**: Ezra rejoiced to see even a **measure of revival** and knew that this was an emblem of God's mercy and favor that should not be despised with disobedience and compromise.

e. **To revive us, to repair the house of our God, to rebuild its ruins, and to give us a wall**: Ezra was impressed by all these signs of God's mercy and favor to His people, signs he had only seen for the first time a few days previously. It made him appreciate how good God had been to His people, and how dangerous it was for them to sin and compromise in response to His goodness.

i. "Some critics take this reference to a wall as an argument for the priority of Nehemiah over Ezra, assuming an allusion to the wall that Nehemiah had repaired in his day. But most scholars agree that the reference here is not to be taken literally." (Yamauchi)

ii. **To give us a wall**: "They had the fence of the king of Persia's favour. They had also God's providence, as a hedge or wall of fire round about them." (Trapp)

iii. "The Jewish commentator Slotki (p. 166) observes poignantly: 'A little grace had been granted by God to his people; a small remnant had found its weary way back to its home and driven a single peg into its soil; a solitary ray of light was shining; a faint breath of freedom lightened their slavery. How graphically Ezra epitomizes Jewish experience in these few words!'" (Yamauchi)

3. (10-14) Ezra fears that God's people are testing His mercy.

And now, O our God, what shall we say after this? For we have forsaken Your commandments, which You commanded by Your servants the

prophets, saying, 'The land which you are entering to possess is an unclean land, with the uncleanness of the peoples of the lands, with their abominations which have filled it from one end to another with their impurity. Now therefore, do not give your daughters as wives for their sons, nor take their daughters to your sons; and never seek their peace or prosperity, that you may be strong and eat the good of the land, and leave *it* as an inheritance to your children forever.' And after all that has come upon us for our evil deeds and for our great guilt, since You our God have punished us less than our iniquities *deserve,* and have given us *such* deliverance as this, should we again break Your commandments, and join in marriage with the people *committing* these abominations? Would You not be angry with us until You had consumed *us,* so that *there would be* no remnant or survivor?

a. **What shall we say after this?** Ezra offered no excuses and not even an explanation. Their conduct was indefensible and in direct disobedience to what God **commanded by** His **servants the prophets**.

i. **That you may be strong**: "Although you may fancy that this way of making leagues and marriages with them is the only way to establish and settle you, yet I assure you it will weaken and ruin you and the contrary course will make you stronger." (Poole)

b. **You our God have punished us less than our iniquities deserve**: As severe as the exile was, Ezra recognized that it was **less than** the people of God deserved. As he looked at their present disobedience, he understood that it was a way of despising the great mercy God had shown in the past and meant they deserved a complete and final judgment.

i. As the tribes of Israel piled sin upon sin before the fall of the northern and southern kingdoms, God still showed remarkable mercy to them. He did not *have to* preserve them in exile; there could have been genocide instead. Furthermore, He did not *have to* bring them back from exile into the Promised Land once again. These were both wonderful examples of God's mercy in the midst of judgment.

ii. "It is a fine revelation of the only attitude in which any man can become a mediator. There is first an overwhelming sense of sin. This is accompanied, and perhaps caused by, that deeper sense of the righteousness and grace of God. It finds expression in agonised and unsparing confession. The passion of the whole movement is evidence of its reality." (Morgan)

4. (15) Ezra calls upon the mercy of God.

O LORD God of Israel, You *are* righteous, for we are left as a remnant, as *it is* this day. Here we *are* before You, in our guilt, though no one can stand before You because of this!"

a. **O LORD God of Israel**: Here Ezra wisely appealed to the LORD as the **God of Israel**. Although God's people had been unfaithful to Him, Ezra still hoped for covenant mercies from the LORD because He was their God.

b. **You are righteous**: Ezra also wisely appealed to God's righteousness, especially in leaving a **remnant** in fulfillment of His prior promises (2 Chronicles 30:6; Isaiah 10:20-22).

i. "Ezra is far too much in earnest simply to wish to help his people to escape from the consequences of their conduct. This would not be salvation. It would be moral shipwreck. The great need is to be saved from the evil conduct itself." (Adeney)

c. **Here we are before You in our guilt**: Ezra wisely did not claim an excuse or a reason for their sin. Israel had sinned and they were *guilty*. The appeal must be made for mercy to the guilty, not as a favor to the deserving (or semi-deserving).

i. We also note that Ezra did not claim special circumstances. He did not tell God that their difficult environment made their present compromise understandable, or seek to excuse their idolatry by listing their other good works or faithfulness. He simply realized that **no one can stand before You because of this!**

ii. "Ezra had not even the heart to plead, as Moses had, that God's name would suffer in such a case. His prayer was naked confession, without excuses, without the pressure of so much as a request." (Kidner)

Ezra 10 – Confession and Repentance

A. The people decide to forsake their sin.

1. (1) The example of Ezra's confession.

Now while Ezra was praying, and while he was confessing, weeping, and bowing down before the house of God, a very large assembly of men, women, and children gathered to him from Israel; for the people wept very bitterly.

a. **While Ezra was praying, and while he was confessing**: The power of Ezra's confession was not merely in the words recorded in Ezra 9:6-15. It was in the *depth of heart* that prompted the prayer, shown here by **weeping, and bowing down before the house of God**. He prayed this prayer and humbled himself on behalf of the people *publicly*, before **a very large assembly of men, women, and children**.

i. **Bowing down before the house of God**: The Hebrew grammar "implies that Ezra kept on 'throwing himself down' on the ground." (Yamauchi)

b. **For the people wept very bitterly**: This shows that the people were also struck by the conviction of sin and their need to confess and repent. They sorrowed over the sin of the covenant community just as Ezra had done.

i. "They could not wash their hands in innocency, they, therefore, washed them in tears; they knew that as the sins of the old world, so of this little world, needeth a deluge." (Trapp)

ii. Through the centuries, one mark of a powerful movement of the Holy Spirit among the people of God is that they are convicted of their sin and feel compelled to confess it and to put it away. The old Puritan John Trapp thought of confession as a purging of sin. "This is the soul's vomit, which is the hardest kind of physic [medicine], but healthsomest. This the devil knows...and, therefore, he holds the lips close, that the heart may not disburden itself by so wholesome evacuation." (Trapp)

iii. "Confession of sins is a neglected doctrine. It only comes into its rightful place in times of revival, when the Holy Spirit comes in doubly-convicting power and makes it impossible for the erring believer to have any peace of mind until the wrong is confessed whenever necessary." (Orr)

iv. In his book, *The Second Evangelical Awakening*, Dr. J. Edwin Orr quoted the observations of a high-ranking army officer concerning the work of the Spirit in his Scottish town: "Those of you who are at ease have little conception of how terrifying a sight it is when the Holy Spirit is pleased to open a man's eyes to see the real state of heart.... Men who were thought to be, and who thought themselves to be good, religious people...have been led to search into the foundation upon which they were resting, and have found all rotten, that they were self-satisfied, resting on their own goodness, and not upon Christ. Many turned from open sin to lives of holiness, some weeping for joy for sins forgiven."

v. William Newton Blair, the author of a book describing the great Korean revival, declares: *"We may have our theories of the desirability or undesirability of public confession of sin. I have had mine, but I know that when the Spirit of God falls upon guilty souls, there will be confession, and no power on earth can stop it."* (Cited in Orr)

vi. The Bible has much to say about the confession of sin, and we can surmise some general guidelines about it:

- Confession should be made to the one sinned against.

- Confession publicly of specific sins should be made within the circle of people affected by those sins.

- Confession of general spiritual need, while being discreet about the specific sin, is appropriate when the circle of the people affected by the sin is either personal or very small.

- Confession should be appropriately specific.

- Confession should be thorough.

2. (2-4) Shechaniah exhorts the people to action.

And Shechaniah the son of Jehiel, *one* of the sons of Elam, spoke up and said to Ezra, "We have trespassed against our God, and have taken pagan wives from the peoples of the land; yet now there is hope in Israel in spite of this. Now therefore, let us make a covenant with our God to put away all these wives and those who have been born to them, according to the advice of my master and of those who tremble at the

commandment of our God; and let it be done according to the law. Arise, for *this* matter *is* your *responsibility*. We also *are* with you. Be of good courage, and do *it.*"

a. **We have trespassed against our God...yet now there is hope in Israel in spite of this**: Shechaniah recognized the severity of their sin, yet he also knew that their present brokenness over their sin was an emblem of the work of God's Spirit among them. Thus, it was a reason for **hope in Israel in spite of this**.

i. It is interesting that Ezra himself did not suggest the course of action that Shechaniah did. Perhaps Ezra was so deeply troubled by the sin of the community that he could not think of a wise response. Perhaps Ezra knew what to do but knew that the suggestion had to come from among the community instead of himself, considering that he was a newcomer to Jerusalem and Judea.

b. **Let us make a covenant with our God to put away all these wives**: Shechaniah advised the *actions* of repentance, more than simply indulging the feelings of brokenness.

i. "One fact to be borne in mind about the issue as a whole is that divorce was permitted in Israel (Deuteronomy 24:1); and broken marriages had been rife at this time for the very opposite of the present reason: *i.e.*, there had been a scandalous number of Jewish wives abandoned in favour of heathen women (Malachi 2:10-16)." (Kidner)

ii. "While divorce is always hateful to God (Malachi 2:16), and a witness to human 'hardness of heart' (Mark 10:5), the situation described in Ezra 9 and 10 was a classic example of one in which the lesser of two evils had to be chosen. If a serious reason for divorce could ever exist, this had a better claim than most to come within that category." (Kidner)

iii. "Marriages made between some prohibited persons; as suppose, between a father and his daughter, a brother and a sister, are not only unlawful, but void marriages, and *ipso facto* null, by the political laws of civil nations. And therefore these marriages with idolatrous and heathen women, being expressly and severely forbidden by God, might well be disannulled." (Poole)

c. **Those who have been born to them**: This was a strong command, because not only would the wives be put away – but also the *children*. Because of this, some commentators (such as Adeney) think that this was excessive zeal in reforming, going beyond God's will and causing great harm. Yet we should see that this was in fact God's will.

i. It was understood in ancient cultures that the women would stay with their children. "'All these women and their children' reflects the fact that in ancient societies, as in ours, mothers were given custody of their children when marriages were dissolved." (Yamauchi)

ii. This arrangement was also, no doubt, mitigated by support from the husbands. "Though by the Jewish laws such marriages were *null* and *void*, yet as the *women* they had taken did not know these laws, their case was deplorable. However, we may take it for granted that each of them received a portion according to the circumstances of their husbands, and that they and their children were not turned away desolate, but had such a provision as their necessities required. *Humanity* must have dictated this, and no law of God is contrary to humanity." (Clarke)

iii. It also seems that because of God's mercy in this difficult situation, there were relatively few children affected (Ezra 10:44).

iv. "That children may and sometimes do suffer, at least temporal evils, for their parents' sins, or upon occasion of them, is most evident, both by the Scripture instances, and by the laws and usages of nations in some cases." (Poole)

d. **Arise, for this matter is your responsibility. We also are with you**: Shechaniah exhorted the guilty people to do what was right, and also stood beside them in support. This was especially meaningful because it seems that although Shechaniah was not guilty of marrying a pagan woman, both his father and his uncles were (Ezra 10:21).

3. (5-8) Ezra issues a proclamation.

Then Ezra arose, and made the leaders of the priests, the Levites, and all Israel swear an oath that they would do according to this word. So they swore an oath. Then Ezra rose up from before the house of God, and went into the chamber of Jehohanan the son of Eliashib; and *when* he came there, he ate no bread and drank no water, for he mourned because of the guilt of those from the captivity.

And they issued a proclamation throughout Judah and Jerusalem to all the descendants of the captivity, that they must gather at Jerusalem, and that whoever would not come within three days, according to the instructions of the leaders and elders, all his property would be confiscated, and he himself would be separated from the assembly of those from the captivity.

a. **Ezra arose, and made the leaders of the priests, the Levites, and all Israel swear an oath**: The counsel of Shechaniah seemed good to Ezra, so he immediately called upon the people to **swear an oath** to **do according to this word**. Significantly, Ezra *began* with the leaders; he expected them to make things right with God first.

b. **He ate no bread and drank no water, for he mourned**: For Ezra, this whole tragedy was as bad as if someone had died. He could not think of himself or his own needs when he knew God was being so greatly dishonored.

> i. We can say that Ezra observed a *complete* fast, abstaining from both food and water. This same kind of fast is rare in the Bible but was observed twice by Moses (Exodus 34:28; Deuteronomy 9:18) and also by the people of Nineveh (Jonah 3:7).

> ii. "The man who sets himself 'to seek, to do, to teach' the law of God invariably brings himself into places where sorrow will be his portion, and intrepid courage necessary." (Morgan)

c. **Whoever would not come within three days...all his property would be confiscated, and he himself would be separated from the assembly**: Ezra was given great civil authority by King Artaxerxes (Ezra 7:26). He put that authority to good use here by enforcing the people to fulfill the oath they had previously made (Ezra 10:5).

B. The spirit of repentance at the assembly of the people.

1. (9-11) Ezra's appeal to the trembling assembly.

So all the men of Judah and Benjamin gathered at Jerusalem within three days. It *was* the ninth month, on the twentieth of the month; and all the people sat in the open square of the house of God, trembling because of *this* matter and because of heavy rain. Then Ezra the priest stood up and said to them, "You have transgressed and have taken pagan wives, adding to the guilt of Israel. Now therefore, make confession to the Lord God of your fathers, and do His will; separate yourselves from the peoples of the land, and from the pagan wives."

a. **So all the men of Judah and Benjamin gathered at Jerusalem within three days**: This was an impressive response to the remarkable call Ezra made in the preceding verses. Their unified response was another evidence of the moving of the Holy Spirit among the people of God.

b. **All the people sat in the open square of the house of God, trembling because of this matter and because of heavy rain**: The willingness of people to forsake normal comforts and to humbly assemble in adverse circumstances was another evidence of the moving of the Holy Spirit among them.

i. This response has been seen again as the Holy Spirit has moved upon the people of God. Orr records that in March of 1859, at the beginning of a great move of God that would bring more than one million souls to conversion in Great Britain, some unordained men with a passion for revival preached at the First Presbyterian Church in Ahoghill, Northern Ireland. Such a large crowd gathered that they had to dismiss the meeting out of fear that the balconies would collapse under the weight of so many people. They took the meeting to the street right outside the church, and in the freezing rain James McQuilkin preached to 3,000 people. Many of the listeners fell to their knees in the wet and muddy street because they were so moved by the conviction of sin under the preaching of these laymen.

c. **You have transgressed...adding to the guilt of Israel**: Ezra's word to the people was clear and strong. Although the moving of the Holy Spirit was evident, it was important to carry the work through to completion and not be satisfied with a partial work.

d. **Now therefore, make confession to the LORD...do His will...separate yourselves**: This was a clear call to both *confession* and *repentance*.

i. We might even say that their *confession* would be vain without corresponding *repentance*. This repentance (the decision to stop one's sinful behavior and to **do His will**) is an essential element of the Christian life.

ii. "Perhaps you have the notion that repentance is a thing that happens at the commencement of the spiritual life, and has to be got through as one undergoes a certain operation, and there is an end of it. If so, you are greatly mistaken; repentance lives as long as faith. Towards faith I might almost call it a Siamese twin. We shall need to believe and to repent as long as ever we live." (Spurgeon)

2. (12-15) The response of the assembly.

Then all the assembly answered and said with a loud voice, "Yes! As you have said, so we must do. But *there are* many people; *it is* the season for heavy rain, and we are not able to stand outside. Nor *is this* the work of one or two days, for *there are* many of us who have transgressed in this matter. Please, let the leaders of our entire assembly stand; and let all those in our cities who have taken pagan wives come at appointed times, together with the elders and judges of their cities, until the fierce wrath of our God is turned away from us in this matter." Only Jonathan the son of Asahel and Jahaziah the son of Tikvah opposed this, and Meshullam and Shabbethai the Levite gave them support.

a. **Yes! As you have said, so we must do**: This was still another evidence of the remarkable moving of the Holy Spirit upon the people. They immediately answered (and **with a loud voice**) in agreement to what Ezra said.

b. **But there are many people.... Nor is this the work of one or two days**: The people asked Ezra for the *time* to make it right. This was necessary because so many people were involved in this sin, yet the principle was agreed upon with very little opposition.

c. **Only Jonathan the son of Asahel**: "Why these four men opposed the measure is unclear. Perhaps they were protecting themselves or their relatives. Perhaps they viewed the measures of separation as too harsh. Less probably they were fanatics who wished no delay in implementing the measure." (Yamauchi)

3. (16-17) Each case is examined individually over a 3-month period.

Then the descendants of the captivity did so. And Ezra the priest, *with certain heads of the fathers' households*, were set apart by the fathers' households, each of them by name; and they sat down on the first day of the tenth month to examine the matter. By the first day of the first month they finished *questioning* all the men who had taken pagan wives.

a. **They sat down on the first day of the tenth month to examine the matter**: Although Ezra was wisely willing to accept the delay because of necessity, he also held the people accountable to do what they agreed to do in the months after the great assembly.

b. **They finished questioning all the men who had taken pagan wives**: The whole process took many weeks because so many men had **taken pagan wives**. The **questioning** was necessary because they needed to examine if any of these wives had genuinely decided to serve the Lord God and to forsake her native religions.

i. If the pagan wife had decided to keep her primary allegiance with her former people and their idols, she could not live among the covenant community and had to be divorced.

ii. To the end of the chapter, there is a list showing that only about 114 of these **pagan wives** refused to embrace the God of Israel and had to be divorced. Yamauchi calculates that it was less than one-half of one percent of the people who were guilty of this pagan intermarriage and who had to divorce their wives. Though it was such a small percentage, it still had to be dealt with strongly – and it was. It also shows that most of the foreign wives joined the people of God in their hearts as well as their homes.

iii. In the New Testament, believers are also instructed to marry within the faith. Marriages to unbelievers are condemned (2 Corinthians 6:14) and widows (as one example of the unmarried) are directly commanded to marry within the faith (1 Corinthians 7:39). However, Paul specifically commanded that if a believer is married to an unbeliever, they are to remain in the marriage, if at all possible, both for the opportunity of a witness to the unbelieving spouse and for the benefit it brings to the children (1 Corinthians 7:12-17).

4. (18-44) The list of those found guilty.

And among the sons of the priests who had taken pagan wives *the following* were found of the sons of Jeshua the son of Jozadak, and his brothers: Maaseiah, Eliezer, Jarib, and Gedaliah. And they gave their promise that they would put away their wives; and *being* guilty, *they presented* a ram of the flock as their trespass offering.

Also of the sons of Immer: Hanani and Zebadiah; of the sons of Harim: Maaseiah, Elijah, Shemaiah, Jehiel, and Uzziah; of the sons of Pashhur: Elioenai, Maaseiah, Ishmael, Nethanel, Jozabad, and Elasah.

Also of the Levites: Jozabad, Shimei, Kelaiah (the same *is* Kelita), Pethahiah, Judah, and Eliezer.

Also of the singers: Eliashib; and of the gatekeepers: Shallum, Telem, and Uri.

And others of Israel: of the sons of Parosh: Ramiah, Jeziah, Malchiah, Mijamin, Eleazar, Malchijah, and Benaiah; of the sons of Elam: Mattaniah, Zechariah, Jehiel, Abdi, Jeremoth, and Eliah; of the sons of Zattu: Elioenai, Eliashib, Mattaniah, Jeremoth, Zabad, and Aziza; of the sons of Bebai: Jehohanan, Hananiah, Zabbai, *and* Athlai; of the sons of Bani: Meshullam, Malluch, Adaiah, Jashub, Sheal, *and* Ramoth; of the sons of Pahath-Moab: Adna, Chelal, Benaiah, Maaseiah, Mattaniah, Bezalel, Binnui, and Manasseh; *of* the sons of Harim: Eliezer, Ishijah, Malchijah, Shemaiah, Shimeon, Benjamin, Malluch, *and* Shemariah; of the sons of Hashum: Mattenai, Mattattah, Zabad, Eliphelet, Jeremai, Manasseh, *and* Shimei; of the sons of Bani: Maadai, Amram, Uel, Benaiah, Bedeiah, Cheluh, Vaniah, Meremoth, Eliashib, Mattaniah, Mattenai, Jaasai, Bani, Binnui, Shimei, Shelemiah, Nathan, Adaiah, Machnadebai, Shashai, Sharai, Azarel, Shelemiah, Shemariah, Shallum, Amariah, *and* Joseph; of the sons of Nebo: Jeiel, Mattithiah, Zabad, Zebina, Jaddai, Joel, *and* Benaiah.

All these had taken pagan wives, and *some* of them had wives *by whom* they had children.

a. **And among the sons of the priests who had taken pagan wives the following were found**: Those who had to put away their wives (because they refused to convert) are listed here. This is a somewhat shameful list, and not a very good way to get one's name recorded in the best-selling book of all time.

i. "None was exempt from the reformation, which was carried out with complete thoroughness. Such action is ever the true outcome, and only satisfactory expression, of sorrow over sin." (Morgan)

ii. Jewish rabbis speculated that the reason why these Jewish men divorced their Jewish wives and married women from the pagan cultures (Malachi 2:10-16) was because the Jewish women who returned from exile had lost their beauty and aged before their time. "When the Jews drew near from the Exile, the faces of the Jewish women had become blackened by the sun. They therefore left them and married heathen wives." (Rabbi Johanan, cited by Yamauchi)

iii. **They presented a ram of the flock**: "This shows that they sinned against knowledge; for a sin of ignorance the oblation was not a ram, but a goat." (Trapp)

iv. **Some of them had wives by whom they had children**: "Whereby he implies that most of their wives were barren; which came to pass by God's special providence, partly to manifest his displeasure against such matches, and partly that the practice of this great and necessary duty might not be encumbered with too many difficulties." (Poole)

b. **All these had taken pagan wives**: As seen before, the greater problem was that these wives *remained* pagan and refused to join the covenant community. Their break with the people of Israel was grounded in *faith*, not in *race*.

i. "Let us at least separate ourselves after the manner of Christ, who frequented the temple, acknowledged the State, accepted invitations to great houses; but his heart and speech always revolved about his Father." (Meyer)

ii. At this point, Ezra disappears from the Biblical record for about thirteen years, after which he appears again in the Book of Nehemiah. His passion then was the same as it was at the end of the Book of Ezra: to transform the people of God by bringing them the word of God.

Nehemiah 1 – Nehemiah's Prayer

A. Nehemiah hears of Jerusalem's crisis condition.

1. Some 1,000 years after the time of Moses and some 400 years before the birth of Jesus, the nation of Israel and the Jewish people were in a desperate state.

a. Their nations were destroyed, first the northern Jewish kingdom of Israel and then the southern Jewish kingdom of Judah. The city of Jerusalem was completely conquered by the Babylonians and the once glorious temple of Solomon was destroyed.

b. When the Babylonians conquered Jerusalem, they deported almost everyone from the city and the region – for some 70 years, Jerusalem was something of a ghost town, with the potential to end up like many ancient cities – completely forgotten except to history.

c. When the Jews were deported to Babylon, they began to make homes for themselves there. They settled down, and many still followed the God of their fathers, but they did it from Babylon, with no desire to return to the land God had promised to Abraham, Isaac, and Jacob.

i. Some of these faithful Jews were raised up to places of prominence in the governments they were deported to. Daniel, Shadrach, Meshach, and Abed-Nego became leaders in Babylon; Esther was made queen in the courts of a Persian king.

d. But after 70 years of captivity in Babylon, they were given the opportunity to return to their homeland, the Promised Land. Out of some two or three million Jews deported from the land, only 50,000 decided to return to the Promised Land – approximately just 2%. But they did return, and in the days of Ezra, they rebuilt the temple and laid a spiritual foundation for Israel once again.

e. The Book of Nehemiah begins 15 years after the Book of Ezra ends, almost 100 years after the first captives came back to the Promised Land

and some 150 years after the city of Jerusalem was destroyed. After this long time, the walls of the city of Jerusalem were still in rubble.

> i. Before this, the citizens of Jerusalem had tried to rebuild the walls but had failed. In Ezra 4:6-23, we see that about 75 years before they tried to rebuild the walls but were stopped by their enemies. No one thought this obstacle could be overcome, so the walls lay in ruins and the people were still vulnerable.

2. (1-3) Nehemiah hears of Jerusalem's condition.

The words of Nehemiah the son of Hachaliah.

It came to pass in the month of Chislev, *in* the twentieth year, as I was in Shushan the citadel, that Hanani one of my brethren came with men from Judah; and I asked them concerning the Jews who had escaped, who had survived the captivity, and concerning Jerusalem. And they said to me, "The survivors who are left from the captivity in the province *are* there in great distress and reproach. The wall of Jerusalem *is* also broken down, and its gates are burned with fire."

a. **In Shushan the citadel**: Nehemiah lived in **Shushan**, the capital city of the Persians, and he lived in the **citadel** – that is, the fortified palace of the Persians. Right away, we know Nehemiah is someone important, living in the palace of the king of Persia.

b. **I asked them concerning the Jews who had escaped, who had survived the captivity, and concerning Jerusalem**: Nehemiah's body was in Persia, but his heart and his interest were in Jerusalem – 800 miles (1,300 km) away. He wanted to know from those returning how the people and the city were doing.

> i. We might think that a prominent man like Nehemiah had more important things to think about than a distant city he had never been to, and a people he was a stranger to. Yet, because his heart was for the things of God, his heart was not for himself, but for others.

> ii. Nehemiah had the heart of Psalm 137:5-6: *If I forget you, O Jerusalem, let my right hand forget its skill! If I do not remember you, let my tongue cling to the roof of my mouth; if I do not exalt Jerusalem above my chief joy.* If Jerusalem was special to God, then it would also be special to Nehemiah.

c. **The wall of Jerusalem is also broken down, and its gates are burned with fire**: The news he received was not encouraging. The people were called **survivors**; this was not a hopeful title. They were in **great distress and reproach**, and the walls of the city itself were **broken down** and the city **gates** were **burned with fire**.

i. The bad state of the people and the bad state of the city walls were intimately connected. In the ancient world, a city without walls was a city completely open and vulnerable to its enemies. They had no defense, no protection at all.

ii. An *unwalled city* was always vulnerable, unable to safely house people and valuables. If there were anything of value in an unwalled city, it could be stolen away easily because there was no defense to stop it.

iii. Those living in an unwalled city lived in constant stress and tension; they never knew when they might be attacked and brutalized. Every man lived in constant fear for his wife and children. The temple could be rebuilt, but never made beautiful, because anything valuable would be taken easily.

iv. No wonder the people lived in constant **distress**, in constant disgrace (**reproach**), living only as **survivors**. God has more for us than to be mere survivors. God not only wants us to be conquerors, but *more than conquerors through Him who loved us* (Romans 8:37).

v. The rebuilding of Jerusalem's walls would also play a role in God's unfolding plan that is crowned in Jesus Christ. The rebuilding of the walls gave security to Israel so they could survive and prosper, remaining a people so they could bring forth the promised Messiah and fulfill other aspects God appointed for them in His plan of the ages.

3. (4) Nehemiah's reaction to the news about Jerusalem and its people.

So it was, when I heard these words, that I sat down and wept, and mourned *for many* days; I was fasting and praying before the God of heaven.

a. **I sat down and wept**: Nehemiah's immediate reaction was extreme. He didn't just feel bad for Jerusalem and its people; right away, there was no strength in his legs (**I sat down**), and he began to weep and to mourn.

i. Like Jesus would later do, Nehemiah wept over Jerusalem. Nehemiah mourned over Jerusalem regarding God's judgment against them in the past. Jesus mourned over Jerusalem regarding God's coming judgment against them (Matthew 23:37-39).

ii. "As is often the case, a brighter flame of zeal burned in the bosoms of sympathisers at a distance than in those of the actual workers, whose contact with hard realities and petty details disenchanted them." (Maclaren)

b. **Mourned for many days**: God was going to use Nehemiah to *do* something *about* this situation. But first, God *did* something *in* Nehemiah. Any great work of God begins with God doing a great work in somebody.

i. God prepared this long ago, with Nehemiah's important position in Persia, with a heart curious about the welfare of Jerusalem and its people. Now we see that he had a heart that broke over their needy state.

ii. God saw the need from heaven, but little would be done until the right man also felt the need. God would do something great to meet that need through Nehemiah.

iii. But there was no way Nehemiah could do this alone. He had to be a *leader* – one who *influences* other people – to get this job done. Nehemiah is a book all about *leadership* – something we obviously need today. Since leadership is *influence*, leadership applies to everyone. Everyone has an area of leadership. In some way, each person is a leader; the question is if they are a good leader or a bad leader.

iv. Leaders must prepare themselves for difficult work because it won't be easy. "There is no winning without warfare; there is no opportunity without opposition; there is no victory without vigilance. For whenever the people of God say, 'Let us arise and build,' Satan says, 'Let me arise and oppose.'" (Redpath)

v. Leaders must have a big vision, and Nehemiah had one. His mentality seemed to be, "Through me, God is going to correct a problem that's been around a hundred and fifty years. Through me, God is going to do something that completely failed before." We must have a big enough vision and goal.

c. **I was fasting and praying before the God of heaven**: Nehemiah's reaction went beyond an immediate emotion. Many times, a concern will come over us in a flush, and then quickly pass. But if it is from the Lord, it will abide and grow, and the burden will remain until the problem that prompted the burden is solved.

i. We should note as well what Nehemiah did *not* do: he did not complain, whine, or "see who could fix this problem." He immediately did what he knew he could do – pray, and intensely seek God in this situation.

d. **The God of heaven**: Nehemiah also had a clear understanding of the God to whom he fasted and prayed. There are many "gods" people trust in but only the **God of heaven** can really meet our needs.

B. Nehemiah's prayer.

1. (5-7) Nehemiah prays to God in humility.

And I said: "I pray, Lord God of heaven, O great and awesome God, *You* who keep *Your* covenant and mercy with those who love You and observe Your commandments, please let Your ear be attentive and Your eyes open, that You may hear the prayer of Your servant which I pray before You now, day and night, for the children of Israel Your servants, and confess the sins of the children of Israel which we have sinned against You. Both my father's house and I have sinned. We have acted very corruptly against You, and have not kept the commandments, the statutes, nor the ordinances which You commanded Your servant Moses.

a. **I pray**: Prayer is essential to leadership. If a vision is so big that only God can accomplish it, then prayer is obviously necessary. If prayer isn't absolutely necessary to accomplish a vision, the goal isn't big enough.

i. It appears that Nehemiah prayed for four months before he did anything (Nehemiah 1:1-4 and 2:1). Later, when the work of rebuilding the walls began, it only took 52 days to finish the job. Yet that 52-day project had a four-month foundation of prayer.

ii. Nehemiah took his pain and stress to God in prayer – and seemingly, was able to leave it there. Prayer will relieve your stress. A man may try to relieve stress through entertainment, but all that does is distract. Entertainment doesn't give any solutions to stress. Prayer gives strength; when God's people wait on Him in prayer, He will renew their strength (Isaiah 40:31).

b. **I pray, Lord God of heaven**: Humility begins by simply understanding that there is a God enthroned in the heavens, and *I am not Him*. Nehemiah recognized exactly who God is, describing Him with many magnificent titles: **Lord God of heaven, O great and awesome God, You who keep Your covenant and mercy with those who love You.**

c. **Please let Your ear be attentive**: Humility also understands my complete dependence on God. When Nehemiah desperately asked God to **hear the prayer of Your servant** (**let Your ear be attentive...Your eyes open**), it reflected his complete dependence on the Lord. Only God could help, and if God would only **hear**, Nehemiah knew He would help.

i. God will allow His people to be fruitless to expose their need for total dependence.

d. **Confess the sins...which we have sinned against You. Both my father's house and I have sinned**: Humility will also confess sin openly. Nehemiah plainly and simply confessed sin, without any attempt at excusing the sin.

i. Believers must always avoid *excusing* themselves in the confession of sin. God's people should not say, "Lord, *if* I sinned" or "Lord, I'm sorry, but You know how hard it was" or other such nonsense. There is great freedom in open, honest confession, without any attempt at excuse or wondering "if" we sinned or not.

ii. "It is useless to ask God to help us to repair the wastes if we do not cast out the sins which have made them. The beginning of all true healing of sorrow is confession of sins." (Maclaren)

e. **Both my father's house and I have sinned. We have acted very corruptly against You**: Humility identifies with the needy. Obviously, Nehemiah was a godly man; but he openly and passionately identified with his **father's house** and prayed by using **we** instead of "they."

i. "You never lighten the load unless first you have felt the pressure in your own soul. You are never used of God to bring blessing until God has opened your eyes and made you see things as they are." (Redpath)

2. (8-10) Nehemiah comes to God, looking to His promises.

Remember, I pray, the word that You commanded Your servant Moses, saying, 'If you are unfaithful, I will scatter you among the nations; but *if* you return to Me, and keep My commandments and do them, though some of you were cast out to the farthest part of the heavens, *yet* I will gather them from there, and bring them to the place which I have chosen as a dwelling for My name.' Now these *are* Your servants and Your people, whom You have redeemed by Your great power, and by Your strong hand.

a. **Remember**: This is a powerful way to come to God, asking Him to remember His promises. Nehemiah said, "Lord, You made a promise to Moses and this nation, I ask You now to fulfill Your promise." Nehemiah quoted from both Leviticus 26 and Deuteronomy 30.

i. This is, no doubt, the secret to great power in prayer: to *plead the promises of God*. We may be a bit annoyed when one of our children comes to us saying "Daddy, you promised"; but our Father in heaven *delights* in it – and often *demands* it before prayer becomes effective.

ii. In Psalm 81:10, God says to His people, *open your mouth wide, and I will fill it*. God will not open His storehouse until we open our mouths in asking Him to perform His promises.

b. **If you return to Me, and keep My commandments and do them**: Nehemiah quoted a *conditional* promise. The condition was returning to God and keeping His commandments. Nehemiah really couldn't know if the nation was keeping the commandments, but he knew that *he* was keeping them. Because he had identified himself with the nation in their sin the nation could also identify itself with Nehemiah in his godly fulfillment of these conditions.

3. (11) Nehemiah prays with a heart ready to *do* something.

O Lord, I pray, please let Your ear be attentive to the prayer of Your servant, and to the prayer of Your servants who desire to fear Your name; and let Your servant prosper this day, I pray, and grant him mercy in the sight of this man."

For I was the king's cupbearer.

a. **Grant him mercy in the sight of this man**: Nehemiah concluded by asking God to bless him as he spoke to the king of Persia about the matter. Nehemiah was going to *do* something about the tragic state of Jerusalem's walls and people, and he knew that without God's intervention, he could do nothing.

i. In his prayer, Nehemiah referred to the king as **this man**. "However powerful Artaxerxes was, he was but 'this man,' not God. The phrase does not indicate contempt or undervaluing of the solid reality of his absolute power over Nehemiah, but simply expresses the conviction that the king, too, was a subject of God's, and that his heart was in the hand of Jehovah, to [mold] as He would." (Maclaren)

b. **Let Your servant prosper this day**: This is a prayer of a man of *action*, not a sideline critic. Nehemiah does not pray "God, make it all better" or "God, get someone *else* moving on this problem." Instead, his prayer is "God, *use me* to make it better."

i. "Recognition of need must be followed by earnest, persistent waiting upon God until the overwhelming sense of world need becomes a specific burden in my soul for one particular piece of work which God would have me do." (Redpath)

ii. "Laying the matter to heart, he did not begin to speak with other people about what they would do, nor did he draw up a wonderful scheme about what might be done if so many thousand people joined in the enterprise; but it occurred to him that he would do something himself." (Spurgeon)

Nehemiah 2 – Nehemiah's Commission

A. Nehemiah the cupbearer.

1. (1-2) Nehemiah stands before the king.

And it came to pass in the month of Nisan, in the twentieth year of King Artaxerxes, *when* **wine** *was* **before him, that I took the wine and gave it to the king. Now I had never been sad in his presence before. Therefore the king said to me, "Why** *is* **your face sad, since you** *are* **not sick? This** *is* **nothing but sorrow of heart."**

So I became dreadfully afraid,

> a. **I took the wine and gave it to the king**: The last verse of Nehemiah 1 told us that Nehemiah was the *king's cupbearer* – a significant position in any ancient royal court. The cupbearer was a personal *bodyguard* to the king, being the one who tasted wine and food before the king did – making certain no one could poison the king.
>
> > i. "The *cupbearer* was a high official in the royal household, whose basic duty of choosing and tasting the wine to demonstrate that it was not poisoned, and of presenting it to the king, gave him frequent access to the king's presence and made him potentially a man of influence." (Kidner)
> >
> > ii. The cupbearer had to be a man of faithful and impressive character in whom the king could place a tremendous amount of trust. If the cupbearer could be turned against the king, assassination would be easy.
> >
> > iii. The cupbearer was a *servant* to the king; he was responsible for choosing most of the foods and wines the king and the court would enjoy.
> >
> > iv. The cupbearer was also a trusted *advisor* to the king; since he was constantly in the king's presence, greatly trusted, and a man of character, it was natural that the cupbearer would often be asked his opinion on different matters coming before the king.

b. **In the month of Nisan, in the twentieth year of King Artaxerxes**: As Nehemiah gave wine to the king, care was given to note the specific day on which this chapter's events began.

i. Why was it so important for God to tell us the date that these things happened? First, to show that Nehemiah prayed and waited for four months with the kind of heart described previously in Nehemiah 1. During those four months, Nehemiah's prayer was likely "LORD, either take this burden from my heart or show me how to be the man to answer this burden."

ii. The date is also important because it establishes the date given to restore Jerusalem and its walls. Daniel 9:25 says that exactly 173,880 days from this day – which was March 14, 445 B.C. – Messiah the prince would be presented to Israel. Sir Robert Anderson, the eminent British astronomer and mathematician, makes a strong case that Jesus fulfilled this prophecy exactly, to the day, entering Jerusalem on A.D. April 6, 32, precisely 173,880 days from Nehemiah 2:1.

c. **I had never been sad in his presence before**: On that day, Nehemiah noted that he had never been sad or depressed in the presence of the king, and on this day when the king took notice, Nehemiah **became dreadfully afraid**. As was true in the courts of many ancient kings, it was forbidden to be sad in the presence of the king. The idea was that the king was such a wonderful person that merely being in his presence was supposed to make a man forget all his problems. When Nehemiah looked sad, it could have been taken as a terrible insult to the king.

i. When the king said, "**This is nothing but sorrow of heart**," Nehemiah knew the king had noticed his sadness, and that the king took it seriously. Nehemiah must have wondered if the next words from the king would be, "Off with his head!"

ii. Nehemiah was also afraid because he knew that he was going to ask the king for something very important. A great deal depended on the king's response to his question.

iii. Nehemiah understood it was not his place to change the king's heart. He prayed and left it up to the LORD, instead of dropping hints and trying to manipulate the situation. Then one day, four months later, the king's heart was different. Believers must not make the mistake of trying to change someone else's heart, instead of leaving it up to the LORD to do it.

2. (3) Nehemiah's response.

And said to the king, "May the king live forever! Why should my face not be sad, when the city, the place of my fathers' tombs, *lies* waste, and its gates are burned with fire?"

a. **May the king live forever**: Nehemiah had probably said these words many times before. This was probably almost a motto among professional cupbearers; since they tasted the wine and food before the king did, they naturally wished the king a good long life.

b. **The city, the place of my fathers' tombs, lies waste, and its gates are burned with fire**: With this, Nehemiah explained why he was sad. Jerusalem was a destroyed, disgraced city.

i. No one had to tell the king this was a disgraceful state of affairs; he would immediately sympathize with Nehemiah's concern for the dignity, safety, and well-being of his people.

ii. Nehemiah's great tact and wisdom was also evident because he told of his concern without specifically mentioning the name of the city. The king would naturally have a bad association with the name "Jerusalem," knowing from history that it was a city rebellious against the Persians and resistant to their rule. By God's goodness and this wise approach, Nehemiah gained the sympathy of the king before he revealed the city he was concerned about.

c. **Why should my face not be sad**: Nehemiah's answer was not only wise; it was also *honest*. Often, when we are visibly depressed or troubled, and when someone asks us about it, we simply reply "Nothing's wrong" or "Oh, I'm alright." At those times, we are often not *honest*.

i. Many people are troubled by this dilemma. No one wants to be a whiner, boring others with our problems when the other person may only be asking out of common courtesy. On the other hand, we know the tremendous value there can be in sharing our concerns with someone else who can pray with us and perhaps share some wisdom from the Bible.

ii. One way to live in this kind of honesty is to seek out others whom we know and trust, and to share our struggles and needs with them. But if we don't know a person well enough to feel confident sharing our personal life, we can still ask them to pray for us in general. They don't need to know all the details to pray because God knows all the details. Also, when someone asks if we are troubled, we can be open to the idea that this person is a special gift to us at this time.

iii. However, we must avoid two traps. First, we must avoid "shopping" for advice – asking many people, telling all of them our problems until we find the advice we want. Second, we must be especially careful of talking to others in a way that puts the problem on other people – people who aren't there to give their side of the story. Nehemiah didn't say to the king, "I'm sad because those incompetents in Jerusalem have had 100 years to build the walls and they haven't done anything. They are a bunch of hardened, uncaring, worthless people." He described the problem without blaming anyone else. When we fail to do this, there's a word for it: *gossip*.

iv. When we are the person whom others ask for prayer or whom others come to for help, it is helpful to guard against the temptation to know every detail of the problem. Of course, it is *interesting* to hear the details of the problems others have, but we do not need to know all the fine points. Our prayer is still valuable if we don't know all the details. We are not less able to lead them to Jesus for His loving care. Some things need to be talked out more than others, but sometimes we want the other person to talk it out more for *us* than for *them*.

3. (4-8) Nehemiah's request.

Then the king said to me, "What do you request?"

So I prayed to the God of heaven. And I said to the king, "If it pleases the king, and if your servant has found favor in your sight, I ask that you send me to Judah, to the city of my fathers' tombs, that I may rebuild it."

Then the king said to me (the queen also sitting beside him), "How long will your journey be? And when will you return?" So it pleased the king to send me; and I set him a time.

Furthermore I said to the king, "If it pleases the king, let letters be given to me for the governors *of the region* beyond the River, that they must permit me to pass through till I come to Judah, and a letter to Asaph the keeper of the king's forest, that he must give me timber to make beams for the gates of the citadel which *pertains* to the temple, for the city wall, and for the house that I will occupy." And the king granted *them* to me according to the good hand of my God upon me.

a. **What do you request?** Immediately, Nehemiah knew God gave him favor with the king. The king's response wasn't "Off with his head!" but "What can I do to help?" Nehemiah knew that four months of prayer were answered.

b. **So I prayed to the God of heaven**: Knowing his prayer had been answered, Nehemiah prayed again. This was not a long, extended prayer (he could have said, "Well king, let me pray about it for a few days and then I'll get back to you"). Instead, this was an immediate, silent prayer of: "Help me, LORD." Nehemiah knew this was an incredible opportunity, and he did not want to miss the chance.

    i. It is wonderful to labor long in prayer, but prayer does not have to be long to be effective. This is especially true when the situation will not allow a long prayer.

c. **I ask that you send me to Judah**: Nehemiah again showed great wisdom as he respectfully asked for a leave of absence and to be *sent* (**you send me**) by the king. He asked the king to share his concern for Jerusalem and to become a partner in getting the city and its people back to where they should be.

    i. Nehemiah's vision was also revealed: **that I may rebuild it**. That was a huge job and a big goal. Nehemiah wasn't going on a mere fact-finding trip, or simply to tell the leaders of Jerusalem what a bad job they were doing. He went to get the work done, trusting in God all the way.

    ii. Again, Nehemiah shows wisdom by referring to Jerusalem without specifically mentioning the city (**send me to Judah, to the city of my father's tombs**). However, Nehemiah was not being deceptive. Although Jerusalem might have historically been a rebellious city to Persia, it was no longer so – and would not be in the future.

    iii. The king wanted to know **when** Nehemiah would **return**, showing that he valued Nehemiah's service. "There are some servants that I know of, who, if they were to go away, their masters would not be particularly anxious that they should come back again." (Spurgeon)

d. **It pleased the king to send me**: Nehemiah's sympathetic heart, his months of prayer, his moment of prayer, his great faith, his big vision, and his wise responses were all answered positively. The king was enthusiastic about supporting Nehemiah in this venture.

    i. Like Jesus would later do, Nehemiah left a throne room to identify with and bring help to the afflicted people of God. As Jesus did, Nehemiah also received a mission from the king and was sent with purpose.

e. **I set him a time**: As a capable leader, Nehemiah clearly had a *plan*. The four months in prayer were not only spent in talking to God, but also in *listening* to Him and developing a Spirit-led plan of action for the time when God would open the door.

    i. Nehemiah knew how long he would need to be gone (**I set him a time**). He knew he would need letters of safe passage from the king (**let letters be given to me**). He knew what kind of materials would be needed (**timber**). He knew what work needed to be done (**the gates of the citadel...the city wall...the house I will occupy**). Nehemiah knew all of this without ever having seen for himself the condition of Jerusalem. Nehemiah knew the needs by carefully and patiently seeking God.

ii. Nehemiah had a plan, and God always works through a plan. The LORD our God is a planning God: *The counsel of the LORD stands forever, the plans of His heart to all generations.* (Psalm 33:11) From the beginning before the worlds were created, God made a plan of salvation which He is carrying out through history.

iii. Sometimes it may seem that God blesses a lack of planning, and sometimes it seems God does a blessed work completely different from what was planned. But in every case, God works through planning – if not our planning, then His planning. As a general principle, God wants to train His people in the work of being planners, just as He is a planner.

iv. *The plans of the diligent lead surely to plenty, but those of everyone who is hasty, surely to poverty.* (Proverbs 21:5) Faith is no substitute for planning. Believers aren't more spiritual for failing to plan and for improvising. There may be times when planning is impossible, but we should never reject planning when it is possible.

f. **He must give me timber**: Nehemiah was also a bold man, not afraid to ask others to help when he knew they had the available resources. Once the king was willing to be a part of his goal (**it pleased the king to send me**), Nehemiah then asked for an official seal of approval on the project (**letters...for the governors**) and for the king to provide resources (**that he must give me timber**).

i. Nehemiah didn't ask in an effort to take advantage of the king. Instead, he showed honor and respect to the king by inviting him to participate in a worthy work. He knew the king was *able* to provide these things and he sensed the king's heart was *willing*. Therefore, Nehemiah showed the king what to do with his willing heart.

g. **And the king granted them to me according to the good hand of my God upon me**: Though this was a pagan king, Nehemiah still understood that God could work through him in a mighty way. God can provide for our needs in totally unexpected or unlikely ways.

B. Nehemiah comes to Jerusalem.

1. (9-10) Arrival and opposition.

Then I went to the governors *in the region* beyond the River, and gave them the king's letters. Now the king had sent captains of the army and horsemen with me. When Sanballat the Horonite and Tobiah the Ammonite official heard *of it,* they were deeply disturbed that a man had come to seek the well-being of the children of Israel.

a. **Then I went**: This is another example of Nehemiah's godly leadership. He actually **went** – he traveled the 800 miles (1,300 km) from Persia to Jerusalem to do the work of building up the walls and the people.

> i. Many people's hearts are touched like Nehemiah's was. They may have the heart for prayer, the wisdom, the vision, the plan, and the faith of a Nehemiah – but they stop short of actually going out and *doing* what needs to be done for the goal to become a reality.

> ii. Sometimes *talking* about something may be substituted for actually doing the thing. It is one thing to stand around with other believers and talk about doing some evangelism; praying about it, planning it, talking about it – it is another thing to actually go out and *do* it. God is in the *doing* of the thing.

> iii. Our spiritual enemies don't mind if *all* God's people do is plan and pray and talk; but when God's people start *doing* something, they take notice.

> iv. Like Jesus would later do, Nehemiah left the comforts of his previous status to come "down" to God's people in ruin.

b. **Beyond the River**: This means "beyond the Euphrates River," an important landmark that separated one region from another. Once a traveler crossed the river, they were on the road to the region of Judea and the city of Jerusalem. At this point, Nehemiah spoke to the **governors** of this region who ruled under the Persians.

c. **Gave them the king's letters**: Nehemiah came prepared. He had letters showing he was truly sent by the king. He had **captains of the army and horsemen** with him. He also had substantial supplies of lumber from the king's forest. Truly, the king of Persia had responded to Nehemiah's invitation to become a partner in the work of rebuilding the walls of Jerusalem.

d. **Sanballat the Horonite...Tobiah the Ammonite**: At the governor's station, Nehemiah met these two enemies of Jerusalem and of anyone who cared for the welfare of the city. **They were deeply disturbed that a man had come to seek the well-being of the children of Israel.**

i. These two would prefer for Jerusalem to be weak and vulnerable. They were indifferent to the ongoing temple worship, but they despised the thought of God's people being strong, secure, and free from stress.

ii. Notice when this opposition came: not at the heart stage, not at the vision stage, not at the prayer stage, not at the planning stage, but when progress came in *doing* something.

iii. Some people fear ever stepping out for the LORD because they know opposition will come. They somehow think their life will be better or easier if they stay in their low, mediocre state before God. It is a sad deception to believe that one can have a better life through a half-hearted commitment to Jesus Christ. Challenging times will come to everyone, but when believers boldly follow and obey God, they are far better equipped to deal with seasons of difficulty.

2. (11-16) Nehemiah makes a secret tour of Jerusalem and her walls.

So I came to Jerusalem and was there three days. Then I arose in the night, I and a few men with me; I told no one what my God had put in my heart to do at Jerusalem; nor was there any animal with me, except the one on which I rode. And I went out by night through the Valley Gate to the Serpent Well and the Refuse Gate, and viewed the walls of Jerusalem which were broken down and its gates which were burned with fire. Then I went on to the Fountain Gate and to the King's Pool, but *there was* no room for the animal under me to pass. So I went up in the night by the valley, and viewed the wall; then I turned back and entered by the Valley Gate, and so returned. And the officials did not know where I had gone or what I had done; I had not yet told the Jews, the priests, the nobles, the officials, or the others who did the work.

a. **So I came to Jerusalem**: After being in Jerusalem **three days**, Nehemiah had not told anyone why he was there or what God had directed him to do (**I told no one what my God had put in my heart to do at Jerusalem**).

i. When Nehemiah came to Jerusalem with a military escort and lumber from the forest of the king of Persia, people would have noticed him – but he didn't say anything about his mission until the time was right. Good leaders learn a sense of God's timing.

ii. Nehemiah traveled to Jerusalem full of heart, full of prayer, full of faith, full of wisdom, full of a big vision, full of support from the king. When he finally got to his destination, he did nothing for three days. Among other things, this was a display of humility. Like Jesus would later do, Nehemiah came humbly to help those afflicted. Like Jesus would later do, Nehemiah lived in glory, came in sacrifice, and did his greatest work after **three days**.

iii. **I told no one**: "It is good to have Christian friends, but it is dangerous to wear your heart on your sleeve. Have a secret place somewhere which nobody knows anything about but you and God." (Redpath)

iv. "You will often find it best not to commit your plans to others. If you want to serve God, go and do it, and then let other people find it out afterwards. You have no need to tell what you are going to do, and, I may add, there is no need for you retelling what you have done, for very, very frequently God withdraws himself when we boast of what is being done." (Spurgeon)

b. **I went out by night through the Valley Gate**: It seems that Nehemiah set out from the west side of the city, then turned towards the south, continuing counterclockwise around the rubble of the city walls, until returning to his starting point.

c. **And viewed the walls of Jerusalem which were broken down and its gates which were burned with fire**: Nehemiah wasn't just sightseeing. Instead, he carefully studied the **broken down** walls and the burned **gates**. The word **viewed** in Nehemiah 2:13 and 2:15 is a medical term that could be used to describe probing a wound to see the extent of its damage.

i. For the first time, Nehemiah saw with his eyes what had been reported to him, and what God had called him to repair. There was no way he could have made this tour with a dry eye, knowing the extent of the damage and the fear, poverty, and insecurity which the broken walls meant in the lives of the people.

d. **The walls of Jerusalem which were broken down and its gates which were burned with fire**: Nehemiah knew the job of rebuilding the walls couldn't go forward unless he saw exactly how bad the situation was.

i. Nehemiah could have focused on all that was right with Jerusalem. They were back in Judah and the forced exile was over. The temple was built. Sacrifice and worship were conducted. Progress was being made, slow as it was. There was much to be thankful for in Jerusalem – but sometimes, one must look at what is wrong, and that is what Nehemiah did.

ii. We deceive ourselves if we only look at what is good. Some have no trouble with this; they *always* find it easy to see what is wrong. They are full of criticism. They believe they have the unique spiritual gift of pointing out what is wrong. Nehemiah teaches us by example that we must look at the broken-down walls and carefully study what is wrong, but only if we have the heart, the prayer, the vision, the passion to be used of God to set it right. There is little use in the kingdom of God for those who offer advice without really knowing the nature of the problem first-hand.

iii. But with the right hearts – hearts ready to *act* – we must take an honest look. "It is utter folly to refuse to believe that things are as bad as they really are. It is vital in any undertaking for God to know the worst, for whenever there is to be a wonderful movement of the Holy Spirit, it begins with someone like Nehemiah who was bold enough to look at facts, to diagnose them, and then to rise to the task." (Redpath)

iv. When we look at other Christians around us, we see that many are strong, joyful, and growing in their relationship with Jesus Christ. Many have victory over sin, and we are thankful for that. But an onlooker might see the figurative walls in their life and notice some broken-down portions. Some among God's people are desperately hurting or are trapped in a cycle of sin and want to get out, but don't know how to ask for help. Some feel like they are on the outside looking in. Some respect God but haven't yet given their lives to Jesus Christ. God can, and will, build up all the broken-down portions of these figurative walls.

v. When we look at our children, we know that we love them, and we care for them. But when we look at them honestly, we see their weaknesses of character and the areas where they fall short. We soberly consider what will become of them if those weaknesses dominate their entire personality. We consider what will happen if they grow up rejecting Jesus, and the possibility of their future ruin unless God uses us to train and nurture their character.

vi. In the same way, when we look at our business, our relationships, our friendships, we should take an honest look, and not only look at what is pretty.

vii. Similarly, we love the church and are thankful for what God does among His people. But when we look honestly, we are probably not satisfied with the impact we have made on our community. We cannot say our efforts have been sufficient; in fact, our impact should be far greater. We think of the financial support and the outreach and the spread of the word of God through the church, and know that it could be more, and that the ministry could go out further and more broadly.

viii. If someone took a tour of your life the same way Nehemiah took a tour of Jerusalem, they might notice many broken down portions in the figurative walls of your life. Proverbs 25:28 says: *Whoever has no rule over his own spirit is like a city broken down, without walls.* Many lives are like a city with broken walls – living with a constant sense of fear, poverty, and insecurity. We should not hide our eyes from these broken-down places; God wants to change them and make the first steps of change right away.

e. **The walls of Jerusalem which were broken down and its gates which were burned with fire**: As much as anything, Nehemiah took time to count the cost before starting the work. He has a *heart*, he has *faith*, he has a *vision* – but before that vision can become a reality, he must see exactly what must be done, and what it will cost – in terms of time, effort, money, and leadership.

3. (17-18) Nehemiah meets with the leaders of Jerusalem.

Then I said to them, "You see the distress that we *are* in, how Jerusalem *lies* waste, and its gates are burned with fire. Come and let us build the wall of Jerusalem, that we may no longer be a reproach." And I told them of the hand of my God which had been good upon me, and also of the king's words that he had spoken to me.

So they said, "Let us rise up and build." Then they set their hands to *this* good *work*.

a. **You see the distress that we are in**: The citizens and leaders of Jerusalem were not sitting around waiting for a hero to rebuild their walls. Probably, they had come to accept that it was an impossible job. It seemed that no one could fix a 100-year-old problem. Years ago, when others had attempted rebuilding the wall, enemies simply stopped them. So, they lived with it.

b. **Then I said to them**: When Nehemiah came to the leaders of the city and explained his vision for the rebuilding of the walls, there was a tremendous amount of importance attached to the meeting. Nehemiah could not do the job by himself, and he would be in a lot of trouble if the leaders didn't support him.

i. No doubt this was something Nehemiah prayed about a lot. He might have prayed something like this, "O LORD, prepare the hearts of the leaders of Jerusalem to support this work You have called me to. Let them see I do not come condemning or criticizing them, only to help. Give me the right words to say and speak to them ahead of time about this work to which You have called me."

c. **The distress that we are in**: Nehemiah *wisely* approached the leaders of Jerusalem. He had to. In the accomplishment of any vision or goal, or at least of a God-sized vision or goal, certain people will be essential to its accomplishment. By all appearances, their help is necessary. Nehemiah's wise approach gives an example to follow.

- Wisely, Nehemiah asked them to notice the obvious: **You see the distress**; sometimes, the obvious is the hardest to see.

- Wisely, Nehemiah did not speak as if he was there to fix *their* problem: **the distress that *we* are in**. Nehemiah owned the problem as his also, even though he might not have. Nehemiah didn't play the blame game. He didn't criticize the leaders of Jerusalem. He simply identified with them regarding the problem.

- Wisely, Nehemiah asked for their partnership: **Come and let *us* build the wall of Jerusalem**. Nehemiah supposed that if God could move upon the heart of a pagan king to partner in this work, He certainly could move upon the hearts of His own people to join in. Nehemiah wasn't there to do it *for* them, but to partner *with* them in the job of restoring Jerusalem and its people.

- Wisely, Nehemiah pointed them to the result: **that we may no longer be a reproach**. This wasn't really about bricks and mortar; it was about removing a condition of shame, fear, poverty, and insecurity among God's people. The hard work involving bricks and mortar would be worth it because it would have a real spiritual impact on all individuals and the community. When David saw Goliath and was outraged that this monster was casting disgrace on the people of God, he simply said, "*Is there not a cause?*" (1 Samuel 17:29) While everyone else was self-focused and calculating the odds, David said, "Let's get the job done. I'm willing for God to use *me* to do it."

- Wisely, Nehemiah encouraged them in the LORD: **I told them of the hand of my God which had been good upon me**. Nehemiah assured the leaders this wasn't *his* project; it was *God's* project. If people sense your vision is really all about *you*, and raising *you* up, and making *you* great, they will rightly be hesitant. But if it is from God, and they can see it, they will be thrilled to partner with you.

- Wisely, Nehemiah gave them confidence by telling of what God had already done: **I told them...of the king's words that he had spoken to me**. Nehemiah could say, "Look, you can know this is of God; the heart of the king of Persia has been touched by the LORD to support this project." If a cause has evidence of God's hand of blessing on it, many people will want to support it. If it looks like only the ambition or effort of man, supporters will rightly hesitate.

d. **And I told them of the hand of my God which had been good upon me**: It is good to notice what Nehemiah *didn't* do; he didn't beg or make deals. Nehemiah had a high calling from God, and asked others to be part of that vision, but he never stopped treating it like a high calling. He wasn't going to be a carnival barker trying to manipulate people into knocking over milk bottles even when they really didn't want to do it.

> i. Nehemiah didn't offer rewards, incentives, or vacations by the Sea of Galilee for the ones who got the job done. Those are all external motivations and aren't God's highest calling. Nehemiah simply said, "Let's take this seriously. We know there's a job to be done, and God is leading us to get it done now." He relied on the Lord and the leaders to create a true *inward* motivation. External motivations like manipulation, guilt, pressure, or carnal rewards can work for a while but are never God's best way of getting things done.

e. **Let us rise up and build**: This response from the leaders of Jerusalem was of God. They said, "Yes, Nehemiah, we're with you." This was even more remarkable considering the ways they might have responded – ways a believer might respond when they are challenged to partner in a work:

- They might have denied the *need* for the walls. "We have survived without those walls for a hundred years now, and we already have the temple."

- They might have seen the project as *too much work*. "Nehemiah, this is a fine work, and we hope it goes well for you, but we can't help you now."

- They might have seen the *opposition as too strong*. "Nehemiah, it is useless to begin this work, because the last time our enemies stopped us."

> i. Like Jesus would later be, Nehemiah was a builder and built something great and important.

f. **Then they set their hands to this good work**: This shows God's hand at work. Nehemiah's *heart*, his *prayer*, his *boldness*, his *big vision*, his *action*, and his *wisdom* were all rewarded. This was a God-inspired thing; God moved the hearts of the leaders to do this.

> i. It is evident that Nehemiah was a great leader because people followed him. The people he was meant to lead were genuinely influenced by his leadership. Like Jesus would later do, Nehemiah brought others into his work and did his greatest work alongside and through others.

4. (19) The opposition rises in response to the work of God.

But when Sanballat the Horonite, Tobiah the Ammonite official, and Geshem the Arab heard *of it*, they laughed at us and despised us, and said, "What *is* this thing that you are doing? Will you rebel against the king?"

a. **But when Sanballat the Horonite, Tobiah the Ammonite official, and Geshem the Arab heard of it**: Things had been going extraordinarily well, so it is not a surprise that opposition came up again. **Sanballat the Horonite** and **Tobiah the Ammonite official** both came to oppose the work.

> i. Many Christians fail to take account of the reality of spiritual opposition to the work God wants to accomplish and are thus defeated in what God would want them to do.

> ii. The Second Person of the Trinity, Jesus Christ, took on humanity to experience spiritual warfare even as God's people do; He knows what it is to be under attack, to be mocked, how to break through to victory. In every attack, Jesus knows how to lead His people to victory.

b. **Sanballat...Tobiah**: These two first surfaced in Nehemiah 2:10; they *were deeply disturbed that a man had come to seek the well-being of the children of Israel.* They had previously made their opinion known; now they will seek to *do* something about the progress Nehemiah is making.

> i. **Tobiah** (a Jewish name) was a man of influence, being associated with the high priest's family, and receiving help from the priests (Nehemiah 13:4). "Tobiah" was a prominent name in priestly families for generations to come. The name "Tobiah" means "Yahweh is good" – a strange name for a man who was an opponent of the work of God.

> ii. **Sanballat** was connected by marriage to priestly families (Nehemiah 13:28). An ancient document from this period refers to Sanballat as "governor of Samaria." (Kidner)

> iii. **The Horonite**: This may mean that **Sanballat** was associated with Moab. Isaiah 15:5 and Jeremiah 48:3-5 mention *Horonaim* as a place in Moab.

> iv. These men were Jews – fellow brothers – of Nehemiah and the citizens of Jerusalem. We might suppose they would support his work, but they did not. Opposition is always difficult, but when it comes from brothers, it is also mixed with the pain of betrayal.

> v. The Bible makes it clear that God's people also have enemies and opponents, but chiefly they are spiritual enemies: *For we do not wrestle against flesh and blood, but against...spiritual hosts of wickedness in heavenly places* (Ephesians 6:12). However, attacks from spiritual enemies can come through flesh-and-blood people (Matthew 16:23). Believers can experience spiritual attack on a direct inward level from spiritual enemies, or through people who are, wittingly or unwittingly, being used as tools by spiritual adversaries.

c. **They laughed at us and despised us**: Sanballat and Tobiah used scorn in their attack. They wanted Nehemiah to feel mocked, stupid, and foolish. **They laughed at us** shows that they displayed their spite (**and despised us**) with a mocking edge.

    i. This scorn may come to us inwardly, through the feeling that we look foolish to everyone. Or the mocking may come through the words of those who are being used by spiritual adversaries, whether they know it or not.

    ii. Many people are turned away from God's will because they experience or fear scorn. Men who were not afraid of death have been manipulated because they did not want to be laughed at. It seems that sooner or later, God will allow every Christian to be tested in this point, whether they regard man or God most highly. Believers must never be more concerned about what people may say about them than what God requires of them.

    iii. The way that Sanballat and Tobiah used laughter and scorn as weapons against the work of God should also make believers reflect on their own use of humor. Some Christians who are otherwise well-meaning are tools of the enemy, all for the sake of a few laughs.

d. **Will you rebel against the king?** This question shows that Sanballat and Tobiah had a low view of God's authority. Their question reveals that they considered the king of Persia to be the highest authority in the land.

    i. First, they were completely ignorant. They didn't know what they spoke about. The king *had* given permission, even if they didn't know it. The king was a *partner* in the work. Many times, those who are being used against us by our spiritual enemies simply don't know what they are talking about.

    ii. Second, they were not concerned with God's authority. Really, it did not matter if the king of Persia was against this work if the God of heaven and earth was for it. One person aligned with God makes a majority. Nehemiah could have rightly turned the question back on them: *Will you rebel against the King of Kings and Lord of Lords?*

    iii. Like Jesus would later experience, Nehemiah was wrongly accused of rebelling against the king (John 19:12-15).

5. (20) Nehemiah's answer to his opponents.

So I answered them, and said to them, "The God of heaven Himself will prosper us; therefore we His servants will arise and build, but you have no heritage or right or memorial in Jerusalem."

a. **So I answered them**: Nehemiah ignored their scorn. His bold, straightforward words revealed that he had not been put on the defensive by their mocking, scornful attack.

> i. When faced with the choice of pleasing man or pleasing God, Nehemiah knew exactly what he would do. Let them mock – he would serve the LORD.

b. **And said to them**: Nehemiah did not give a point-by-point reply. He did not show the document proving the king's support of the project. If he had, Sanballat and Tobiah would have just claimed it was a forgery or would have come up with another objection. Nehemiah knew that hearts which refuse to be convinced will *never* be convinced.

c. **The God of heaven Himself will prosper us**: Nehemiah instead proclaimed his confidence in God. "It doesn't matter if you are against us. God's work will succeed."

> i. Nehemiah didn't put the work on hold while a crisis response team decided on the best way to answer Sanballat and Tobiah. He wasn't going to let them sidetrack him. He had a work to do, and he was going to do it. If a believer stops the work they should be doing in order to focus completely on their enemies, then their adversaries have won.

> ii. **Will prosper us**: There is a touch of holy boldness in Nehemiah's response. "You may attempt to stop our work, but you will not succeed. God is with us. He isn't with you. You will fail. We will prosper under the hand of the God of heaven."

d. **We His servants will arise and build**: Nehemiah proclaimed *who he was* and *what he would do*.

> i. Nehemiah and his followers were **servants** of God. Sanballat and Tobiah felt confident because they were servants of the king, but Nehemiah was a servant of God.

> ii. Nehemiah and his followers had a job to do. Not for a moment did he doubt that this was God's will. They had agreed to **rise up and build** (Nehemiah 2:18), and they would do it.

> iii. In facing our enemies, we must keep in mind *who we are* and *what we should do*. Failure to recognize these truths will always lead to defeat. These are exactly the things spiritual adversaries want believers to forget. Therefore, it was good for Nehemiah to simply say, **we His servants will arise and build**.

e. **You have no heritage or right or memorial in Jerusalem**: Nehemiah proclaimed the truth about his enemies. They may have been Jews by birth; they may have been legal citizens of Jerusalem; they may have owned property in the city. But their hearts showed that they had no **heritage or right or memorial** in God's city.

i. Nehemiah sized up these two men more quickly than many believers often might. He knew they weren't in favor of him or Jerusalem, or even of God at all – though they may have claimed to be. It was as if Nehemiah said, "You don't belong here. God is doing a great work, and you don't want to be part of it. Just move on."

ii. Believers can say the same to their spiritual adversaries: "You have no heritage or right or memorial in me. I belong to Jesus Christ. You don't belong here. You may as well move on because I'm not going anywhere."

iii. This opposition did not immediately melt away. Believers often wish that the opposition would just go away if they did everything right, like Nehemiah did here. But it didn't. Sanballat and Tobiah opposed the work all that they could, *but they didn't stop it*. God's work was accomplished, and Nehemiah's adversaries were proven completely wrong.

Nehemiah 3 – The Building of the Walls

A. The record of the builders.

1. (1-2) Builders near the Sheep Gate.

Then Eliashib the high priest rose up with his brethren the priests and built the Sheep Gate; they consecrated it and hung its doors. They built as far as the Tower of the Hundred, *and* consecrated it, then as far as the Tower of Hananel. Next to *Eliashib* the men of Jericho built. And next to them Zaccur the son of Imri built.

a. **They built…. built…. built**: Nehemiah 3 is all about work – how individuals pitched in and did the work together, coordinated and led by Nehemiah.

b. **And built the Sheep Gate**: The work is described in reference to the gates of the wall. The gates were the critical entry and exit points to the city, and the places most likely to see an enemy attack. Therefore, the work started at each gate and worked out from there.

i. The **Sheep Gate** was so named because it was the gate where shepherds brought their flocks to sell them. Up until a few years ago, this gate was being used for this same purpose in Jerusalem.

c. **Eliashib the high priest**: This was the first worker mentioned. He **rose up** to do the work with the other priests, and they worked at rebuilding the **Sheep Gate** and the section of wall near there.

i. **Eliashib the high priest** acted as a godly leader should; he was out in front of the work, leading by example. He did not act as if he was too "spiritual" for the hard work of rebuilding the walls.

ii. If someone is a leader, others are looking hard at them and will follow their example. If they are slow to work, they will be also; if they are full of discouragement and doubt, they will follow that pattern. There is a good reason why **Eliashib** was first mentioned, and why the rest of the chapter is filled with the names of more than 50 others that followed his example in the work.

iii. In a wonderful way, the servant **high priest** named **Eliashib** is a beautiful picture of the High Priest to come, who was and is the ultimate servant: Jesus the Messiah.

d. **They consecrated it**: The idea behind consecration is to recognize something as special, as uniquely set apart for God's glory and service. These city gates were made especially for God. Nehemiah and Eliashib knew that God wanted *everything* set apart exclusively for Him, including these city walls and gates.

i. By honoring God at the beginning of the work, they were effectively saying: "All of this work belongs to You, LORD. This is a special work done for You."

ii. This is a great secret to joy and success in life: to do everything as if doing it for the LORD. *And whatever you do in word or deed, do all in the name of the Lord Jesus, giving thanks to God the Father through Him.* (Colossians 3:17)

e. **Next to Eliashib the men of Jericho built**: Every man's work was important, and although these men did not work on a gate, they did the important job of building up the walls of protection and security for Jerusalem. Each person or family was given individual responsibility for their work.

2. (3-5) Builders near the Fish Gate.

Also the sons of Hassenaah built the Fish Gate; they laid its beams and hung its doors with its bolts and bars. And next to them Meremoth the son of Urijah, the son of Koz, made repairs. Next to them Meshullam the son of Berechiah, the son of Meshezabel, made repairs. Next to them Zadok the son of Baana made repairs. Next to them the Tekoites made repairs; but their nobles did not put their shoulders to the work of their Lord.

a. **The Fish Gate**: This gate got its name because of the nearby fish market. The **sons of Hassenaah** did the work of rebuilding the gate while others helped.

b. **Made repairs**: According to Kidner, the word for **repairs** is the Hebrew word *chazaq*, used 35 times in this chapter alone. It has the idea of strengthening, encouraging, of making something strong. These are principles that have application to far more than *material* gates and walls.

i. The Bible says that people must be *built up* and *repaired*. In Ephesians 4:12, God says the purpose of the church is *for the equipping of the saints*, and the idea behind *equipping* is to prepare, strengthen, and make something able to be used. God's people come together as Christians to strengthen one another, to make each other strong and able to live for Jesus and serve Him outside the gatherings of the church.

ii. It's wonderful to consider that Jesus Himself was a builder (Mark 6:3). Of all the professions the Son of God could have chosen, He chose to be a builder. Nehemiah points to Jesus, who is building His people into a beautiful building for the glory of God (1 Corinthians 3:9, Ephesians 2:20-22, 1 Peter, 2:5).

c. **Next to them the Tekoites made repairs**: The **Tekoites** did their work. The people of the city of Tekoa were more than willing to work – **but their nobles did not put their shoulders to the work of their Lord**. For the most part, people joined in – but not *everybody*. These **nobles** from the city of Tekoa thought they were above the hard work, so they didn't join in.

i. Literally, the idea in the Hebrew is that they wouldn't submit – they would not "bend their necks" to what the LORD wanted them to do. The real issue was submission. Maybe they thought they had a better plan, or maybe they didn't like how Nehemiah was doing it. Whatever their reason, it is likely that they later regretted it because they stand in infamy as the only people mentioned in this chapter who *did not* join in the work.

ii. Perhaps Nehemiah wanted to record the *names* of each of these nobles, but the LORD gave him the mercy to refer to them in only a general way.

3. (6-12) Builders near the Old Gate.

Moreover Jehoiada the son of Paseah and Meshullam the son of Besodeiah repaired the Old Gate; they laid its beams and hung its doors, with its bolts and bars. And next to them Melatiah the Gibeonite, Jadon the Meronothite, the men of Gibeon and Mizpah, repaired the residence of the governor *of the region* beyond the River. Next to him Uzziel the son of Harhaiah, one of the goldsmiths, made repairs. Also next to him Hananiah, one of the perfumers, made repairs; and they fortified Jerusalem as far as the Broad Wall. And next to them Rephaiah the son of Hur, leader of half the district of Jerusalem, made repairs. Next to them Jedaiah the son of Harumaph made repairs in front of his house. And next to him Hattush the son of Hashabniah made repairs.

Malchijah the son of Harim and Hashub the son of Pahath-Moab repaired another section, as well as the Tower of the Ovens. And next to him was Shallum the son of Hallohesh, leader of half the district of Jerusalem; he and his daughters made repairs.

a. **Moreover Jehoiada the son of Paseah and Meshullam the son of Besodeiah repaired the Old Gate**: Among the repairers of the **Old Gate** and its nearby walls was **Uzziel, the son of Harhaiah, one of the goldsmiths**. Alongside him was **Hananiah, one of the perfumers**.

  i. These were men of different professions, not professional builders. They were not trained for this kind of work. It would have seemed they had an easy excuse to not do anything, but they jumped in and did the work. **They fortified Jerusalem**, even though many would not think them qualified or able.

  ii. The most important ability in the work of the LORD is *availability*. The one with few gifts and little talent, who has passion and drive to see God's work done, will accomplish far more than a gifted and talented person who doesn't have the passion and drive to do the LORD's work.

  iii. "Viggo Olsen, who helped rebuild ten thousand houses in war-ravaged Bangladesh in 1972, derived unexpected inspiration from reading a chapter ordinarily considered one of the least interesting in the Bible: 'I was struck...that no expert builders were listed in the "Holy Land brigade." There were priests, priests' helpers, goldsmiths, perfume makers, and women, but no expert builders or carpenters were named.'" (Yamauchi)

b. **The Broad Wall**: Today the remains of this **Broad Wall** are on display in Jerusalem and the wall is broad, more than 20 feet (6 meters) wide. Critics attempt to deny the accuracy of biblical history, but the archaeologist's shovel confirms the truth of the Bible again and again.

  i. In a sermon on this text, Charles Spurgeon used Jerusalem as a symbol or type of the church and said there is a **broad wall** around the church, one that speaks of *separation, security*, and *enjoyment*. The character and benefits of a **broad wall** should also mark the individual Christian life.

  ii. "My business is to say to those of you who profess to be the Lord's people, *take care that you maintain a broad wall of separation between yourselves and the world*. I do not say that you are to adopt any peculiarity of dress, or to take up some singular style of speech.... The separation which we plead for is moral and spiritual. Its foundation is laid deep in the heart, and its substantial reality is very palpable in the life." (Spurgeon)

c. **Rephaiah the son of Hur, leader of half the district of Jerusalem**: Here was another **leader** who knew the value of example and active involvement in the work. **Rephaiah** didn't expect others to do the work as he sat idle; he joined in the work himself.

d. **Jedaiah the son of Harumaph made repairs in front of his house**: Several times in the Nehemiah 3, it speaks of those who worked on the section right in front of their **house**. Often, believers need to give attention to the work of God in their own homes. If the work needs to be done anywhere, it needs to be done in one's own home.

i. The names of the men who are said to have **made repairs in front of his house** are interesting:

- Nehemiah 3:10 mentions **Jedaiah**, and his name means *he who calls unto God*. Our homes must be places of prayer, where the family calls on God.

- Nehemiah 3:23 mentions *Benjamin*, and his name means *son of my right hand*, speaking of a protector. Our homes must be places of protection and peace.

- Nehemiah 3:29 mentions *Zadok*, and his name means *justice*. Our homes must be places of justice and integrity, especially with integrity regarding our marital vows and promises.

- Nehemiah 3:30 mentions *Meshullam*, and his name means *devoted*. Our homes must be places of devotion and separation to God.

e. **Malchijah son of Harim**: This man is mentioned in Ezra 10:31 as one of the men who was confronted by Ezra for the sin of taking a pagan wife. That happened many years before this, so **Malchijah** got things right with God and now, years later, he served Him.

i. A believer should never let a past failure get in the way of serving God. Repent, set it right, make a stand for righteousness – and get on serving the LORD.

f. **Shallum the son of Hallohesh...he and his daughters made repairs**: *Everyone* who could help did help in the repairs.

i. With the great number of different people working on the walls, it was imperative that they all work with the same mind, otherwise the wall would not be uniform and would fail as a strong defense. Yet each section was a little different because different people worked on each section.

ii. In the same way, in the family of God, the work must be done with a common vision and mindset – *the mind of Christ*, as Paul described in 1 Corinthians 2:16. When believers work together in one accord, with each person offering their distinctive gifts, the work of God gets done in a glorious way.

4. (13) Builders near the Valley Gate.

Hanun and the inhabitants of Zanoah repaired the Valley Gate. They built it, hung its doors with its bolts and bars, and *repaired* **a thousand cubits of the wall as far as the Refuse Gate.**

5. (14) Builders near the Refuse Gate.

Malchijah the son of Rechab, leader of the district of Beth Haccerem, repaired the Refuse Gate; he built it and hung its doors with its bolts and bars.

6. (15-25) Builders near the Fountain Gate.

Shallun the son of Col-Hozeh, leader of the district of Mizpah, repaired the Fountain Gate; he built it, covered it, hung its doors with its bolts and bars, and repaired the wall of the Pool of Shelah by the King's Garden, as far as the stairs that go down from the City of David. After him Nehemiah the son of Azbuk, leader of half the district of Beth Zur, made repairs as far as *the place* **in front of the tombs of David, to the man-made pool, and as far as the House of the Mighty.**

After him the Levites, *under* **Rehum the son of Bani, made repairs. Next to him Hashabiah, leader of half the district of Keilah, made repairs for his district. After him their brethren,** *under* **Bavai the son of Henadad, leader of the** *other* **half of the district of Keilah, made repairs. And next to him Ezer the son of Jeshua, the leader of Mizpah, repaired another section in front of the Ascent to the Armory at the buttress. After him Baruch the son of Zabbai carefully repaired the other section, from the buttress to the door of the house of Eliashib the high priest. After him Meremoth the son of Urijah, the son of Koz, repaired another section, from the door of the house of Eliashib to the end of the house of Eliashib.**

And after him the priests, the men of the plain, made repairs. After him Benjamin and Hasshub made repairs opposite their house. After them Azariah the son of Maaseiah, the son of Ananiah, made repairs by his house. After him Binnui the son of Henadad repaired another section, from the house of Azariah to the buttress, even as far as the corner. Palal the son of Uzai *made repairs* **opposite the buttress, and on the tower which projects from the king's upper house that** *was* **by the court of the prison. After him Pedaiah the son of Parosh** *made repairs.*

a. **By the King's Garden**: Charles Spurgeon preached a beautiful sermon on this text, where he spoke of six different gardens of the King:

- Eden
- Gethsemane
- The garden tomb
- The human heart
- The church as a whole
- The garden of paradise in heaven

7. (26-27) Builders near the Water Gate.

Moreover the Nethinim who dwelt in Ophel *made repairs* as far as *the place* in front of the Water Gate toward the east, and on the projecting tower. After them the Tekoites repaired another section, next to the great projecting tower, and as far as the wall of Ophel.

a. **The Tekoites repaired another section**: The section of wall near the Water Gate saw some remarkable service. Apparently, the **Tekoites** weren't satisfied with the significant work they had done before, so they went on to do even more work. They didn't allow the bad example of their nobles who refused to work (Nehemiah 3:5) keep them from working above and beyond the call of duty.

8. (28-30) Builders near the Horse Gate.

Beyond the Horse Gate the priests made repairs, each in front of his *own* house. After them Zadok the son of Immer made repairs in front of his *own* house. After him Shemaiah the son of Shechaniah, the keeper of the East Gate, made repairs. After him Hananiah the son of Shelemiah, and Hanun, the sixth son of Zalaph, repaired another section. After him Meshullam the son of Berechiah made repairs in front of his dwelling.

a. **Shemaiah the son of Shechaniah, the keeper of the East Gate**: Apparently the gate in front of his house was in good condition, so he pitched in and helped at the **Horse Gate**. His unselfishness was a great example.

b. **Meshullam the son of Berechiah made repairs in front of his dwelling**: The Hebrew word for **dwelling** is actually *chamber* – it refers to a singular room. **Meshullam** had only one small room, yet he was devoted to God and to the work of rebuilding the walls. It is better to be devoted to God in one small room than to have a mansion and have a heart cold towards God.

9. (31-32) Builders near the Miphkad (muster or assembly) Gate.

After him Malchijah, one of the goldsmiths, made repairs as far as the house of the Nethinim and of the merchants, in front of the Miphkad Gate, and as far as the upper room at the corner. And between the

upper room at the corner, as far as the Sheep Gate, the goldsmiths and the merchants made repairs.

B. Observations on Nehemiah 3.

1. This chapter shows the need for believers to work together to accomplish something.

a. It pleased God to see His people working together in one accord, with one heart and one mind. God will put believers into situations where they *must* work together and learn how to lead, how to follow, and how to operate with one heart and mind.

b. The wall was continuous. Any gap compromised the entire structure. Therefore, each breach in the wall was potentially dangerous, even if someone did not think so. Furthermore, the wall could never be strong if someone was tearing it down at a different section.

2. The work done was a reflection of each family – almost everyone mentioned is mentioned as the *son of* someone.

a. It is in the family that our children learn how to work. Parents must be committed to teaching their children how to be hard workers. In a spiritual sense, our hard work – or lack of it – is a reflection of our spiritual family. Each Christian should be a good reflection of their spiritual family.

3. Evidence of Nehemiah's leadership.

a. Nehemiah was an effective leader because he made each man accountable for his work. Each man had a section of wall he was responsible for, and it was known he was responsible for it. No one wanted it to be seen that they were a poor worker in God's cause.

i. By giving each man responsibility for the work, they helped ensure the work would be done correctly. It made each man accountable.

b. Nehemiah was an effective leader because he noted who did the work and who didn't – the list demonstrates this.

c. Nehemiah was an effective leader because he organized the work for maximum efficiency. Everyone had their section, and the work was organized around the gates, the places most needful of the work.

d. Nehemiah was an effective leader because he knew where to start. He began with the spiritual aspect of the work (the high priest's work is mentioned first), and by consecrating everything to God.

e. Nehemiah was an effective leader because he got both "high" and "low" people to join together in doing the work. The leaders and the high priest worked together with the man who lived in a single room.

f. Nehemiah was an effective leader because he was willing to let people try new things – goldsmiths, priests, and perfumers all became construction workers.

g. Nehemiah was an effective leader because he made people focus on their own house first.

h. Nehemiah was an effective leader because he didn't disqualify people because of past sin and compromise.

4. Seeing Jesus in the building work.

a. Jesus is a builder, greater than Nehemiah (Mark 6:3; 1 Corinthians 3:9, Ephesians 2:20-22, 1 Peter 2:5). Like Jesus, Nehemiah revived a dead work.

b. Jesus is the servant High Priest, greater than Eliashib.

c. Jesus is the Messiah, whose birth was made possible by the work of building the wall and establishing security for the vulnerable people of God.

Nehemiah 4 – Enemies Try to Stop the Work

A. Sanballat and Tobiah ridicule the work of God.

1. (1-3) The attempt to discourage the workers.

But it so happened, when Sanballat heard that we were rebuilding the wall, that he was furious and very indignant, and mocked the Jews. And he spoke before his brethren and the army of Samaria, and said, "What are these feeble Jews doing? Will they fortify themselves? Will they offer sacrifices? Will they complete it in a day? Will they revive the stones from the heaps of rubbish—*stones* that are burned?"

Now Tobiah the Ammonite *was* beside him, and he said, "Whatever they build, if even a fox goes up *on it,* he will break down their stone wall."

a. **But it so happened, when Sanballat heard that we were rebuilding the wall, that he was furious and very indignant**: Sanballat and Tobiah were first *deeply disturbed* when they heard a man wanted to help the people of Jerusalem (Nehemiah 2:10). Then they used scorn and intimidation to prevent the work from starting (Nehemiah 2:19). Now that the work had begun, they were **furious and very indignant**.

i. "There never was a good work yet but what there were some to oppose it, and there never will be till the Lord comes." (Spurgeon)

b. **And mocked the Jews**: The nature of their discouraging attack is evident. They used a mocking, sarcastic tone and **mocked the Jews…. these feeble Jews…. will they…. will they…. will they…. if even a fox goes up on it, he will break down their stone wall**.

i. **Will they offer sacrifices?** This has the idea of, "Will they seek God through sacrifice and expect Him to miraculously build the walls? Will they pray the walls into existence?" **Will they complete it in a day?** This has the idea of, "Do they have any idea what they are taking on? This isn't an easy project."

ii. Like most attacks of discouragement, there is a trace of truth in the words of the enemy. As builders, the Jews were **feeble**. They would not **complete it in a day**. They didn't have the best materials to work with. A lying, discouraging attack will often have *some* truth in it, but it will neglect the great truth: that *God is with us and has promised to see us through.*

iii. Sanballat and Tobiah sought to bring discouragement through criticism. Charles Swindoll pointed out that many people took part in the sarcastic, mocking criticism – and observed "critics run with critics." One mark of a leader is to be able to measure criticism. Leaders must not allow themselves to be run down by critical remarks, and need to remain sensitive to God's voice in the midst of criticism.

iv. Discouragement is a powerful weapon, because it directly opposes faith. Where faith believes God and His love and promises, discouragement looks for and believes the worst. It tends forget about who God is and what He has promised to do.

v. There was also a mocking element to their opposition. "The enemies of God's people generally take to sneering. It is a very easy way of showing opposition…. No doubt these questions were thought to be very witty and very sarcastic. The enemies of Christ are generally good hands at this kind of thing." (Spurgeon)

c. **He will break down their stone wall**: Tobiah made a huge mistake. He called the wall *their* **stone wall**; it wasn't **their** wall at all, but God's – he was criticizing God's wall, God's work.

i. Critics who bring only discouragement often miss what God is doing; because they don't like the wall, they can't believe it is God's work. In the same way, the church is God's church; Jesus loves His bride. A believer should always be careful about the way they talk about Jesus' bride.

d. **Furious and very indignant, and mocked the Jews**: Because Nehemiah and the workers did in fact have legal protection from the king (proven by the *letters* mentioned in Nehemiah 2:7), Sanballat and Tobiah had no authority to actually stop the work. All they could do was discourage the Jews from continuing the work.

i. The exact same attack comes into the lives of believers who are legally set free by their King, yet at times they are discouraged from completing the work God gave them to do.

ii. Believers work differently when they are believing compared to when they are discouraged. Believers pray differently under faith or under discouragement. Believers read and hear the word differently under faith or under discouragement. It is no wonder that Satan works so hard to keep God's people from faith and keep them in discouragement.

iii. *Now the just shall live by faith; but if anyone draws back, My soul has no pleasure in him. But we are not of those who draw back to perdition, but of those who believe to the saving of the soul.* (Hebrews 10:38-39)

2. (4-5) Nehemiah comes against the discouraging attack with prayer.

Hear, O our God, for we are despised; turn their reproach on their own heads, and give them as plunder to a land of captivity! Do not cover their iniquity, and do not let their sin be blotted out from before You; for they have provoked *You* to anger before the builders.

a. **Hear, O our God**: Nehemiah's response was a great example. He didn't debate, he didn't form a committee, he didn't even deal with the two enemies directly. Instead, he took it to God in prayer.

i. For Nehemiah, prayer was a first resource, not a last resort. When times of opposition come, God wants us to rely on Him – and the purest way of expressing our reliance on God is through prayer. Like Jesus would later do, Nehemiah found strength and comfort to fulfill God's will in difficult circumstances through prayer.

b. **Hear, O our God, for we are despised**: In his prayer, Nehemiah first asked for God's attention and mercy. God did care about Nehemiah and the work of rebuilding, but Nehemiah needed God to *display* it and he also needed to *sense* God's presence and care.

c. **Turn their reproach on their own heads...give them as plunder.... do not cover their iniquity**: Nehemiah next asked God to fight their enemies for them. He depended on God to fight the battle. God gave him a work to do, and he would not be distracted from it.

i. This prayer seems rather severe, but prayers in the Psalms are even more severe: *Break their teeth in their mouth, O God* (Psalm 58:6). *Let their dwelling place be desolate; let no one live in their tents* (Psalm 69:25). It is proper for the children of God to pray such a prayer because they are giving their violent inclinations over to God and letting *Him* deal with them.

ii. If a believer is angry with someone or has a real enemy, they can deal with them in prayer. We don't pray evil over our enemies; we simply turn them over to a good and just God who knows exactly what to do with them.

d. **They have provoked You to anger**: Finally, Nehemiah's prayer gave God a reason to show mercy and to come against His enemies. Nehemiah recognized that this was *God's* cause, not his own.

3. (6) The result after the attack and Nehemiah's defense in prayer: the work continues with greater strength.

So we built the wall, and the entire wall was joined together up to half its *height*, for the people had a mind to work.

a. **So we built the wall**: God answered Nehemiah's prayer by giving them all **a mind to work**. A **mind to work** is a gift from God, and no significant job will ever be accomplished until people come together with **a mind to work**.

i. This is exactly what Satan wants to destroy with his attacks – the **mind to work**. He wants to make us feel defeated, or passive, or self-focused, or discouraged.

ii. "Critics demoralize. Leaders encourage. When the critics spoke, the workmen heard them and were demoralized. But when the capable leader stepped up and said, 'Let's look at it God's way, stay at the job,' the crew members were back in there." (Swindoll)

iii. **So we built the wall**: "You half expected to read, 'So we stopped building the wall, and answered Sanballat and Tobiah.' Not a bit of it. They kept to their work and let these two men scoff as they pleased." (Spurgeon)

b. **For the people had a mind to work**: The immediate answer to this prayer was not that their enemies changed. The prayer was answered by the people of God doing the work. Nehemiah's prayer asked God to take care of his enemies, and God answered by taking care of His people.

i. Believers often miss God's answer to their prayers when they pray for Him to do a work in the lives of others they conflict with, yet He answers by moving in their own lives, and they resist this work. It is as if He tried to give **a mind to work** in a situation, but a believer resisted it.

c. **The entire wall was joined together up to half its height**: The work was half finished. It was an exciting, but dangerous time; much had been done, but much was left to do. Fatigue and discouragement were ready to set in, if given an opportunity.

B. Sanballat and Tobiah plan to lead a violent attack against the work.

1. (7-8) The conspiracy to attack the work.

Now it happened, when Sanballat, Tobiah, the Arabs, the Ammonites, and the Ashdodites heard that the walls of Jerusalem were being restored and the gaps were beginning to be closed, that they became very angry, and all of them conspired together to come *and* attack Jerusalem and create confusion.

a. **The gaps were beginning to be closed**: The wall was only half as high as it should be, but it was almost continuous now. Therefore, the enemies of the work **became very angry**.

i. It must be that the work of God often makes the enemy of our soul angry. He must often rage against the progress being made by God's people in touching a lost world for Jesus Christ. It's not a bad thing to make the devil angry.

b. **All of them conspired together to come and attack**: As the work progressed, the enemies became more serious. They were no longer simply complaining or mocking but threatening and planning for violence.

i. On the one hand, this was serious: the wall was built to protect against attacks of violence, and now it seemed that the very building of the wall might prompt an attack to come. It would have been easy for the people to fear and to think perhaps all their work would be made useless.

ii. On the other hand, this wasn't serious at all. It is to be noted that they *didn't attack* – they just talked about it. Sanballat and Tobiah were hoping that the *threat* of attack would be enough. Satan uses the same strategy of fear against God's people. If they are paralyzed by a threat, the threat has worked, even when nothing actually happens.

iii. **All of them conspired**: "It has always struck me as a very startling thing, that you have never heard of any division among the devils in hell. There are no sects among the devils; they seem to work together with an awful unanimity of purpose in their wicked design. In this one thing they seem to excel the family of God. Oh, that we were as hearty and united in the service of God as wicked men are in the service of Satan!" (Spurgeon)

c. **And create confusion**: This was an important strategy of Satan – to create confusion among the people of God. Confused people will never move forward and fulfill God's work. They are usually confused because they are distracted by the tricks of their enemies instead of focusing on God and His promises.

2. (9) The attack is guarded against by prayer and watching.

Nevertheless we made our prayer to our God, and because of them we set a watch against them day and night.

a. **Nevertheless we made our prayer to our God**: Nothing would make them stop depending on God through prayer. They might have given up, believing the continued attack was a failure on God's part to answer their earlier prayers, but they had more trust in God than that.

i. God allowed the attack to go on, even though He could have instantly swept it away. God allowed it to continue because He was delighted that His people drew closer to Him with a deeper trust than ever before. God did His perfect work *both* in building up the walls and His people.

ii. **Nevertheless**: "If we pull it to pieces, we get three words, never the less; when certain things happen, we will pray never the less; on the contrary, we will cry to our God all the more. Sanballat sneered; but we prayed never the less, but all the more because of his sneers. Tobiah uttered a cutting jest; but we prayed never the less, but all the more because of his mocking taunt." (Spurgeon)

b. **We set a watch**: They also knew that prayer didn't mean they were to do *nothing*. They used sanctified common sense to do what was necessary, protecting against attack, using willing servants of God to *be* the wall until the wall was built.

i. It isn't hard to imagine some super-spiritual among them saying, "Now Nehemiah, we don't need to **set a watch**. We have prayed, and God will protect us." Nehemiah would probably respond, "Yes, God will protect us, and He will as He finds us doing our duty before Him. Set the guard."

ii. When a believer sees an area of their Christian life that needs particular attention, it isn't enough to pray. They need to set a watch as well – giving special attention and accountability to that area of their life until they are walking in consistent victory.

iii. Prayers do not replace our actions; rather, they make our actions effective for God's work. In Nehemiah's day and in every generation since, both prayer and watching are important. "One will help the other. Prayer will call out the watchman, prayer will incite him to keep his eyes open, prayer will be the food to sustain him during the night, prayer will be the fire to warn him. On the other hand, watching will help prayer, for watching proves prayer to be true. Watching excites prayer, for every enemy we see will move us to pray more earnestly." (Spurgeon)

c. **Day and night**: This shows that Nehemiah was determined. He wouldn't let the security of daylight or the sleepiness of night keep him from the work. This sent a powerful message.

> i. It sent a message to the people of God saying, "We are committed. This is going to succeed, because God is with us and will enable us to overcome every obstacle."

> ii. It sent a message to the enemies saying, "You will not succeed. God's work is going on and will not be stopped. We will make whatever sacrifices necessary to see it done – weary days, sleepless nights, it doesn't matter."

> iii. It sent a message to God: "We trust in You, and our faith is a living faith – a faith of actions, not just words. We love and trust You, LORD."

C. Challenges from the inside and the outside.

1. (10) The challenge from the inside: discouragement among the people because the work seemed too big.

Then Judah said, "The strength of the laborers is failing, and *there is* so much rubbish that we are not able to build the wall."

a. **Then Judah said**: Judah was supposed to be the strongest, bravest tribe. It was the tribe of great kings and, ultimately, the Messiah Himself. It was a challenging discouragement to have this word come from the tribe of Judah.

> i. Nehemiah and the Jews rebuilding Jerusalem had been standing strong in the face of attack; but now that the rebuilding work was at the halfway point, and the wall was almost continuous, particular challenges arose.

> ii. "Judah, instead of being lion-hearted, made a noise more like a mouse than a lion…. Poor Judah! He ought to have been bolder and braver; but he was not. It is the same to-day; some who seem to be pillars, prove very weak in the hour of trial, and by their cowardice discourage the rest." (Spurgeon)

b. **The strength of the laborers is failing**: The halfway point (mentioned in Nehemiah 4:6) is a dangerous place. Much remains to be done, but fatigue sets in because much has already been done.

> i. It isn't enough to just begin well. Many a team has had a great first half – only to lose in the final minutes. The rebuilding work has gone very well, and many obstacles have been overcome – but the job isn't done yet, the game isn't over yet, and victory is not yet certain.

c. **There is so much rubbish**: The work of rebuilding the walls meant not only construction but cleaning and hauling away the rubbish. The ruins of the walls, lying in waste for 100 years, had become a collecting point for all kinds of rubbish.

i. Clearing away the rubbish was not an option – it had to be done. The destroyed parts of the wall and the accumulated rubbish had to be cleared away so the walls could be rebuilt upon their foundations. If they didn't do this, the walls wouldn't stand at all.

ii. In our Christian life, nothing much can be built for God's glory unless the rubbish is swept away as well. Taking out the garbage can be discouraging work, but it must be done.

iii. "Now, this, it seems to me, is intended, or at least may justifiably be used, for a type of the work which God's people have to carry on in the name of Jesus, and in the power of his Spirit, in the world. We have to build the wall of the church for God, but we cannot build it, for there is so much rubbish in our way. This is true, first, *of the building of the church, which is the Jerusalem of God*; and this is equally true *of the temple of God, which is to be built in each one of our hearts*." (Spurgeon)

iv. Spurgeon described the kind of **rubbish** that a believer may need to deal with: "Ah, brethren, much more of such rubbish remains in us. Oh, the rubbish of pride, of unbelief, of evil lustings, of anger, of despondency, of self-exaltation!" To these Spurgeon added the rubbish of legalism, bad habits, worldly associations, self-promotion, and perfectionism.

d. **We are not able to build the wall**: So, the excavation work had to start. Before they could build the walls up, they had to tear down and clear away the rubbish. They had to go down before they could go up.

i. It was difficult because often the work of building is a lot easier – or more fun – than clearing away the rubbish.

ii. It was difficult because as the mound of rubbish was torn down, the city was even more vulnerable than before. Some probably thought, "Don't take away the rubbish; our enemies are near, and you are merely clearing a path for them to come in."

iii. It was difficult because there have always been those who will defend any heap of rubbish, no matter how useless it is. "My grandfather lived with that pile of rubbish, and if it was good enough for him, it is good enough for us today." This is bad thinking; the old should be cleared away, so that building can begin on the true foundation.

iv. It was difficult because the strength of the laborers was failing.

The heart of the people as shown in verse 10 must have been a discouragement for Nehemiah; it's easy to lead when they followers are full of enthusiasm and have a heart to work. But what happens when the excitement begins to fade?

2. (11) The challenge from the outside: the enemies plan a surprise attack.

And our adversaries said, "They will neither know nor see anything, till we come into their midst and kill them and cause the work to cease."

a. **And our adversaries said**: Verse 10 may mark the lowest point in the spirits of those doing the work. Things were already in a bad state, and the discouraged workers felt like giving up. *Now* the enemy planned its raid on the workers, to crush those rebuilding the walls.

b. **They will neither know nor see anything**: It is doubtful whether these enemies knew exactly how discouraged the people of God were. But certainly, the counsels of spiritual darkness in high places knew – and the attack was planned.

i. We can almost imagine the spiritual ranks of darkness suggesting to the adversaries of God's people: "Now is the time to attack. Do not delay, and you will crush them." They knew that Israel's state of discouragement made a victory for evil possible.

ii. The attacks believers suffer from spiritual forces of darkness are just as strategically timed. Our spiritual adversaries know when we are discouraged, tired, angry, or proud in our self-confidence.

c. **They will neither know nor see anything**: Often, attacks from the adversary are successful only if they come as a surprise. When God's people are on guard, the enemy sees little victory.

d. **Kill them and cause the work to cease**: The enemies of God's people paid a back-handed compliment by saying this. They knew by now the only way to get them to stop serving God and doing His work was to **kill them**.

i. This cannot be said of every servant of God today. For many, the devil does not have to kill them because discouragement, compromise, money, relationships, frustration, or trouble get them to stop serving God.

3. (12) God allows the Jews to be warned about the coming attack.

So it was, when the Jews who dwelt near them came, that they told us ten times, "From whatever place you turn, *they will be* upon us."

a. **The Jews who dwelt near them came**: This is a wonderful example of the power and goodness of God. The enemies of God and His people did their best, but God was always in control. The enemies did not know there were faithful Jews listening to their plotting.

b. **They told us ten times**: It is easy to picture this scene, and see the informants repeatedly saying, "An attack is coming, and our enemies will defeat us." **From whatever place you turn, they will be upon us!**

i. Those who overheard the plan didn't have the wisdom to know what to do in response. They were in a panic, and they were probably troubled that Nehemiah didn't join in the panic.

4. (13-14) Nehemiah organizes the defense.

Therefore I positioned *men* behind the lower parts of the wall, at the openings; and I set the people according to their families, with their swords, their spears, and their bows. And I looked, and arose and said to the nobles, to the leaders, and to the rest of the people, "Do not be afraid of them. Remember the Lord, great and awesome, and fight for your brethren, your sons, your daughters, your wives, and your houses."

a. **Therefore**: These verses tell us what Nehemiah did, but what Nehemiah *could* have done in this situation may also be considered.

i. He could have done *nothing* – and even been spiritual about it. "Well brother, we're just trusting in the Lord. We prayed about it and believe that the Lord will deliver us somehow."

ii. He could have *panicked* – and started thinking it was his job alone to defend against the attack.

iii. He could have doubted God. Instead, he *wisely and calmly trusted God* amid the storm. He did the practical things God would have him do to gain the victory.

b. **Their swords, their spears, and their bows**: Nehemiah commanded them to bring out their armor. It was time to get serious, to put on the full armor, and to get ready to fight with every resource they had.

i. **According to their families**: "I like the common-sense of Nehemiah. He kept families together." (Spurgeon)

ii. **Swords, spears, bows**: In contrast to Jesus, Nehemiah fought with weapons of earthly warfare; Jesus fought with heavenly and spiritual weapons.

c. **Do not be afraid of them. Remember the Lord, great and awesome**: Nehemiah put things in perspective. The challenge was great but there was no reason for fear. He who was *in them* was greater than he who was in the world (1 John 4:4).

d. **Fight for your brethren, your sons, your daughters, your wives, and your houses**: Nehemiah reminded them what they were fighting for. Believers fight most effectively for the Lord when they keep in mind how much there is to lose.

5. (15) The enemies shrink back.

And it happened, when our enemies heard that it was known to us, and *that* God had brought their plot to nothing, that all of us returned to the wall, everyone to his work.

a. **When our enemies heard that it was known to us, and that God had brought their plot to nothing**: Once they saw the defenses of the people of God, the enemies shrunk back. They didn't want a battle because they knew they would lose. What the enemies wanted was for the people of God to hand them an easy victory by failing to watch and be ready.

b. **All of us returned to the wall, everyone to his work**: *This* was the victory. Defending against the attack was not a victory; the people of God would not be at peace and would not live in security until the wall was rebuilt. Getting on with the work was the victory.

i. When believers are under spiritual attack it is easy to feel that just enduring the storm is the victory. It isn't. The attack often comes to prevent *progress and work* for the LORD. Victory is enduring the attack *and* continuing the progress and work for the LORD.

6. (16-18) The sword and the trowel.

So it was, from that time on, *that* half of my servants worked at construction, while the other half held the spears, the shields, the bows, and *wore* armor; and the leaders *were* behind all the house of Judah. Those who built on the wall, and those who carried burdens, loaded themselves so that with one hand they worked at construction, and with the other held a weapon. Every one of the builders had his sword girded at his side as he built. And the one who sounded the trumpet *was* beside me.

a. **So that with one hand they worked at construction, and with the other held a weapon**: Some of the servants did the work of defending and some did the work of building. The workers had a sword at their side and a trowel in their hands to get the work done. The kingdom of God is built with both a sword and a trowel, a sword to come against every spiritual force of wickedness in high places, and a trowel to do the work of building up the people of God.

i. "God's workers must be prepared for warfare as well as building. There have been epochs in which that necessity was realised in a very sad manner; and the Church on earth will always have to be the Church militant. But it is well to remember that building is the end, and fighting is but the means. The trowel, not the sword, is the natural instrument." (Maclaren)

b. **The one who sounded the trumpet**: In addition to the sword and the trowel, Nehemiah also made use of the **trumpet**. It was used to sound the alarm and was an expression of the watchfulness previously mentioned (Nehemiah 4:9).

7. (19-23) Plans are made to keep a ready defense.

Then I said to the nobles, the rulers, and the rest of the people, "The work is great and extensive, and we are separated far from one another on the wall. Wherever you hear the sound of the trumpet, rally to us there. Our God will fight for us."

So we labored in the work, and half of *the men* held the spears from daybreak until the stars appeared. At the same time I also said to the people, "Let each man and his servant stay at night in Jerusalem, that they may be our guard by night and a working party by day." So neither I, my brethren, my servants, nor the men of the guard who followed me took off our clothes, *except* that everyone took them off for washing.

a. **The work is great and extensive, and we are separated far from one another**: Nehemiah knew they had to keep in communication if the work was going to be done. The trumpets were a new way of communication to meet the challenge.

b. **Wherever you hear the sound of the trumpet, rally to us there**: They stayed ready to sound the alarm at the slightest notice. They would not be caught off guard.

c. **From daybreak until the stars appeared**: They dedicated themselves to the work all the more, working hard from sunrise until past dark, even spending the night out at the job site to protect against attack.

d. **So neither I, my brethren, my servants, nor the men of the guard who followed me took off our clothes**: They kept their clothes on all the time because they did not want to be caught unprepared. They were always ready to respond to the blast of a trumpet.

i. Christians need to be armed with the same attitude today. They need to always be ready, always clothed with the righteousness of Jesus Christ, always wearing the armor of God, and ready for that final trumpet blast that will gather us together with our LORD.

Nehemiah 5 – The Work Is Threatened Internally

A. Financial problems threaten the work.

1. (1) A **great outcry of the people** stops the work of rebuilding the wall.

And there was a great outcry of the people and their wives against their Jewish brethren.

> a. **And there was**: Chapter four ended on a note of great victory. The people of God were doing the work of God, and they did it despite all obstacles. They worked with a sword in one hand and a trowel in the other, and they would not let their enemies stop them. But in this section of chapter five, there is no mention of working on the wall, which indicates that the work had stopped.

> b. **Against their Jewish brethren**: The work stopped because of *strife among God's people*. The enemy could not stop the work of God by direct attack, but the work stopped when God's people weren't unified and working together.

>> i. **A great outcry of the people and their wives against their Jewish brethren** meant one group fought against another. When God's people fight one another, they are neither fighting the real enemy nor getting God's work done.

2. (2-5) The reason for strife among God's people: money problems.

For there were those who said, "We, our sons, and our daughters *are* many; therefore let us get grain, that we may eat and live."

There were also *some* who said, "We have mortgaged our lands and vineyards and houses, that we might buy grain because of the famine."

There were also those who said, "We have borrowed money for the king's tax *on* our lands and vineyards. Yet now our flesh *is* as the flesh of our brethren, our children as their children; and indeed we are forcing our sons and our daughters to be slaves, and *some* of our daughters

have been brought into slavery. *It is* **not in our power** *to redeem them,* **for other men have our lands and vineyards."**

a. **We, our sons, and our daughters are many; therefore let us get grain, that we may eat and live**: Nehemiah is not primarily a book about money; it is a book about rebuilding the walls of Jerusalem and bringing God's people into a place of peace, security, and blessing. Yet money problems directly affected the rebuilding work.

i. Most of the time money problems affect a building project because there isn't enough money to do the work. But the job of rebuilding the walls of Jerusalem seems to have been paid for by the king of Persia, who provided the necessary building materials for Nehemiah (Nehemiah 2:8) and sent him with royal guards (Nehemiah 2:9).

ii. Nehemiah's money problems were different; they were money problems among the people that harmed the unity of the people of God.

b. **Let us get grain, that we may eat**: People had money problems because they worked hard on the walls and did not spend the same time on providing for the needs of their households.

i. If a believer wants to spend much time in directly ministering to the needs of God's people and in spreading the gospel, in most cases it will affect their ability to provide. Ministry takes time, and time spent on ministry is time someone isn't making money. If a believer gets to the place where the ministry is their way of making a living, they should be used to not making a lot of money, or the transition will be rather difficult.

c. **Because of the famine**: People had money problems because there was a famine, which made food more expensive. It was so expensive that some mortgaged their property to provide food.

i. A famine is no one's fault; many of the financial problems people face are really not the fault of anyone. Yet there may be a failing in how the problems are addressed.

d. **For the king's tax**: People had money problems because the government kept taxing them even though they weren't working as much, and the cost of living went up.

i. These taxes were not the fault of those who were hurt by them. Neither Nehemiah nor the people acted as if these taxes were unfair, yet they were still a hardship.

e. **We have borrowed money…. indeed we are forcing our sons and our daughters to be slaves**: People had financial problems because the loans they had taken out to live cost interest, and some were in default. Therefore, some people had to give their children as servants to their lenders to pay off the debt.

i. As will be indicated later (Nehemiah 5:11, *the hundredth part*), the rich were taking advantage of the crisis to make money off the poor, charging 12% interest a year.

ii. It isn't unusual for money problems to create strife and completely disrupt what God wants to do. If Nehemiah and his people did not find a way to do what God wanted them to do with regard to their money and money problems, the work of God would be stopped – without a single arrow being fired by the enemies of God.

iii. Believers sometimes want to separate their dealings with money from their walk with God. This is a huge deception from Satan. Buying a house is a spiritual decision, not just a financial one. Taking a job, choosing a career, deciding how much money to make – these are all matters that will directly affect a believer's walk with God, both now and in the future.

iv. If a believer doesn't handle their money with the right heart, and make financial decisions with an eye to eternity, they can make mistakes that will affect the work of God in their lives for years and years.

v. Being a giver is essential to handling money with the right heart before God. Being a giver to the work of the Lord helps us always remember that God and His kingdom come first. The New Testament says our giving should be regular, thoughtful, proportional, and private (1 Corinthians 16:1-4); that it must be generous, freely and cheerfully given (2 Corinthians 9:7).

vi. Money problems are rarely only about money. We often think if we just had more money, our money problems would go away. This can be seen as untrue by looking at the lives of many of those who win a lottery or come into unexpected riches. If they had money problems before – if they didn't know how to handle their money and glorify God with it – they won't know after. The same problems will soon show up again, often bigger than ever.

3. (6) Nehemiah's immediate reaction: anger.

And I became very angry when I heard their outcry and these words.

a. **And I became very angry**: Nehemiah became angry because these money problems were caused, in part, by the greed of those who wanted to make a profit from the money troubles of others, something the Law of Moses clearly said was wrong (Exodus 22:25).

b. **I became very angry when I heard their outcry**: Nehemiah became angry because these money problems led to a lack of unity among the people of God. This unity was more precious than any amount of money.

i. Like Jesus would later do (Matthew 21:12-13), Nehemiah became **angry** when God's people were being cheated and treated unjustly.

c. **I heard their outcry and these words**: No mention was made about the work on the walls. Nehemiah got angry because these money problems stopped the work of the LORD in rebuilding the walls. It must have frustrated him that they could stand so strong against an enemy but fall so quickly because of these kinds of problems.

4. (7-11) Nehemiah's wise response: confronting those who were in the wrong.

After serious thought, I rebuked the nobles and rulers, and said to them, "Each of you is exacting usury from his brother." So I called a great assembly against them. And I said to them, "According to our ability we have redeemed our Jewish brethren who were sold to the nations. Now indeed, will you even sell your brethren? Or should they be sold to us?"

Then they were silenced and found nothing *to say*. Then I said, "What you are doing *is* not good. Should you not walk in the fear of our God because of the reproach of the nations, our enemies? I also, *with* my brethren and my servants, am lending them money and grain. Please, let us stop this usury! Restore now to them, even this day, their lands, their vineyards, their olive groves, and their houses, also a hundredth of the money and the grain, the new wine and the oil, that you have charged them."

a. **After serious thought**: This was great leadership from Nehemiah. He was a man passionate enough to get angry, but wise enough not to act until he had considered the matter carefully.

b. **I rebuked the nobles and rulers**: Nehemiah was no coward. When people were in the wrong, he confronted them. He told the truth, and from the result (Nehemiah 5:12-13), we can judge that he must have told the truth in love.

i. Nehemiah teaches us that a leader should deal with problems directly. Nehemiah did this directly, but not alone. He also **called a great assembly against them**. "Some persons are deaf to the voice of justice until it is repeated loudly by thousands of their fellow-men." (Spurgeon)

c. **Each of you is exacting usury from his brother**: Usury is interest that is either too high or should not be charged at all. The Bible says it is wrong to make money off someone's financial need; if someone needs money for the most basic needs of life, they should be given money, not loaned it at interest.

i. Of course, loaning money at interest is permitted for things that are not absolute necessities. Yet God's people must always use great wisdom and self-control in borrowing money.

d. **We have redeemed our Jewish brethren**: Nehemiah noted that when Judah was conquered, many Jews were sold as slaves to foreigners and many of them had been bought out of slavery by other Jews. Because of this, it was very wrong to have Jews being sold into slavery to other Jews in order to pay off high-interest loans.

e. **Should you not walk in the fear of our God**: Many business deals go wrong before God because there is no regard for God's will or wisdom. The only concern is whether a deal can be made, and if it will turn a profit, not whether it is right or wrong.

f. **Restore now to them, even this day**: Nehemiah was not asking the nobles and the rulers to just feel bad, or to just stop what they were doing; they had to set right the wrong they had done. If money had been charged unfairly or collateral was taken unfairly, restitution had to be made.

5. (12-13) The response of the rulers and nobles who had done wrong.

So they said, "We will restore *it*, and will require nothing from them; we will do as you say."

Then I called the priests, and required an oath from them that they would do according to this promise. Then I shook out the fold of my garment and said, "So may God shake out each man from his house, and from his property, who does not perform this promise. Even thus may he be shaken out and emptied."

And all the assembly said, "Amen!" and praised the LORD. Then the people did according to this promise.

a. **We will restore it**: This was good. Nehemiah wisely told the truth in love, confronting these brothers; and they received the rebuke, doing the right thing and admitting they had been wrong.

i. Their teachable spirit, open to correction, was impressive; too few are willing to admit they are wrong and to do what is right – especially if money is involved.

b. **So may God shake out each man...who does not perform this promise**: Nehemiah wisely knew their words were not enough. Their words had to be followed through with real action – and it was: **the people did according to this promise**.

i. Nehemiah assured accountability through the oaths and public record of these dealings. God's people often need accountability to help them do what is right. The spirit may be willing, but the flesh is often weak.

B. Nehemiah's godly example.

1. (14-16) Nehemiah did not tax the people.

Moreover, from the time that I was appointed to be their governor in the land of Judah, from the twentieth year until the thirty-second year of King Artaxerxes, twelve years, neither I nor my brothers ate the governor's provisions. But the former governors who *were* before me laid burdens on the people, and took from them bread and wine, besides forty shekels of silver. Yes, even their servants bore rule over the people, but I did not do so, because of the fear of God. Indeed, I also continued the work on this wall, and we did not buy any land. All my servants *were* gathered there for the work.

a. **Neither I nor my brothers ate the governor's provisions**: Nehemiah was a great example of putting the work of God ahead of his own personal interest. He certainly had the right to tax the people for his support (others had done it before him), but he didn't claim that right because it wouldn't help the work of God.

i. Like Jesus would later do (Matthew 20:28), Nehemiah did not come to be served, but to serve others.

ii. The apostle Paul is another great example of someone who had the right to be supported but didn't claim that right because it was better for the cause of the gospel (1 Corinthians 9:1-15).

iii. Should ministers be supported today? It is all a question of what is better for the cause of the gospel. If it is better for a minister to be able to devote himself full-time to the care and teaching of God's people, he should be supported. If it is better for him not to be supported that way, he shouldn't. There's something wrong with a minister who will only minister to God's people if the money is right.

b. **Because of the fear of God**: Nehemiah did what was right before God, not what was "right" for his own cares and concerns – because he knew he would have to answer to God.

c. **I did not do so, because of the fear of God**: Nehemiah could say this because it didn't matter to him what others did, how the crowd acted, or what the rest of the world thought. He lived by another standard. Believers should have an even higher standard than Nehemiah. When confronted by the sin this world takes for granted, we can say *I did not do so, because of the love of Jesus*.

2. (17-18) Nehemiah's example of generosity.

And at my table *were* one hundred and fifty Jews and rulers, besides those who came to us from the nations around us. Now *that* which was prepared daily *was* one ox *and* six choice sheep. Also fowl were prepared for me, and once every ten days an abundance of all kinds of wine. Yet in spite of this I did not demand the governor's provisions, because the bondage was heavy on this people.

a. **And at my table were one hundred and fifty Jews and rulers**: Nehemiah refrained from taking when he could have, and gave when he didn't have to. He received a lot of food from the king's provisions, which he could have sold for his own profit. Instead, he gave them away to be the example of generosity – regularly feeding as many as 150 people.

i. Like Jesus would later do (Matthew 14:15-21), Nehemiah extravagantly fed a multitude.

b. **Yet in spite of this I did not demand the governor's provisions**: Nehemiah could have taken more (**the governor's provisions**), but he didn't. Therefore, Nehemiah set an example by what he did not *take* and by what he did not *keep*.

c. **Because the bondage was heavy on this people**: Nehemiah, in his own life, lived the way he told the nobles and rulers to live –not taking personal advantage of another's need. Nehemiah set an example of godly leadership by never expecting more of his followers than he expected of himself.

3. (19) Nehemiah's prayer, asking God to remember his good deeds.

Remember me, my God, for good, *according to* all that I have done for this people.

a. **Remember me, my God**: Some think that Nehemiah was wrong for saying all the good things he did. Jesus clearly taught us that our good works must not be done to show others how spiritual we are.

i. Matthew 6:1-4: *Take heed that you do not do your charitable deeds before men, to be seen by them. Otherwise you have no reward from your Father in heaven. Therefore, when you do a charitable deed, do not sound a trumpet before you as the hypocrites do in the synagogues and in the streets, that they may have glory from men. Assuredly, I say to you, they have their reward. But when you do a charitable deed, do not let your left hand know what your right hand is doing, that your charitable deed may be in secret; and your Father who sees in secret will Himself reward you openly.*

b. **Remember me, my God, for good**: In his prayer, Nehemiah did not look for praise from man, but from God. In fact, Nehemiah probably originally intended that no one else see any part of this book, because it was written as a diary.

i. In our own private time with the LORD, it is entirely appropriate – and right – to say, "*Remember me, my God, for good*" and have confidence in God's promise of heavenly reward, instead of the praise of men.

c. **According to all that I have done for this people**: We should be glad that God took this personal diary of Nehemiah and gave it to us. It shows us that a leader must first lead by example, and that Nehemiah could advise others on right living because his own walk was right. His public words and private actions said the same thing.

Nehemiah 6 – The Walls Completed

A. Nehemiah is attacked in three phases.

1. (1-4) The snare of the enemy's friendship.

Now it happened when Sanballat, Tobiah, Geshem the Arab, and the rest of our enemies heard that I had rebuilt the wall, and *that* there were no breaks left in it (though at that time I had not hung the doors in the gates), that Sanballat and Geshem sent to me, saying, "Come, let us meet together among the villages in the plain of Ono." But they thought to do me harm.

So I sent messengers to them, saying, "I *am* doing a great work, so that I cannot come down. Why should the work cease while I leave it and go down to you?"

But they sent me this message four times, and I answered them in the same manner.

a. **Our enemies heard that I had rebuilt the wall**: The wall was almost finished – the gaps were closed, but the gates were not yet hung. For the enemies of Nehemiah, and the work of God, this was a "now-or-never" time. If they didn't do something immediately to stop the work, the walls would be completely finished.

b. **Come, let us meet together among the villages in the plain of Ono**: At this time, Sanballat, Tobiah, and Geshem tried to arrange a meeting with Nehemiah – by all appearances, a friendly meeting, perhaps even a reconciliation or a vacation. Their invitation may have had the sense of a break for a few days of rest and relaxation out on the plain of Ono.

c. **But they thought to do me harm**: Nehemiah was able to see through the outward appearance, and to understand what Sanballat's friendly offer was all about.

i. "Whether you be a pastor or a teacher or evangelist or Sunday school leader, or whatever your position may be in Christian leadership, let me say that there will always be those who are friendly to your face, but plan your downfall behind your back. Beware of the fawning, flattering Christian who is always fluttering around you, and who behind your back will be the first to rejoice when you go down." (Redpath)

d. **But they thought to do me harm**: Nehemiah was equipped with *discernment*.

i. Discernment is the ability to judge matters according to God's view of them, and not according to their outward appearance. We are often deceived by outward appearances, *For the LORD does not see as man sees; for man looks at the outward appearance, but the LORD looks at the heart.* (1 Samuel 16:7)

ii. Many people confuse being discerning with being negative or cynical. Discernment is equally able to see the good which others might miss as well as the bad by which others may be deceived through outward appearances.

iii. Christians today suffer a great deal because they lack discernment. They follow leaders and teachers who have a good appearance, but don't walk in the nature of Jesus. They accept something blindly because it looks good or sounds good, without carefully judging it against the whole counsel of God's word. We might even picture Nehemiah going to the word of God and equipping himself with discernment. Perhaps he read Proverbs 27:6: *Faithful are the wounds of a friend, but the kisses of an enemy are deceitful.* That passage alone would remind him to not look to outward appearances, but to judge soberly.

iv. How can discernment be developed? First, if a believer wants to see things as God sees them, they must get to know His word. Second, a believer must develop spiritual maturity; Hebrews 5:12-14 says that discernment is something spiritual babies don't have (a baby will stick *anything* in his mouth). Third, discernment can be given as a gift from the Holy Spirit (1 Corinthians 12:10). Seek Him for it.

v. Without discernment, a believer can think a dangerous invitation from an enemy is really an offer of reconciliation. They can think presumption is faith. They can think our own noble desires are God's promises. They can think God is saying "now" when He is saying "later" or that He is saying "later" when He is saying "now." They can think someone is a person of character or a spiritual leader when they are doing damage to God's people.

e. **Why should the work cease while I leave it and go down to you?** Using discernment, Nehemiah would not only escape their trap; he wouldn't even be distracted from his work.

i. If the enemy can *distract* God's people, then he has won; if believers start majoring on minors, and minoring on majors, they will lose their effectiveness for the work of the LORD.

ii. Nehemiah was *persistent* in his discernment; the request came four times, and each time Nehemiah stood fast and didn't fall for it.

f. **I am doing a great work, so that I cannot come down. Why should the work cease while I leave it and go down to you?** Discernment gave Nehemiah *focus*; he knew what God wanted him to be doing, and he did it. He wouldn't be sidetracked by things that sounded good but weren't of the LORD for him.

i. Anyone doing a work for God must contend with a hundred different noble causes, and a hundred things that might look good – and be good – but they are not what they are called to do at that time. Discernment gives us focus.

2. (5-9) The subtlety of the enemy's slander.

Then Sanballat sent his servant to me as before, the fifth time, with an open letter in his hand. In it *was* written:

It is reported among the nations, and Geshem says, *that* you and the Jews plan to rebel; therefore, according to these rumors, you are rebuilding the wall, that you may be their king. And you have also appointed prophets to proclaim concerning you at Jerusalem, saying, *"There is* a king in Judah!" Now these matters will be reported to the king. So come, therefore, and let us consult together.

Then I sent to him, saying, "No such things as you say are being done, but you invent them in your own heart."

For they all *were trying to* make us afraid, saying, "Their hands will be weakened in the work, and it will not be done."

Now therefore, *O God,* strengthen my hands.

a. **It is reported among the nations, and Geshem says**: Sanballat's slander began the way many verbal attacks do, as a report of what others have reportedly said.

i. Vague accusations often sound like, "Everyone is talking about" or "A number of people are saying." Such vague words can very easily give the wrong impression.

ii. What Sanballat accused Nehemiah of was *false.* If a thousand nations reported it, it would not make it true. A popular lie may be more dangerous, but it does not become more true because it is popular.

b. **The Jews plan to rebel...that you may be their king.... you have also appointed prophets to proclaim**: These lies probably outraged Nehemiah. He had worked hard and trusted God greatly, so this work would be done with the blessing of the king. Nehemiah had also accepted great personal sacrifice to demonstrate that he was not in this for himself. The idea of "appointing prophets" to say what the leader wanted to hear was offensive to Nehemiah. He was being accused of the very things he had sacrificed in order to be blameless.

    i. The enemy of our souls knows which accusations will annoy and bother us the most. Often, believers can't stop such attacks, but they can learn how to defend against them and deal with them.

c. **These matters will be reported to the king. So come, therefore, and let us consult together**. Now Sanballat made a plain threat. Nehemiah wouldn't be deceived into coming to this meeting (he had too much discernment for that); so now he tried slander against Nehemiah.

d. **You invent them in your own heart**: Nehemiah replied by calmly and straightforwardly telling Sanballat that he was a liar, and by carrying on with the work.

    i. Nehemiah did not mount an elaborate defense, trying to prove Sanballat wrong point by point. He wasn't going to waste his time. Men like Sanballat are not satisfied with facts, explanations, or evidence. Such enemies will not be satisfied unless their demands are obeyed, which Nehemiah refused to do.

    ii. Sanballat would not be defeated by being told he was a liar. He didn't care if the whole world thought he was a liar, if *he could only cause the work to stop*. Thankfully, Nehemiah was steadfast.

e. **They all were trying to make us afraid**: Nehemiah had the discernment to see the slander strategy was all about fear, and he wouldn't give in to it. No enemy can make us afraid; all they can do is try to make us choose fear – but it is up to us to refuse it.

    i. Many people live paralyzed by the fear of what others are saying about them, or what they might say about them. Instead, we should forget about what they think. In these situations, people will talk regardless. There is little we can do about it, besides determining *not* to be made afraid.

    ii. One of Benjamin Franklin's proverbs from *Poor Richard's Almanac* wisely says: "Since I cannot govern my own tongue, tho' within my own teeth, how can I hope to govern the tongues of others?"

iii. "No man can lead a work of God if he allows himself to be governed by what other people think. He is to secure help, fellowship, prayer, advice, and he is foolish not to take it; but if his ultimate decisions are based on popular opinion he is going to fail." (Redpath)

f. **Now therefore, O God, strengthen my hands**: Believers must do what Nehemiah did – pray for God's strength and power in their lives. We cannot overcome slander or fear of our enemies in our own strength. It will be said, *not by might nor by power, but by* the Spirit of God (Zechariah 4:6).

3. (10-14) The scandal of the enemy's religion.

Afterward I came to the house of Shemaiah the son of Delaiah, the son of Mehetabel, who *was* a secret informer; and he said, "Let us meet together in the house of God, within the temple, and let us close the doors of the temple, for they are coming to kill you; indeed, at night they will come to kill you."

And I said, "Should such a man as I flee? And who *is there* such as I who would go into the temple to save his life? I will not go in!" Then I perceived that God had not sent him at all, but that he pronounced *this* prophecy against me because Tobiah and Sanballat had hired him. For this reason he *was* hired, that I should be afraid and act that way and sin, so *that* they might have *cause* for an evil report, that they might reproach me.

My God, remember Tobiah and Sanballat, according to these their works, and the prophetess Noadiah and the rest of the prophets who would have made me afraid.

a. **Afterward I came to the house of Shemaiah**: This man **Shemaiah** was said to be a prophet (**he pronounced this prophecy**), but he was not. Shemaiah offered Nehemiah a protected place in the temple. The idea was that although Nehemiah was said to be threatened, he could find refuge in the temple.

i. It may sound reasonable – and one might even take some Scripture to support it: Psalm 61:4 says, *I will abide in Your tabernacle forever; I will trust in the shelter of Your wings.* Nehemiah needed discernment now more than ever.

b. **Should such a man as I flee?** Nehemiah, knowing the heart of God as it is revealed in the whole counsel of God's word, had discernment. Shemaiah tried to create fear in Nehemiah and attempted to get him to disobey God based on this fear.

i. Only priests were allowed in the temple, and Nehemiah was not a priest. He would have been disobeying God if he had done what

Shemaiah suggested. In 2 Chronicles 26, King Uzziah – who was not a priest – went into the temple, and God instantly struck him with leprosy.

ii. "He seeks to persuade Nehemiah into an easy-going, compromising religion that will shirk persecution, that will carry no cross, and that is governed by fear of the opinions of other people." (Redpath)

iii. Like Jesus would later refuse to do, Nehemiah would not disobey or dishonor God to save his own life.

c. **Let us meet together in the house of God**: Shemaiah knew how to use religious talk, but it was still a trap. If Nehemiah had believed Shemaiah's religious talk, he would have sinned and given others reason to find fault with him and discredit him.

d. **And who is there such as I who would go into the temple to save his life? I will not go in**: Nehemiah stood bravely against this religious deception. In his commitment to obedience, God revealed to him the heart of Shemaiah – who was no true prophet. Instead, he was on Sanballat's payroll.

e. **My God, remember Tobiah and Sanballat**: Best of all, instead of lashing out against Shemaiah and his fellow false-religionists, he simply committed these wicked men – and the situation – to God. If God could take good care of Nehemiah, then He could also take care of Shemaiah according to divine wisdom.

i. Nehemiah's response to the three-fold attack of pretended friendship, slander, and false religion makes us admire him as a leader. But we can love and admire Jesus far more.

ii. "Come down to the plain of Ono," they said to Nehemiah. People also said to Jesus, "come down from the cross" (Matthew 27:42). But Jesus was doing a great work – the greatest work – on the cross and would not be stopped.

iii. They slandered Nehemiah, but he didn't defend himself. He spoke the truth and trusted in God. Jesus was also slandered yet did not challenge His critics – He spoke the truth and trusted in His Father in heaven.

iv. A false prophet offered Nehemiah an easy way out, but it was a way of fear and disobedience. Nehemiah would have none of it. Jesus was also offered a way out of crucifixion – if Jesus would just worship Satan, all the kingdoms of the world would be delivered to Him. Jesus rejected this seemingly easier way.

B. Completion of the wall.

1. (15-16) The wall is completed in 52 days.

So the wall was finished on the twenty-fifth *day* of Elul, in fifty-two days. And it happened, when all our enemies heard *of it,* and all the nations around us saw *these things,* that they were very disheartened in their own eyes; for they perceived that this work was done by our God.

a. **So the wall was finished on the twenty-fifth day of Elul, in fifty-two days**: The amount of time it took to finish the job was remarkably short. The walls were in ruins for more than 100 years, and then they were set right in a period of only 52 days.

i. Why hadn't the wall been completed in the preceding 100 years? It wasn't that no one saw the problem; it wasn't that walls were not wanted. Many people saw broken walls and knew how they ruined the lives of the people of Jerusalem, but no one got past the place of just *wishing* Jerusalem had walls.

ii. Finally, there came a man who did more than wish Jerusalem had walls; he grieved, he ached, he prayed, he planned, he asked boldly, he went, he fought, he encouraged, he stood strong, and he saw the job through to completion. But he also had people around him with the same kind of heart.

iii. Believers often have such small ideas of how God can use them. God used a man named Nehemiah to set right a 100-year-old problem in less than two months – and the same God sits on a throne in heaven and works through His people today.

iv. Like Jesus would later do, Nehemiah completed a work that many thought was impossible. The "impossible" work of Jesus was to reconcile God with man through His sacrificial death and victorious resurrection.

b. **In fifty-two days**: At the beginning, when he saw the need, Nehemiah prayed for four months (the difference in time between Nehemiah 1:1 and 2:1). But the work itself took less than two months. Nehemiah spent more time laboring in prayer than was needed to build the wall.

i. This shows that the spiritual battle was greater than the material battle. We are often told this, but it can be hard to believe.

c. **And all the nations around us saw these things...they were very disheartened in their own eyes**: When the wall was finished, their enemies **were very disheartened**. It is a glorious thing to dishearten the enemies of God's people and to let them be discouraged for a while.

i. The battles were hard; the work was big; there were challenges from within and without. But the job was now finished, and victory was sweet.

ii. In contrast to the work of Jesus Christ, Nehemiah completed a wall between Jew and Gentile. Jesus broke down the wall between Jew and Gentile (Ephesians 2:14).

d. **They perceived that this work was done by our God**: Their enemies were disheartened not just because the wall was finished, but especially because it was evident that God did the work. When something has the fingerprints of God on it, all of our enemies notice.

i. The enemy is *only* disheartened when God does the work. If it is the product of man's efforts, they just laugh. Men might be fooled, and see a work of man and be impressed, but angels in heaven (and every demon in hell) know what things have been done by man and what things have been done by God.

ii. A strong, secure people of Jerusalem were a witness to the surrounding nations. Many believers live Christian lives unworthy of notice, because their lives are like broken walls, giving no security, peace, or stability. Let the LORD do a building work, and others will notice.

2. (17-19) The work is finished despite some who were friends with the enemy Tobiah.

Also in those days the nobles of Judah sent many letters to Tobiah, and *the letters of* **Tobiah came to them. For many in Judah were pledged to him, because he was the son-in-law of Shechaniah the son of Arah, and his son Jehohanan had married the daughter of Meshullam the son of Berechiah. Also they reported his good deeds before me, and reported my words to him. Tobiah sent letters to frighten me.**

a. **Also in those days the nobles of Judah sent many letters to Tobiah**: Tobiah was the man who had opposed the rebuilding work with Sanballat.

- In Nehemiah 2:10, Tobiah was disturbed that Nehemiah came to rebuild the walls.

- In Nehemiah 2:19 and 4:3, Tobiah mocked Nehemiah's work.

- In Nehemiah 4:7, Tobiah was angry that the work was being done.

- In Nehemiah 6:1-2, Tobiah was one of the men who tried to get Nehemiah to stop the work and come to the plain of Ono where he could be attacked.

b. **For many in Judah were pledged to him**: The **nobles of Judah** had no trouble being friends to such a man, because he had family ties to many in the tribe of Judah. In fact, they tried to recommend him to Nehemiah (**they reported his good deeds before me**).

> i. These Jewish brothers of Nehemiah could not see what was so plain to Nehemiah. Perhaps they did not see much of the evil work of Tobiah first-hand, so they had a hard time believing reports about it. We imagine them saying, "He's always been nice to us; look at all the good he has done."

> ii. It is also possible they just didn't have the shepherd's heart and shepherd's eyes which Nehemiah had. Nehemiah was called by God to protect God's people and God's work; he was watching and on guard in a way that others were not.

> iii. Also, in the case of these nobles, there was self-interest at work. They had financial dealings with Tobiah that they wanted to protect. "His numerous binding agreements (**pledged to him**) within the Jewish community were probably trading contracts, facilitated by marriage connections." (Kidner)

c. **They reported his good deeds before me, and reported my words to him**: Undoubtedly, they saw Nehemiah as the guilty party. They thought that Tobiah's deeds were good, and that Nehemiah spoke against Tobiah without cause. For example, in Nehemiah 4:4, Nehemiah prayed that the evil Tobiah had planned would be turned back upon him, and that Tobiah would be captured and carried away.

> i. Nehemiah had to be willing to be seen (by some) as the guilty party in order to do what was right by the people of God. He could see what the nobles of Judah could not. He knew that Tobiah's **good deeds** were not the whole story, because all the while, Tobiah was sending frightening letters to Nehemiah. Those letters were not one of Tobiah's good deeds.

> ii. "Tobiah's friends acted as a Fifth Column. They attempted both to propagandize on behalf of Tobiah and to act as an intelligence system for him. Tobiah himself kept on trying to frighten Nehemiah." (Yamauchi)

d. **Tobiah sent letters to frighten me**: Nehemiah wrote no more about this situation. He wasn't going to demand that the nobles change their minds about Tobiah but neither would he deny what he knew to be true about Tobiah. He seems willing to let it go and let God take care of it.

i. Nehemiah had a work to do, and that work did not include attacking people like Tobiah. He could leave the Tobiahs alone, if they weren't attacking the work of God.

Nehemiah 7 – The Wall Guarded

A. Watchmen provided for the walls.

1. (1-2) The appointment of Hanani and Hananiah.

Then it was, when the wall was built and I had hung the doors, when the gatekeepers, the singers, and the Levites had been appointed, that I gave the charge of Jerusalem to my brother Hanani, and Hananiah the leader of the citadel, for he *was* a faithful man and feared God more than many.

a. **Then it was, when the wall was built**: Everything was in order – both practically (**the wall...hung the doors...the gatekeepers**) and spiritually (**the singers...the Levites**); the work was completed and set right.

i. The singers and the Levites were there to lead the people in worship. The walls were not rebuilt so the people of Jerusalem could look at nice walls; they were rebuilt so they could worship God with greater glory and freedom than ever before.

ii. Every victory in our lives should take us deeper into praise. If we are not praising God more and more deeply with each passing year, are we really having much victory? Maybe we are making it *through* tough times – but coming out more bitter and sour than ever. That is not God's victory. His victory leads to a sweeter spirit and to deeper praise.

b. **I gave the charge of Jerusalem**: Nehemiah wasn't in this for political glory. He had done a work, and now he could let it go. God would still use him in Jerusalem, but he knew it wasn't his place to stay in authority.

c. **Hanani**: This was Nehemiah's brother, and the one who first told him about the sad state of affairs in Jerusalem (Nehemiah 1:2). His initiative and concern made him well qualified to govern.

d. **He was a faithful man and feared God more than many**: This described **Hananiah**, who was the co-leader of Jerusalem. Faithfulness and the fear of God are what God requires in a man or woman to use them greatly.

i. Many people who don't seem to be especially gifted – they can't sing, they can't remember many Bible verses, they don't have a knack for teaching, and so forth – can still be used greatly of God if they are faithful and fear God. On the other hand, many remarkably gifted people may see little fruit in serving God if they are not faithful and do not fear God.

3. (3) A watch set on the walls.

And I said to them, "Do not let the gates of Jerusalem be opened until the sun is hot; and while they stand *guard,* let them shut and bar the doors; and appoint guards from among the inhabitants of Jerusalem, one at his watch station and another in front of his own house."

a. **Do not let the gates of Jerusalem be opened until the sun is hot; and while they stand guard**: A tremendous victory had been won – the walls were rebuilt. Yet, the walls would not protect themselves. Diligent watchmen needed to be appointed to guard the walls.

i. The gates were to be opened late and closed early – it was a time for high security.

b. **Appoint guards from among the inhabitants of Jerusalem**: In the Christian life, often a victory is won and later lost because there was no guard. An enemy may come in because we are not watching. Walls can be climbed if there is no one there to stop the enemy, but an enemy is easily turned back from a wall by a guard.

B. List of the returned families.

1. (4-5) The need to develop Jerusalem.

Now the city *was* large and spacious, but the people in it *were* few, and the houses *were* not rebuilt. Then my God put it into my heart to gather the nobles, the rulers, and the people, that they might be registered by genealogy. And I found a register of the genealogy of those who had come up in the first *return,* and found written in it:

a. **The people in it were few, and the houses were not rebuilt**: Now that the walls were rebuilt, Nehemiah still wanted to see how he could be a blessing to the people of God and the city of God. He noticed that the population was low and there were many abandoned houses.

b. **Then God put it into my heart**: Nehemiah wanted Jerusalem to grow and prosper. But before that could happen, he must first know who was already with him. Just as when he toured the broken-down walls in Nehemiah 2:11-16, he needed to clearly understand the problem. So, he took a census and looked at the registry first written by Ezra in Ezra 2:1-70.

2. (6-73) The citizens of Jerusalem who returned from the Babylonian captivity.

These *are* the people of the province who came back from the captivity, of those who had been carried away, whom Nebuchadnezzar the king of Babylon had carried away, and who returned to Jerusalem and Judah, everyone to his city.

Those who came with Zerubbabel *were* Jeshua, Nehemiah, Azariah, Raamiah, Nahamani, Mordecai, Bilshan, Mispereth, Bigvai, Nehum, and Baanah.

The number of the men of the people of Israel: the sons of Parosh, two thousand one hundred and seventy-two;
the sons of Shephatiah, three hundred and seventy-two;
the sons of Arah, six hundred and fifty-two;
the sons of Pahath-Moab, of the sons of Jeshua and Joab, two thousand eight hundred and eighteen;
the sons of Elam, one thousand two hundred and fifty-four;
the sons of Zattu, eight hundred and forty-five;
the sons of Zaccai, seven hundred and sixty;
the sons of Binnui, six hundred and forty-eight;
the sons of Bebai, six hundred and twenty-eight;
the sons of Azgad, two thousand three hundred and twenty-two;
the sons of Adonikam, six hundred and sixty-seven;
the sons of Bigvai, two thousand and sixty-seven;
the sons of Adin, six hundred and fifty-five;
the sons of Ater of Hezekiah, ninety-eight;
the sons of Hashum, three hundred and twenty-eight;
the sons of Bezai, three hundred and twenty-four;
the sons of Hariph, one hundred and twelve;
the sons of Gibeon, ninety-five;
the men of Bethlehem and Netophah, one hundred and eighty-eight;
the men of Anathoth, one hundred and twenty-eight;
the men of Beth Azmaveth, forty-two;
the men of Kirjath Jearim, Chephirah, and Beeroth, seven hundred and forty-three;
the men of Ramah and Geba, six hundred and twenty-one;
the men of Michmas, one hundred and twenty-two;
the men of Bethel and Ai, one hundred and twenty-three;
the men of the other Nebo, fifty-two;
the sons of the other Elam, one thousand two hundred and fifty-four;
the sons of Harim, three hundred and twenty;
the sons of Jericho, three hundred and forty-five;

the sons of Lod, Hadid, and Ono, seven hundred and twenty-one;
the sons of Senaah, three thousand nine hundred and thirty.

The priests: the sons of Jedaiah, of the house of Jeshua, nine hundred
and seventy-three;
the sons of Immer, one thousand and fifty-two;
the sons of Pashhur, one thousand two hundred and forty-seven;
the sons of Harim, one thousand and seventeen.

The Levites: the sons of Jeshua, of Kadmiel,
and of the sons of Hodevah, seventy-four.

The singers: the sons of Asaph, one hundred and forty-eight.

The gatekeepers: the sons of Shallum,
the sons of Ater,
the sons of Talmon,
the sons of Akkub,
the sons of Hatita,
the sons of Shobai, one hundred and thirty-eight.

The Nethinim: the sons of Ziha,
the sons of Hasupha,
the sons of Tabbaoth,
the sons of Keros,
the sons of Sia,
the sons of Padon,
the sons of Lebana,
the sons of Hagaba,
the sons of Salmai,
the sons of Hanan,
the sons of Giddel,
the sons of Gahar,
the sons of Reaiah,
the sons of Rezin,
the sons of Nekoda,
the sons of Gazzam,
the sons of Uzza,
the sons of Paseah,
the sons of Besai,
the sons of Meunim,
the sons of Nephishesim,
the sons of Bakbuk,
the sons of Hakupha,
the sons of Harhur,

the sons of Bazlith,
the sons of Mehida,
the sons of Harsha,
the sons of Barkos,
the sons of Sisera,
the sons of Tamah,
the sons of Neziah,
and the sons of Hatipha.

The sons of Solomon's servants: the sons of Sotai,
the sons of Sophereth,
the sons of Perida,
the sons of Jaala,
the sons of Darkon,
the sons of Giddel,
the sons of Shephatiah,
the sons of Hattil,
the sons of Pochereth of Zebaim,
and the sons of Amon.
All the Nethinim, and the sons of Solomon's servants, *were* three
hundred and ninety-two.

And these *were* the ones who came up from Tel Melah, Tel Harsha,
Cherub, Addon, and Immer, but they could not identify their father's
house nor their lineage, whether they *were* of Israel: the sons of
Delaiah,
the sons of Tobiah,
the sons of Nekoda, six hundred and forty-two;
and of the priests: the sons of Habaiah,
the sons of Koz,
the sons of Barzillai, who took a wife of the daughters of Barzillai the
Gileadite, and was called by their name.
These sought their listing *among* those who were registered by
genealogy, but it was not found; therefore they were excluded from the
priesthood as defiled. And the governor said to them that they should
not eat of the most holy things till a priest could consult with the Urim
and Thummim.

Altogether the whole assembly *was* forty-two thousand three hundred
and sixty, besides their male and female servants, of whom *there were*
seven thousand three hundred and thirty-seven; and they had two
hundred and forty-five men and women singers. Their horses were
seven hundred and thirty-six, their mules two hundred and forty-five,

their camels four hundred and thirty-five, *and* donkeys six thousand seven hundred and twenty.

And some of the heads of the fathers' *houses* gave to the work. The governor gave to the treasury one thousand gold drachmas, fifty basins, and five hundred and thirty priestly garments. Some of the heads of the fathers' *houses* gave to the treasury of the work twenty thousand gold drachmas, and two thousand two hundred silver minas. And that which the rest of the people gave *was* twenty thousand gold drachmas, two thousand silver minas, and sixty-seven priestly garments.

So the priests, the Levites, the gatekeepers, the singers, *some* of the people, the Nethinim, and all Israel dwelt in their cities.

When the seventh month came, the children of Israel *were* in their cities.

> a. **These are the people…who returned to Jerusalem and Judah**: This list was important because each of these people was important to God, in that they did what so few of their fellow Jews did – they took the trouble to return back to the land of Israel after they had already set down roots for seventy years in the Babylonian empire.

> > i. These are people who had a pioneer spirit; they were willing to endure hardship and discomfort because they had a call from God that was more important than their own comfort. Life was easier in Babylon, but it was better in Jerusalem.

> b. **These are the people**: Since only about 2% of the Jews who were carried away into exile by the Babylonians came back, the ones who did have the pioneer spirit are worthy of mention – and they are mentioned *twice* in God's eternal word (here and in Ezra 2).

> > i. It would be wonderful to have your name in the Bible (at least in a positive light). Though we are too late for that privilege, God does have a *book of remembrance* (Malachi 3:16), and surely the names of God's faithful pioneers will be in it.

> > ii. In Nehemiah's list several things were important.

> > > • Every individual was important (specific names were mentioned).

> > > • Which families they came from was important (many family heads were named).

> > > • Their gifts to support the work were important (they were specifically listed towards the end of the chapter).

c. **These sought their listing among those who were registered by genealogy, but it was not found**: Some men could not be priests until their lineage was determined. In the Old Testament, one could not be a priest unless it was established that they were descended from Aaron, the brother of Moses and the first high priest over Israel.

d. **When the seventh month came, the children of Israel were in their cities**: This list flows beautifully after the completion of the work because it reminds us that the work was really all about these people.

i. The walls weren't all that important; what was important was the benefit the walls provided for God's people, enabling them to live in peace and security.

ii. The building work wasn't all that important; what was important was the benefit the building gave to God's people. The building project taught them to work hard, to work together, to work through adversity and attack, and to work till the wall was done.

Nehemiah 8 – The Spirit of God, Working through the Word of God, Brings Revival

J. Edwin Orr defined revival as: "The Spirit of God working through the Word of God, in the lives of the people of God." This chapter is a wonderful example of this principle.

A. Hearing God's word sparks revival.

1. (1-3) The people gather and ask Ezra to read God's word.

Now all the people gathered together as one man in the open square that *was* in front of the Water Gate; and they told Ezra the scribe to bring the Book of the Law of Moses, which the LORD had commanded Israel. So Ezra the priest brought the Law before the assembly of men and women and all who *could* hear with understanding on the first day of the seventh month. Then he read from it in the open square that *was* in front of the Water Gate from morning until midday, before the men and women and those who could understand; and the ears of all the people *were attentive* to the Book of the Law.

a. **They told Ezra the scribe to bring the Book of the Law**: This demonstrates that the Spirit of God was at work even before the reading of God's word. People do not gather **together as one man** for the things of God unless the Spirit of God has moved them, and they do not desire God's word unless the Spirit of God has moved them.

i. "The walls were completed; but the true defence of Israel was in God, and the condition of His defending was Israel's obedience to His law." (Maclaren)

ii. If someone attends to the hearing of the word of God, it is evidence that the Spirit of God is working with them. But it is still important to cooperate with that work and not resist it. Believers need to cooperate and flow with the work of God's Spirit if the word of God is going to do its full work in them.

154

b. **The Book of the Law of Moses**: This refers to the first five books of the Bible (Genesis, Exodus, Leviticus, Numbers, and Deuteronomy). This was Israel's instruction manual for how to walk before God.

c. **Ezra the scribe…. Ezra the priest**: Ezra was the man responsible for having the temple rebuilt, and for returning God's people to worship. Nehemiah, in all his work of rebuilding the walls, just carried on the work that Ezra had begun.

> i. It is evident that Ezra cared about God's word because he was a **scribe** – someone who copied the Bible by hand. He was a man devoted to God Himself because he was a godly **priest**. Like Jesus would later be, Ezra was a man devoted to God's word.

d. **All who could hear with understanding**: This shows us *who* needed to hear the word of God. Everyone who could understand it needed to hear it.

e. **Then he read from it in the open square**: Ezra read God's word from daylight to midday. For some six hours, he read God's word and the people listened.

> i. This was a move of the Spirit of God. People who will be **attentive to the Book of the Law** for six hours are people touched by the Spirit of God.

> ii. **From morning** is literally, "from the light." These people gathered from dawn to hear God's word. They were willing to sacrifice their sleep to hear it – they *wanted* it, and like Jacob (Genesis 32:26) they would not let go until they had their blessing.

> iii. "This scene was in the truest sense a 'revival.' We may learn the true way of bringing men back to God; namely, the faithful exposition and enforcement of God's will and word." (Maclaren)

2. (4-6) How God's word was received.

So Ezra the scribe stood on a platform of wood which they had made for the purpose; and beside him, at his right hand, stood Mattithiah, Shema, Anaiah, Urijah, Hilkiah, and Maaseiah; and at his left hand Pedaiah, Mishael, Malchijah, Hashum, Hashbadana, Zechariah, *and* Meshullam. And Ezra opened the book in the sight of all the people, for he was *standing* above all the people; and when he opened it, all the people stood up. And Ezra blessed the LORD, the great God. Then all the people answered, "Amen, Amen!" while lifting up their hands. And they bowed their heads and worshiped the LORD with *their* faces to the ground.

a. **So Ezra...stood on a platform**: They had taken the time to build a wooden platform, so that the word of God could be heard. They did practical things in order for God's word to have the greatest effect.

> i. There are practical things believers can do also to help God's word have the greatest effect; when a room is comfortable, low in distractions, and the preacher is clearly heard, it helps God's word have the greatest impact.

> ii. But by far, the greatest preparation must happen in the heart. Believers must come, willing to forget about themselves and their agenda, and submit to God's word – not the preacher's word, but God's word.

b. **At his right hand...and at his left hand**: On the right hand and left hand of Ezra were men who were supporting him in his ministry of teaching God's word. The ministry of God's word has the greatest effect when people can see men who are in support of it and obedience to it.

c. **When he opened it, all the people stood up**: They had *respect* for God's word. They recognized it for what it was – the word of God, not the word of man. They honored it.

> i. This is evidence of two things. First, that the Spirit of God is at work; second, that something good is going to happen.

d. **Then all the people answered**: This work of the word of God and the Spirit of God had three immediate results.

- The people *thanked God* (by saying **Amen** when Ezra blessed the LORD).
- The people prayed (by **lifting up their hands**).
- The people worshipped (by bowing down before Him).

> i. Thanksgiving, prayer, and praise are all good measures of how the Spirit of God and the word of God are working in us.

3. (7-8) God's word is presented so the people may understand.

Also Jeshua, Bani, Sherebiah, Jamin, Akkub, Shabbethai, Hodijah, Maaseiah, Kelita, Azariah, Jozabad, Hanan, Pelaiah, and the Levites, helped the people to understand the Law; and the people *stood* in their place. So they read distinctly from the book, in the Law of God; and they gave the sense, and helped *them* to understand the reading.

a. **Helped the people to understand the Law**: Special men were appointed to help the people **understand** God's word. After the reading, they needed to understand it, because it would do little good if it was not understood.

i. *Understanding* needs to be the first goal of any preacher or teacher. When a preacher stands before God's people, there are some things to remember:

- If people leave knowing five helpful hints to a better life, but do not have a greater understanding of God's word, the preacher has failed.

- If people leave having been amused by humor, entertained by anecdotes, or captivated by dramatic stories, but do not have a greater understanding of God's word, the preacher has failed.

- If people leave motivated to action, or praying a prayer, but this is not based on a greater understanding of God's word, the preacher has failed.

- If people leave admiring the preacher, but do not have a greater understanding of God's word, the preacher has failed – and will be held to account before God.

b. **Helped the people to understand the Law**: It is important to see why God's people need special help in understanding God's word.

i. First, because the things of God are spiritually discerned and not intellectually discerned. The Holy Spirit uses gifted teachers to bring spiritual discernment to us, helping us to understand what God's word says.

ii. Second, because it was first written in a different language, in a different culture, in a different place, and at a far distant time. Teachers help us understand it all in our own day.

iii. Third, because our minds are often slow to understand things that will convict our hearts. We often need it spelled out for us.

iv. Finally, understanding isn't only necessary for those who haven't become familiar with the Bible. Sometimes if we have heard it ten times before, we still don't really understand it. When an art restorer cleans a painting, he reveals things that were always there, but the colors weren't as bright, and the details weren't as clear, because they were obscured – when the painting is clean, the real impact of the painter's work can be seen.

c. **They read distinctly**: The preacher must speak in a clear, easy-to-understand way. His main goal is to make the people understand, not to impress or entertain them.

d. **They gave the sense, and helped them to understand the reading**: The preacher must communicate the sense of the passage of Scripture, and not his own agenda or favorite personal topics. The people must leave understanding God's word better, not understanding the preacher's opinions better.

B. Response to God's word prompts revival.

1. (9-11) The people respond with weeping.

And Nehemiah, who *was* the governor, Ezra the priest *and* scribe, and the Levites who taught the people said to all the people, "This day *is* holy to the LORD your God; do not mourn nor weep." For all the people wept, when they heard the words of the Law.

Then he said to them, "Go your way, eat the fat, drink the sweet, and send portions to those for whom nothing is prepared; for *this* day *is* holy to our LORD. Do not sorrow, for the joy of the LORD is your strength."

So the Levites quieted all the people, saying, "Be still, for the day *is* holy; do not be grieved."

a. **All the people wept, when they heard the words of the Law**: The word of God was doing its intended work. 2 Timothy 3:16 tells us two things that the word of God is profitable for: *reproof* and *correction*. Sometimes it hurts to be reproved and corrected, and these tears were evidence of some of that pain.

b. **Do not mourn nor weep**: Ezra, Nehemiah, and the Levites did not want the people to mourn, even though it is a good thing to be sad under the conviction of the Holy Spirit through the word of God. Yet if the sense of conviction is greater than the sense that God is doing a good and holy work, then tears are not good.

i. Our knowledge of our sin should never be bigger than our knowledge of Jesus as our Savior. We are great sinners, but He is a greater Savior.

ii. Therefore, **the joy of the Lord is your strength** – even when a believer is being convicted of sin. When God's people are convicted of sin, they can know that God is doing a work in them, so they can be glad and take joy.

c. **Do not sorrow, for the joy of the LORD is your strength**: The people *felt* sad because they were aware of their own sin. But they could walk in **joy** because God was doing a great work. Our emotions are not beyond our control; believers can do God's will even when they don't feel like it.

i. Maclaren paraphrased the idea like this: "You will have no more power for obedience, you will not be fit for your work, if you fall into a desponding state. Be thankful and glad; and remember that the purest worship is the worship of God-fixed joy, 'the joy of the Lord is your strength.'"

ii. Spurgeon considered some sources of the **joy of the LORD**, where it comes from.

- It springs from God and has God as its object.

- It comes from a deep sense of reconciliation to God, of acceptance with God, and beyond that, of adoption and close relationship to God.

- It comes from an assurance that all the future, whatever it may be, is guaranteed by divine goodness.

iii. Spurgeon considered some instances of when and why the **joy of the LORD** comes:

- Joy comes for every Christian when he enters into actual fellowship with God.

- Joy comes for every Christian when he has the honor of being allowed to serve God.

- Joy comes to give strength against temptation and for Christian service.

d. **The joy of the LORD is your strength**: If Israel in the days of the Nehemiah found **strength** in the LORD's **joy**, it should mark the life of the Christian even more. Believers today relate to God on a better covenant and live in light of the finished work, sacrifice, and resurrection of Jesus Christ.

i. Repeatedly, Christians are commanded to rejoice.

- *…we also rejoice in God through our Lord Jesus Christ, through whom we have now received the reconciliation* (Romans 5:11)

- *Finally, my brethren, rejoice in the Lord* (Philippians 3:1)

- *Rejoice in the Lord always. Again I will say, rejoice!* (Philippians 4:4)

- *Rejoice always* (1 Thessalonians 5:16)

- *…you rejoice with joy inexpressible and full of glory* (1 Peter 1:8)

2. (12) The people choose to rejoice.

And all the people went their way to eat and drink, to send portions and rejoice greatly, because they understood the words that were declared to them.

a. **They understood the words that were declared to them**: They went away praising God because understanding God's word brings a sweet sense of joy.

3. (13) The leaders gather for more study of God's word.

Now on the second day the heads of the fathers' *houses* **of all the people, with the priests and Levites, were gathered to Ezra the scribe, in order to understand the words of the Law.**

a. **The heads of the fathers' houses of all the people, with the priests and Levites**: Leaders have a special need to understand and walk in God's word. Their ignorance or disobedience affects far more than themselves – it affects everyone they have an influence on.

4. (14-18) The people keep the Feast of Tabernacles.

And they found written in the Law, which the LORD had commanded by Moses, that the children of Israel should dwell in booths during the feast of the seventh month, and that they should announce and proclaim in all their cities and in Jerusalem, saying, "Go out to the mountain, and bring olive branches, branches of oil trees, myrtle branches, palm branches, and branches of leafy trees, to make booths, as *it is* **written." Then the people went out and brought** *them* **and made themselves booths, each one on the roof of his house, or in their courtyards or the courts of the house of God, and in the open square of the Water Gate and in the open square of the Gate of Ephraim. So the whole assembly of those who had returned from the captivity made booths and sat under the booths; for since the days of Joshua the son of Nun until that day the children of Israel had not done so. And there was very great gladness. Also day by day, from the first day until the last day, he read from the Book of the Law of God. And they kept the feast seven days; and on the eighth day** *there was* **a sacred assembly, according to the** *prescribed* **manner.**

a. **And they found written in the Law, which the LORD had commanded by Moses**: This was beautiful, simple obedience. Their attitude was, "God said it, so we will do it." Even though tradition did not tell them to keep the Feast of Tabernacles (it had not been done **since the days of Joshua**), they relied on God's word, not on tradition.

b. **That the children of Israel should dwell in booths during the feast of the seventh month**: The Feast of Tabernacles was all about remembering how God had blessed and provided for Israel in the wilderness during the Exodus. They could see God's blessing and provision for them in their present circumstances, and it made something old seem brand new to them.

c. **And there was very great gladness**: Because of their great obedience to God's word, there was **very great gladness**. Believers are often deceived into thinking the path of gladness is in doing what they want to do, but gladness and freedom come only through obedience.

d. **Day by day, from the first day until the last day, he read from the Book of the Law of God**: This revival began by the Spirit of God working through the word of God, and it continued on in the same way.

Nehemiah 9 – Israel Confesses Their Sin

A. A repentant nation gathers.

1. (1) An assembly of humble repentance.

Now on the twenty-fourth day of this month the children of Israel were assembled with fasting, in sackcloth, and with dust on their heads.

> a. **The children of Israel were assembled**: After the wall was completed and functioning, after the people had heard and obeyed God's word, after the Holy Spirit had already done a significant work in the lives of people – now there came a scene of dramatic, humble repentance.

> b. **Assembled with fasting**: Fasting showed their lowly, humble state. They considered themselves so poor before God that they took no food. They also wanted to say, "we are so troubled by our sin that food seems unimportant."

> c. **In sackcloth**: They were wearing rough fabric, like a burlap bag. Again, this was to show their complete poverty of spirit before God. They also wanted to say, "we are so troubled by our sin that the normal comforts of life are unimportant."

> d. **With dust on their heads**: This meant they took little handfuls of dirt and cast them on their heads. This also was to show their lowly state before God.

>> i. All of this reflects a humble attitude of heart – humble not only towards God, but also humble towards man. They did this publicly, and others would see them in this public state.

>> ii. Surely there were those among them who said, "I won't humiliate myself and join in." Others must have said, "I'll do it, just so others can see that I'm spiritual too." But there were many, if not most, who came to God with truly humble, repentant hearts.

2. (2) An assembly to separate themselves.

Then those of Israelite lineage separated themselves from all foreigners; and they stood and confessed their sins and the iniquities of their fathers.

a. **Then those of Israelite lineage separated themselves from all foreigners**: Those who were of the pure line of Israel came to confess the sin of their nation; they confessed **their sins and the iniquities of their fathers**.

b. **Confessed their sins**: This was important. They had to realize and admit that they had missed God's mark.

i. The English word *sin* comes from the idea "to miss the mark." In an archery tournament, if one did not hit the target in the right place, they would say they "sinned." A sin might miss the target by an inch, or it might miss it by ten feet – but it was still a sin either way. We sin when we do what God has told us not to do (communicated to us either by His word, our conscience, or through legitimate authority), or when we do *not* do what God has told us to do (telling us in God's word, in conscience, or by proper authority). Not all sin is the same, but all sin *is* sin.

c. **And the iniquities of their fathers**: This was also important because they had to admit that not only were they sinners, but that they came from sinful ancestors. This was especially important in Israel, where there was a tradition of glorifying their forefathers.

i. This does not mean there was some type of "generational curse" that had to be broken. God does not punish the children for their father's sin, and it is *evil* to say He does (Ezekiel 18). We do recognize that people raised in an environment of sin may very well repeat those same sins, but not because they *must* – it is because their environment made it an easy choice to make.

d. **They stood and confessed**: It should not seem strange that after such great victories, in both the physical restoration of the wall and the spiritual restoration of the people, there was such humble repentance. This shows that repentance isn't something believers "finish" after coming to Jesus. It is something that grows as we grow closer to Jesus.

i. "Repentance grows as faith grows. Do not make any mistake about it; repentance is not a thing of days and weeks, a temporary penance to be got over as fast as possible! No, it is the grace of a lifetime, like faith itself. Repentance is the inseparable companion of faith." (Spurgeon)

ii. "How often the discovery of something new in the loveliness of the Lord Jesus has brought with it the discovery of some new corruption in our own hearts.... God will never plant the seed of His life upon the soil of a hard, unbroken spirit. He will only plant that seed where the conviction of His Spirit has brought brokenness, where the soil has been watered with the tears of repentance as well as the tears of joy." (Redpath)

iii. This great, humble gathering of God's people took place only two days after the end of the joyful celebration of the feast of tabernacles. They had drawn close to God, and now God was drawing them even closer.

3. (3) An assembly to hear God's word and to worship Him.

And they stood up in their place and read from the Book of the Law of the LORD their God *for one*-fourth of the day; and *for another* fourth they confessed and worshiped the LORD their God.

a. **They stood up in their place and read from the Book of the Law**: The humble repentance and confession of sin would have been an incomplete work if it were not for hearing the word and worship. God does not show His people their sin just so that they will humbly confess it, but so that they can walk on in what is right before Him.

i. "In the light of the previous chapter we may take it that the reading was no mere stream of words, but punctuated with explanatory comments and applications to the present situation." (Kidner)

b. **They confessed and worshiped the LORD their God**: This brokenness of heart led them to humbly come before God and hear His word. A sure first step of revival is brokenness of heart.

B. The prayer of repentance.

1. (4-5a) Those leading the congregation.

Then Jeshua, Bani, Kadmiel, Shebaniah, Bunni, Sherebiah, Bani, *and* Chenani stood on the stairs of the Levites and cried out with a loud voice to the LORD their God. And the Levites, Jeshua, Kadmiel, Bani, Hashabniah, Sherebiah, Hodijah, Shebaniah, *and* Pethahiah, said:

a. **Then Jeshua, Bani**: This mentions those Levites and leaders gathered to lead the people in their humble confession. It shouldn't surprise us, or make us feel like failures, if we must be led into confession and repentance.

b. **Stood on the stairs of the Levites and cried out with a loud voice**: Obviously, all eight of these men did not pray the following prayer at the same time. Perhaps it was written out and they took turns, perhaps it was spontaneously prayed in succession, or perhaps (and according to tradition), Ezra prayed this prayer.

i. The following prayer is thought to be the longest prayer in the Bible – and yet takes only six and one-half minutes to say. Prayer does not need to be long to be glorious and effective.

2. (5b-6) Praise to the God of all creation.

"Stand up *and* bless the Lord your God
Forever and ever!

"Blessed be Your glorious name,
Which is exalted above all blessing and praise!
You alone *are* the Lord;
You have made heaven,
The heaven of heavens, with all their host,
The earth and everything on it,
The seas and all that is in them,
And You preserve them all.
The host of heaven worships You.

a. **You have made heaven**: After the encouragement to praise, Ezra gave a reason to praise – because this is the great God who made it all. Looking at the glory of God's creation gives us a reason to praise Him, to humble ourselves before Him, and to trust Him.

b. **The host of heaven worships You**: God wants us to praise Him, to humble ourselves before Him, and to trust Him – and He gives us good reason to. We sometimes want our own reasons, but God gives us plenty of His own reasons.

3. (7-8) Praise to the God who chose Abraham and made a covenant with him and his descendants.

"You *are* the Lord God,
Who chose Abram,
And brought him out of Ur of the Chaldeans,
And gave him the name Abraham;
You found his heart faithful before You,
And made a covenant with him
To give the land of the Canaanites,
The Hittites, the Amorites,
The Perizzites, the Jebusites,
And the Girgashites—
To give *it* to his descendants.
You have performed Your words,
For You *are* righteous.

a. **You have performed Your words**: This says to God, "Lord, You promised this land to Abraham and his descendants, and now here we are. Your promise is indeed true."

4. (9-15) Praise to the God who delivered Israel from Egypt and provided for them in the wilderness.

"You saw the affliction of our fathers in Egypt,
And heard their cry by the Red Sea.
You showed signs and wonders against Pharaoh,
Against all his servants,
And against all the people of his land.
For You knew that they acted proudly against them.
So You made a name for Yourself, as *it is* **this day.**
And You divided the sea before them,
So that they went through the midst of the sea on the dry land;
And their persecutors You threw into the deep,
As a stone into the mighty waters.
Moreover You led them by day with a cloudy pillar,
And by night with a pillar of fire,
To give them light on the road
Which they should travel.

"You came down also on Mount Sinai,
And spoke with them from heaven,
And gave them just ordinances and true laws,
Good statutes and commandments.
You made known to them Your holy Sabbath,
And commanded them precepts, statutes and laws,
By the hand of Moses Your servant.
You gave them bread from heaven for their hunger,
And brought them water out of the rock for their thirst,
And told them to go in to possess the land
Which You had sworn to give them.

   a. **You saw the affliction of our fathers in Egypt**: A second sure sign of revival (following brokenness of heart) is reflection on the goodness of God. When our pride is cast down, and our hearts are humble before God, we can begin to see Him for who He is – and when we see God's character, we recognize how good He is.

5. (16-17a) The sinful response of man to God's goodness.

"But they and our fathers acted proudly,
Hardened their necks,
And did not heed Your commandments.
They refused to obey,
And they were not mindful of Your wonders
That You did among them.

But they hardened their necks,
And in their rebellion
They appointed a leader
To return to their bondage.

> a. **But they and our fathers**: This was a terrible response to the great and good works of God on behalf of Israel. God had been so good to Israel, **but they and our fathers acted proudly**. Our sin is bad enough; but considering that we sin against a God who has only treated us well is far, far, worse.

> b. **Hardened their necks…. refused to obey…were not mindful**: This is a third sure sign of revival – recognition of our own sinfulness. When believers humbly seek God, and see His goodness, they can't help but to notice their own sinfulness – the blackness of their sin stands out against the brightness of God's purity and goodness.

6. (17b-21) God's gracious reply to rebellious Israel.

But You *are* God,
Ready to pardon,
Gracious and merciful,
Slow to anger,
Abundant in kindness,
And did not forsake them.

"Even when they made a molded calf for themselves,
And said, 'This *is* your god
That brought you up out of Egypt,'
And worked great provocations,
Yet in Your manifold mercies
You did not forsake them in the wilderness.
The pillar of the cloud did not depart from them by day,
To lead them on the road;
Nor the pillar of fire by night,
To show them light,
And the way they should go.
You also gave Your good Spirit to instruct them,
And did not withhold Your manna from their mouth,
And gave them water for their thirst.
Forty years You sustained them in the wilderness,
They lacked nothing;
Their clothes did not wear out
And their feet did not swell.

a. **But You are God, ready to pardon, gracious and merciful, slow to anger, abundant in kindness, and did not forsake them**: God's gracious answer to the rebellion of Israel was glorious. **Ready to pardon** is especially wonderful, indicating that there is nothing keeping God from pardoning us except our refusal to come to Him through Jesus. **He** is **ready to pardon**, if believers are ready to receive it.

i. **Ready to pardon**: "Not a God who may possibly pardon; neither a God who upon strong persuasion and earnest pleadings may, at length be induced to forgive; not one who, perchance, at some remote period after we have undergone a long purgation may manifest a mercy which is now in the background, but a God 'ready to pardon,' – willing and more than willing – ready, standing prepared." (Spurgeon)

b. **Even when they made a molded calf for themselves**: This was God's gracious response to Israel – even after they made the golden calf and worshiped it, He still did not forsake them. He still provided the cloud by day and the pillar of fire by night, He still guided them by His Spirit, He still fed them and gave them water. Together it all shows not how special Israel was, but how special God is.

c. **You sustained them in the wilderness**: God is impressively patient with the sinner; He somehow holds back His terrible judgment against those people who deserve it so badly. God's provision for Israel **in the wilderness** shows that He is also patient with His own people, even when they act in ungrateful ways.

i. "God's mercy with a sinner is only equaled and perhaps outmatched by His patience with the saints, with you and me." (Redpath)

7. (22-31) The cycle of Israel's relationship with God.

"Moreover You gave them kingdoms and nations,
And divided them into districts.
So they took possession of the land of Sihon,
The land of the king of Heshbon,
And the land of Og king of Bashan.
You also multiplied their children as the stars of heaven,
And brought them into the land
Which You had told their fathers
To go in and possess.
So the people went in
And possessed the land;
You subdued before them the inhabitants of the land,
The Canaanites,
And gave them into their hands,

With their kings
And the people of the land,
That they might do with them as they wished.
And they took strong cities and a rich land,
And possessed houses full of all goods,
Cisterns *already* dug, vineyards, olive groves,
And fruit trees in abundance.
So they ate and were filled and grew fat,
And delighted themselves in Your great goodness.

"Nevertheless they were disobedient
And rebelled against You,
Cast Your law behind their backs
And killed Your prophets, who testified against them
To turn them to Yourself;
And they worked great provocations.
Therefore You delivered them into the hand of their enemies,
Who oppressed them;
And in the time of their trouble,
When they cried to You,
You heard from heaven;
And according to Your abundant mercies
You gave them deliverers who saved them
From the hand of their enemies.

"But after they had rest,
They again did evil before You.
Therefore You left them in the hand of their enemies,
So that they had dominion over them;
Yet when they returned and cried out to You,
You heard from heaven;
And many times You delivered them according to Your mercies,
And testified against them,
That You might bring them back to Your law.
Yet they acted proudly,
And did not heed Your commandments,
But sinned against Your judgments,
'Which if a man does, he shall live by them.'
And they shrugged their shoulders,
Stiffened their necks,
And would not hear.
Yet for many years You had patience with them,
And testified against them by Your Spirit in Your prophets.

Yet they would not listen;
Therefore You gave them into the hand of the peoples of the lands.
Nevertheless in Your great mercy
You did not utterly consume them nor forsake them;
For You *are* God, gracious and merciful.

a. **So they ate and were filled and grew fat, and delighted themselves in Your great goodness**: The cycle began with God showing His goodness to His people (**You gave them kingdoms and nations**) and with God's people being blessed.

b. **Nevertheless they were disobedient and rebelled against You**: Then, in the time of comfort and abundance, God's people turned from Him.

c. **Therefore You delivered them into the hand of their enemies**: Next, God brought correction – a "wake-up call" to His people.

d. **And in the time of their trouble...they cried out to You, You heard from heaven...You gave them deliverers**: As a result, God's people turned back to Him.

e. **But after they had rest, they again did evil before You**: Having been blessed and satisfied, God's people **again did evil** and turned away from Him, continuing the cycle.

f. **Nevertheless in Your great mercy You did not utterly consume them nor forsake them; for You are God, gracious and merciful**: As this process continues, the motions of each cycle get deeper and deeper – but God doesn't change.

i. Believers sometimes feel as if God has become tired of them; that they can't ask Him to forgive them for something He has forgiven them for so many times before. But God never gets tired of His people, and never turns away the repentant heart.

8. (32-37) A plea to God for intervention.

**"Now therefore, our God,
The great, the mighty, and awesome God,
Who keeps covenant and mercy:
Do not let all the trouble seem small before You
That has come upon us,
Our kings and our princes,
Our priests and our prophets,
Our fathers and on all Your people,
From the days of the kings of Assyria until this day.
However You *are* just in all that has befallen us;
For You have dealt faithfully,**

But we have done wickedly.
Neither our kings nor our princes,
Our priests nor our fathers,
Have kept Your law,
Nor heeded Your commandments and Your testimonies,
With which You testified against them.
For they have not served You in their kingdom,
Or in the many good *things* that You gave them,
Or in the large and rich land which You set before them;
Nor did they turn from their wicked works.

"Here we *are*, servants today!
And the land that You gave to our fathers,
To eat its fruit and its bounty,
Here we *are*, servants in it!
And it yields much increase to the kings
You have set over us,
Because of our sins;
Also they have dominion over our bodies and our cattle
At their pleasure;
And we *are* in great distress.

a. **The great, the mighty, and awesome God, who keeps covenant and mercy**: Because of who God is, and because of who they were (rebellious and wicked), they needed God to do the work of saving them from their enemies.

i. In Nehemiah's day, Israel was not an independent nation – they were a province of the Persian Empire and were under heavy taxes and obligations. Therefore, they asked God to honor His **covenant** and to show His **mercy**, and to deliver them once again from this oppression.

b. **You are just in all that has befallen us**: This gives a good description of what real confession is all about. It recognizes that God is right, and we are wrong (**but we have done wickedly**). Confession is agreeing with God about both things.

i. "It is a tremendous moment in a Christian's life when he can honestly look up into the face of God and say, 'Yes, Lord, You are right and I am wrong,' when he stops arguing with God, and drops his controversy. He says, 'Lord, yes. I've got what I deserved in this situation. You are right; I am wrong.' That is the thing for which God has been working in your life and mine from the very moment of our conversion." (Redpath)

9. (38) Conclusion: a point of decision.

"And because of all this,
We make a sure *covenant,* and write *it;*
Our leaders, our Levites, *and* our priests seal *it.*"

a. **We make a sure covenant**: Israel needed to come to this place, knowing who God is and knowing who they were, they made a *covenant* with God – even writing it down – to commit themselves to His ways.

b. **We make a sure covenant, and write it**: The fourth sure sign of revival – after brokenness of heart, after reflection on God's goodness, after recognition of our sinfulness, is *a renewal of our obedience*. We come to a place of decision, so this work of God is not just a wonderful experience, but something that shapes our future.

i. God's work in us often must come to a place of decision – where He wants us to make a stand for Him, and to reject some other things. If *you* need to reach a point of decision, consider these self-examination questions from Alan Redpath:

What about my relationship with men?

Am I consciously or unconsciously creating the impression that I am a better man than I really am? Is there the least suspicion of hypocrisy in my life? Am I honest in all my words and acts? Do I exaggerate?

Am I reliable? Can I be trusted? Do I confidentially pass on what was told to me in confidence? Do I grumble and complain in the church?

Am I jealous, impure, irritable, touchy, distrustful? Am I self-conscious, self-pitying, or self-justifying? Am I proud? Do I thank God I am not as other people? Is there anyone I fear, or dislike, or criticize, or resent? If so, what am I doing about it?

What about my devotion to God?

Does the Bible live to me? Do I give it time to speak to me? Do I go to bed in time and do I get up in time?

Am I enjoying my prayer life today? Did I enjoy it this morning? When I am involved in a problem in life, do I talk about it or pray about it?

Am I disobeying God in anything, or insisting upon doing something about which my conscience is very uneasy?

When did I last speak to someone else with the object of trying to win him for Christ?

Am I a slave to books, dress, friends, work, or what others think? How do I spend my spare time?

Nehemiah 10 – Israel's Covenant with God

A. Roster of those who signed the covenant.

1. (1-8) Nehemiah and the priests sign the covenant.

Now those who placed *their* seal on *the document were*:

Nehemiah the governor, the son of Hacaliah, and Zedekiah, Seraiah, Azariah, Jeremiah, Pashhur, Amariah, Malchijah, Hattush, Shebaniah, Malluch, Harim, Meremoth, Obadiah, Daniel, Ginnethon, Baruch, Meshullam, Abijah, Mijamin, Maaziah, Bilgai, *and* Shemaiah. These *were* the priests.

a. **Those who placed their seal on the document**: At the end of Nehemiah chapter 9, the people had come to a place of decision, and now, collectively, the nation was going to do something about it by entering into a covenant.

i. Nehemiah 9:38 gives the sense of this: *And because of all this, we make a sure covenant and write it; our leaders, our Levites, and our priests seal it.*

ii. In Nehemiah 9:38, *make a covenant* is literally translated "*cut* a covenant." This phrasing was used because covenants were not made in the ancient world, they were *cut*. Almost always an animal was sacrificed as part of "signing" the covenant. A covenant always cost something, and our point of decision will cost us something – the self-life, comfort, ease, some of the passing pleasures of this world.

b. **Those who placed their seal on the document**: It was wonderful for the nation as a whole to feel that something had to be done about the sin problem among them. But it was meaningless unless individuals came forward to say, "*we* will do something about this." Here were 84 leaders willing to put their names on the line for the covenant before God.

c. **On the document**: These people in Nehemiah's day knew the customs of making covenants, and they knew how important covenants were to God. They remembered that God made a covenant with Abraham, promising that both a nation and the Messiah would descend from him; God made a covenant with Moses and the nation of Israel when He gave them the law at Mount Sinai; God made a covenant with King David, promising the Messiah would come from his family. But the greatest covenant, the new covenant instituted by the Messiah, was yet to come.

> i. Like Jesus would later do in perfection, Nehemiah did in part: he established a new covenant with the people of God.

2. (9-13) The Levites who signed the covenant.

The Levites: Jeshua the son of Azaniah, Binnui of the sons of Henadad, *and* Kadmiel.

Their brethren: Shebaniah, Hodijah, Kelita, Pelaiah, Hanan, Micha, Rehob, Hashabiah, Zaccur, Sherebiah, Shebaniah, Hodijah, Bani, *and* Beninu.

3. (14-27) The civic leaders who signed the covenant.

The leaders of the people: Parosh, Pahath-Moab, Elam, Zattu, Bani, Bunni, Azgad, Bebai, Adonijah, Bigvai, Adin, Ater, Hezekiah, Azzur, Hodijah, Hashum, Bezai, Hariph, Anathoth, Nebai, Magpiash, Meshullam, Hezir, Meshezabel, Zadok, Jaddua, Pelatiah, Hanan, Anaiah, Hoshea, Hananiah, Hasshub, Hallohesh, Pilha, Shobek, Rehum, Hashabnah, Maaseiah, Ahijah, Hanan, Anan, Malluch, Harim, *and* Baanah.

B. The terms of the covenant.

1. (28-29) The making of the covenant with God.

Now the rest of the people—the priests, the Levites, the gatekeepers, the singers, the Nethinim, and all those who had separated themselves from the peoples of the lands to the Law of God, their wives, their sons, and their daughters, everyone who had knowledge and understanding— these joined with their brethren, their nobles, and entered into a curse and an oath to walk in God's Law, which was given by Moses the servant of God, and to observe and do all the commandments of the LORD our Lord, and His ordinances and His statutes:

> a. **Now the rest of the people**: The previously mentioned 84 leaders sealed the covenant, but **the rest of the people** – that is, **everyone who had knowledge and understanding** – also made the covenant with God.

> b. **Entered into a curse and an oath to walk in God's Law**: In making the covenant, they agreed to accept a curse from God if they did not obey His **Law**. They accepted the curse as a form of His correction, to bring them back to obedience.

i. Many of us have done a similar thing. We probably didn't pray "God, curse me if I disobey You." But many of us have prayed, "Lord, whatever it takes I want to follow You. Whatever it takes I want to be Your man/woman." Those prayers are essentially the same, and it's a good thing to pray.

c. **Their wives, their sons, and their daughters, everyone who had knowledge and understanding**: They made this covenant publicly; although its most significant meaning was between the individual and God, it was also important that other people be witness to the covenant. A public covenant meant accountability.

2. (30) The first point of decision: faithfulness to God in romantic relationships.

We would not give our daughters as wives to the peoples of the land, nor take their daughters for our sons;

a. **We would not give our daughters as wives to the peoples of the land**: This promise was addressed to parents. This is because in that day, *parents* made the marriage decisions, not the people getting married.

i. If this covenant were to be repeated today, it wouldn't be focused on the parents, but on the individuals who wanted to get married.

b. **We would not give our daughters as wives to the peoples of the land**: This preserved the important principle that a follower of God should only marry another similarly committed follower of God. It is obvious by experience and observation that it is important to carefully and prayerfully choose your spouse.

i. Many of us have remarkable stories of how we came together with our mate – some stories are romantic, and others are rather strange. Once a couple comes together, God wants to make that marriage something special before Him, and desires to draw the couple closer together as they draw closer to God, just like the sides of a triangle draw closer as they go higher up.

ii. Even if one is not now married, it is important to make the same kind of covenant. If you have given your life to serving Jesus Christ, there will be difficulties if you marry someone who has given their life to something else. If you are in that situation now, God can do great things, but you should never knowingly choose to be in that place from the beginning.

iii. The whole idea of marriage is closely connected to the idea of *covenant*. Malachi 2:14 says, *Yet she is your companion, and your wife by covenant.* Marriage is a covenant, between the husband and wife, between them and all family and witnesses, but most importantly, between them and God.

iv. When we understand marriage as a covenant, we have something to bind husband and wife together that is *stronger* than society's expectations, *more constant* than romantic love, and *more certain* than happy times.

3. (31) The second point of decision: faithfulness to God in business dealings.

If **the peoples of the land brought wares or any grain to sell on the Sabbath day, we would not buy it from them on the Sabbath, or on a holy day; and we would forego the seventh year's** *produce* **and the exacting of every debt.**

a. **If the peoples of the land brought wares or any grain to sell on the Sabbath day**: Under the Old Testament law, God said that no one could buy or sell anything on the Sabbath day. These citizens of Jerusalem had been breaking this law, but now they covenanted with God to obey it.

b. **We would not buy it from them on the Sabbath**: The motive for breaking this law was clear. They could make more money selling on seven days of the week instead of six days. This was a covenant to only make money in ways that were obedient and glorifying to God.

i. This is a great challenge for the church today as some people's careers offer the opportunity to earn money in ways that are wrong in God's sight. We need to have the same heart Nehemiah and Israel had here, and covenant before God to only make money in ways that are obedient and glorifying to Him.

ii. Many of us – as was true in Nehemiah's day – slip into these practices subtly. We don't wake up in the morning saying we're going to cut corners, cheat others, and defraud the system. We do it because we think we *need* to – bills need to be paid, the kids need things, and so on. Then we do it because it *works*. But we don't really need to; if we trust God, He will take care of us. We should never trust our slick ways of doing business more than we trust God in heaven.

4. (32-39) The third point of decision: faithfulness to God in the support of the LORD's work.

Also we made ordinances for ourselves, to exact from ourselves yearly one-third of a shekel for the service of the house of our God: for the showbread, for the regular grain offering, for the regular burnt offering of the Sabbaths, the New Moons, and the set feasts; for the holy things, for the sin offerings to make atonement for Israel, and all the work of the house of our God. We cast lots among the priests, the Levites, and

the people, for bringing the wood offering into the house of our God, according to our fathers' houses, at the appointed times year by year, to burn on the altar of the LORD our God as *it is* written in the Law.

And *we made ordinances* to bring the firstfruits of our ground and the firstfruits of all fruit of all trees, year by year, to the house of the LORD; to bring the firstborn of our sons and our cattle, as *it is* written in the Law, and the firstborn of our herds and our flocks, to the house of our God, to the priests who minister in the house of our God; to bring the firstfruits of our dough, our offerings, the fruit from all kinds of trees, *the* new wine and oil, to the priests, to the storerooms of the house of our God; and to bring the tithes of our land to the Levites, for the Levites should receive the tithes in all our farming communities. And the priest, the descendant of Aaron, shall be with the Levites when the Levites receive tithes; and the Levites shall bring up a tenth of the tithes to the house of our God, to the rooms of the storehouse. For the children of Israel and the children of Levi shall bring the offering of the grain, of the new wine and the oil, to the storerooms where the articles of the sanctuary *are, where* the priests who minister and the gatekeepers and the singers *are;* and we will not neglect the house of our God.

a. **To exact from ourselves yearly one-third of a shekel for the service of the house of our God**: They laid down a yearly tax to support the workings of the temple. They required people to bring wood to the temple on a rotating basis. They committed themselves to obey the command to bring the firstborn, the firstfruits, and the tithe (ten percent of the produce of their land) to the house of God.

i. They simply did two things. First, they agreed to give as God had commanded (the firstborn, firstfruits, and the tithe). Second, they agreed to give as the special need required (the one-third of a shekel tax and the wood).

ii. Firstborn and firstfruits were risky ways to give, because your land might not yield much more produce, and your cow or ewe might not give birth again – yet the first still belonged to God and was given to the priests. God promised to bless this giving of the firstfruits and firstborn in faith: *Honor the LORD with your possessions, and with the firstfruits of all your increase; so your barns will be filled with plenty, and your vats will overflow with new wine.* (Proverbs 3:9-10).

b. **We will not neglect the house of our God**: If before they covenanted to make money only in ways that would glorify God, here they covenanted to spend their money in ways that would glorify God – beginning with giving to the LORD.

c. **We will not neglect the house of our God**: Simply said, the Bible says believers need to be givers. It is not so much for the sake of those they give to, but because giving sets the heart right about material things. God Himself is the greatest giver.

> i. If you hold on to money so tightly that you will not be a giver, then you have revealed where your heart is when it comes to money.

> ii. The New Testament speaks with great clarity on the principle of giving: that giving should be regular, planned, proportional, and private (1 Corinthians 16:1-4); that it must be generous, freely and cheerfully given (2 Corinthians 9).

> iii. If a believer is reluctant to be a giver as the Bible says they should, it would be good for them to talk with those who do give after God's pattern. Ask them if it has been a blessing or a curse in their life to give as God says to. God promises He will never owe anything to His people, and they cannot out-give God – though the return is often far better than money.

Nehemiah 11 – The Citizens of Jerusalem

A. Recruiting citizens of Jerusalem.

1. (1) Those who will live in Jerusalem.

Now the leaders of the people dwelt at Jerusalem; the rest of the people cast lots to bring one out of ten to dwell in Jerusalem, the holy city, and nine-tenths *were to dwell* in *other* cities.

a. **To bring one out of ten to dwell in Jerusalem**: It wasn't enough to see the city walls rebuilt and the spiritual renewal of the people of Jerusalem; now they concerned themselves with getting more people into the city.

i. For a city to prosper and be great, it must be populated. For more than seventy years, Jerusalem had been nothing but a ghost town. Over a period of eighty or so years it had been repopulated, with a new temple built (under Ezra) and the walls rebuilt (under Nehemiah). But the city still needed more people.

ii. Nehemiah understood that the bigger the population of Jerusalem, the greater would be the resources for defense and strength in battle. He didn't rebuild the walls just to see some conquering army come and break them down again.

b. **Now the leaders of the people dwelt at Jerusalem**: It was good that the **leaders of the people** set the example by living in Jerusalem. Leaders must set the pattern by their lives. They had no right to expect the people to live in Jerusalem if they themselves were not living there.

c. **One out of ten**: The rest of the people submitted themselves to a lottery system, in which one out of ten would be selected to move from the surrounding regions into the city of Jerusalem. So, in the end, at least ten percent of Judah's population would live in Jerusalem.

2. (2) Blessing the citizens of Jerusalem.

And the people blessed all the men who willingly offered themselves to dwell at Jerusalem.

a. **And the people blessed all the men**: Apart from the leaders (who had a special obligation) and those selected in the lottery (who were also obligated), there were **all the men who willingly offered themselves to dwell at Jerusalem**. These men had a special blessing.

i. They had a unique pioneer spirit. They had the ability to endure some measure of hardship or discomfort to accomplish a greater work for God's kingdom.

ii. It was in these days of the rebuilding of Jerusalem that God asked an important question through the prophet Zechariah: *For who has despised the day of small things?* (Zechariah 4:10). The answer is, "Many of us have despised those days." But the people who offered themselves to **willingly** live at Jerusalem, to take what is small and build it up before the LORD, had decided not to despise the day of small things.

b. **To dwell at Jerusalem**: If such a blessing was reserved for those who willingly offered to live in Jerusalem, there was something distinct about the challenge of living in Jerusalem.

i. To live in Jerusalem, they had to re-order their view of material things. They had to give up land in their previous region and take up new business in Jerusalem.

ii. To live in Jerusalem, they had to re-arrange their social priorities, certainly leaving some friends and family behind in their old villages.

iii. To live in Jerusalem, they had to have a mind to endure the problems in the city. It had been a ghost town for 70 years, and was now basically a slightly rebuilt, somewhat repopulated ghost town. The city didn't look beautiful and glorious, and it still needed work.

iv. To live in Jerusalem, they had to live knowing they were a target for the enemy. There were strong walls of protection, but since Jerusalem was now a notable city with rebuilt walls, the fear was more from whole armies than bands of robbers.

v. The Bible says there is a city coming down from heaven to earth, when God is done with this earth as we know it, called the *New Jerusalem* (Revelation 21:2). People don't want to be citizens of the New Jerusalem for the same reasons many didn't want to be citizens of Nehemiah's Jerusalem.

B. Roster of those living in Jerusalem and in Judea.

1. (3-24) Leaders who lived in Jerusalem.

These *are* the heads of the province who dwelt in Jerusalem. (But in the cities of Judah everyone dwelt in his own possession in their cities—

Israelites, priests, Levites, Nethinim, and descendants of Solomon's servants.) Also in Jerusalem dwelt *some* of the children of Judah and of the children of Benjamin.

The children of Judah: Athaiah the son of Uzziah, the son of Zechariah, the son of Amariah, the son of Shephatiah, the son of Mahalalel, of the children of Perez; and Maaseiah the son of Baruch, the son of Col-Hozeh, the son of Hazaiah, the son of Adaiah, the son of Joiarib, the son of Zechariah, the son of Shiloni. All the sons of Perez who dwelt at Jerusalem *were* four hundred and sixty-eight valiant men.

And these are the sons of Benjamin: Sallu the son of Meshullam, the son of Joed, the son of Pedaiah, the son of Kolaiah, the son of Maaseiah, the son of Ithiel, the son of Jeshaiah; and after him Gabbai *and* Sallai, nine hundred and twenty-eight. Joel the son of Zichri *was* their overseer, and Judah the son of Senuah *was* second over the city.

Of the priests: Jedaiah the son of Joiarib, and Jachin; Seraiah the son of Hilkiah, the son of Meshullam, the son of Zadok, the son of Meraioth, the son of Ahitub, *was* the leader of the house of God. Their brethren who did the work of the house *were* eight hundred and twenty-two; and Adaiah the son of Jeroham, the son of Pelaliah, the son of Amzi, the son of Zechariah, the son of Pashhur, the son of Malchijah, and his brethren, heads of the fathers' *houses, were* two hundred and forty-two; and Amashai the son of Azarel, the son of Ahzai, the son of Meshillemoth, the son of Immer, and their brethren, mighty men of valor, *were* one hundred and twenty-eight. Their overseer *was* Zabdiel the son of *one of* the great men.

Also of the Levites: Shemaiah the son of Hasshub, the son of Azrikam, the son of Hashabiah, the son of Bunni; Shabbethai and Jozabad, of the heads of the Levites, *had* the oversight of the business outside of the house of God; Mattaniah the son of Micha, the son of Zabdi, the son of Asaph, the leader *who* began the thanksgiving with prayer; Bakbukiah, the second among his brethren; and Abda the son of Shammua, the son of Galal, the son of Jeduthun. All the Levites in the holy city *were* two hundred and eighty-four.

Moreover the gatekeepers, Akkub, Talmon, and their brethren who kept the gates, *were* one hundred and seventy-two.

And the rest of Israel, of the priests *and* Levites, *were* in all the cities of Judah, everyone in his inheritance. But the Nethinim dwelt in Ophel. And Ziha and Gishpa *were* over the Nethinim.

Also the overseer of the Levites at Jerusalem *was* Uzzi the son of Bani, the son of Hashabiah, the son of Mattaniah, the son of Micha, of the sons of Asaph, the singers in charge of the service of the house of God. For *it was* the king's command concerning them that a certain portion should be for the singers, a quota day by day. Pethahiah the son of Meshezabel, of the children of Zerah the son of Judah, *was* the king's deputy in all matters concerning the people.

a. **These are the heads of the province**: This extensive list includes tribal leaders (of the tribes of Judah and Benjamin), military men, priests, Levites, gatekeepers, and civil and royal servants.

b. **Who dwelt in Jerusalem**: All these notable men and their families took the lead by choosing to settle in Jerusalem, setting a good example for all God's people.

2. (25-36) Jewish villages and towns throughout Judea.

And as for the villages with their fields, *some* of the children of Judah dwelt in Kirjath Arba and its villages, Dibon and its villages, Jekabzeel and its villages; in Jeshua, Moladah, Beth Pelet, Hazar Shual, and Beersheba and its villages; in Ziklag and Meconah and its villages; in En Rimmon, Zorah, Jarmuth, Zanoah, Adullam, and their villages; in Lachish and its fields; in Azekah and its villages. They dwelt from Beersheba to the Valley of Hinnom.

Also the children of Benjamin from Geba *dwelt* in Michmash, Aija, and Bethel, and their villages; in Anathoth, Nob, Ananiah; in Hazor, Ramah, Gittaim; in Hadid, Zeboim, Neballat; in Lod, Ono, *and* the Valley of Craftsmen. Some of the Judean divisions of Levites *were* in Benjamin.

Nehemiah 12 – Dedication of the Wall

A. Priestly and Levitical families.

1. (1-11) Priests and Levites in the days of Zerubbabel, the high priest.

Now these *are* the priests and the Levites who came up with Zerubbabel the son of Shealtiel, and Jeshua: Seraiah, Jeremiah, Ezra, Amariah, Malluch, Hattush, Shechaniah, Rehum, Meremoth, Iddo, Ginnethoi, Abijah, Mijamin, Maadiah, Bilgah, Shemaiah, Joiarib, Jedaiah, Sallu, Amok, Hilkiah, *and* Jedaiah.

These *were* the heads of the priests and their brethren in the days of Jeshua.

Moreover the Levites *were* Jeshua, Binnui, Kadmiel, Sherebiah, Judah, *and* Mattaniah *who led* the thanksgiving *psalms,* he and his brethren. Also Bakbukiah and Unni, their brethren, *stood* across from them in *their* duties.

Jeshua begot Joiakim, Joiakim begot Eliashib, Eliashib begot Joiada, Joiada begot Jonathan, and Jonathan begot Jaddua.

2. (12-21) Priests in the days of Joiakim.

Now in the days of Joiakim, the priests, the heads of the fathers' *houses were:* of Seraiah, Meraiah; of Jeremiah, Hananiah; of Ezra, Meshullam; of Amariah, Jehohanan; of Melichu, Jonathan; of Shebaniah, Joseph; of Harim, Adna; of Meraioth, Helkai; of Iddo, Zechariah; of Ginnethon, Meshullam; of Abijah, Zichri; *the son* of Minjamin; of Moadiah, Piltai; of Bilgah, Shammua; of Shemaiah, Jehonathan; of Joiarib, Mattenai; of Jedaiah, Uzzi; of Sallai, Kallai; of Amok, Eber; of Hilkiah, Hashabiah; *and* of Jedaiah, Nethanel.

3. (22-26) Levites during the reign of Darius the Persian.

During the reign of Darius the Persian, a record *was also kept* of the Levites and priests *who had been* heads of their fathers' *houses* in the days of Eliashib, Joiada, Johanan, and Jaddua. The sons of Levi,

the heads of the fathers' *houses* until the days of Johanan the son of Eliashib, *were* written in the book of the chronicles.

And the heads of the Levites *were* Hashabiah, Sherebiah, and Jeshua the son of Kadmiel, with their brothers across from them, to praise *and* give thanks, group alternating with group, according to the command of David the man of God. Mattaniah, Bakbukiah, Obadiah, Meshullam, Talmon, and Akkub *were* gatekeepers keeping the watch at the storerooms of the gates. These *lived* in the days of Joiakim the son of Jeshua, the son of Jozadak, and in the days of Nehemiah the governor, and of Ezra the priest, the scribe.

B. The dedication ceremony.

1. (27-29) Gathering the Levites for the dedication ceremony.

Now at the dedication of the wall of Jerusalem they sought out the Levites in all their places, to bring them to Jerusalem to celebrate the dedication with gladness, both with thanksgivings and singing, *with* cymbals and stringed instruments and harps. And the sons of the singers gathered together from the countryside around Jerusalem, from the villages of the Netophathites, from the house of Gilgal, and from the fields of Geba and Azmaveth; for the singers had built themselves villages all around Jerusalem.

a. **They sought out the Levites in all their places, to bring them to Jerusalem**: The Levites had many responsibilities in the life and worship of Israel, but one of the most important jobs they had was to lead the people in songs of worship and praise to God.

b. **To celebrate the dedication with gladness, both with thanksgivings and singing**: They often sang with musical instruments. Here **cymbals and stringed instruments and harps** are specifically mentioned.

i. There are at least twenty-two different musical instruments mentioned in the Bible, including the harp, the lyre (an ancient guitar), horns, trumpets, flutes, tambourines, drums, cymbals, and bells.

ii. The Levites were specially appointed to use these instruments to lead the people in worshiping God through singing.

c. **Sons of the singers...the singers had built themselves villages**: There were also specifically appointed singers. The singers in Nehemiah's day had a close-knit bond, both by families and living arrangements.

i. Since the job of these singers was to lead the people in worship of God, they had to be good singers; but more importantly, they had to be people of worship themselves.

ii. There is a huge difference between being a great singer and being a great leader of songs of worship to God. Worship should be excellent, but it isn't entertainment. The goal isn't to give the people a good feeling (though that may happen), but to give glory and honor to God.

2. (30) The ceremonies for purification.

Then the priests and Levites purified themselves, and purified the people, the gates, and the wall.

a. **Then the priests and Levites purified themselves**: They did this *first*. They could not effectively lead the people in worship of God unless they walked in purity before the Lord.

b. **And purified the people**: This was their next step. They brought cleansing to the people in the way the Bible described, knowing that only a purified people could really worship and praise God.

i. Some might silently object here; they might say, "I know a person who goes to church and seems to be lost in beautiful praise and worship to God, and I also know their life is rather impure outside the church walls. It appears they are worshiping God, but they are personally impure."

ii. Something is wrong there; probably, their worship is not true worship of God in spirit and in truth, but instead a "soulish" experience. All that inwardly moves a person in a deep way is not necessarily of God's Spirit; it can be of the soul. One of the great works of the word of God is to divide between that which is truly spiritual and that which is merely soulish (Hebrews 4:12).

iii. Without purity, believers can't worship God in spirit and in truth, as Jesus commanded (John 4:24). Psalm 24:3-4 asks, *Who may ascend into the hill of the Lord? Or who may stand in His holy place? He who has clean hands and a pure heart*, and it means it in the sense of bringing praise to God.

iv. Believers can be made pure and clean before God today, right now, by doing what the Bible says to do – not in following an Old Testament ceremony, but by receiving the word of the New Testament: *If we confess our sins, He is faithful and just to forgive us our sins and to cleanse us from all unrighteousness.* (1 John 1:9)

c. **The gates, and the wall**: Finally, their surroundings were purified. Purified surroundings help us to walk consistently in purity. The homes and offices of many Christians could benefit from purification and cleansing.

3. (31-43) Two choirs lead Jerusalem in joyful praise.

So I brought the leaders of Judah up on the wall, and appointed two large thanksgiving choirs. *One* went to the right hand on the wall toward the Refuse Gate. After them went Hoshaiah and half of the leaders of Judah, and Azariah, Ezra, Meshullam, Judah, Benjamin, Shemaiah, Jeremiah, and some of the priests' sons with trumpets—Zechariah the son of Jonathan, the son of Shemaiah, the son of Mattaniah, the son of Michaiah, the son of Zaccur, the son of Asaph, and his brethren, Shemaiah, Azarel, Milalai, Gilalai, Maai, Nethanel, Judah, *and* Hanani, with the musical instruments of David the man of God. Ezra the scribe *went* before them. By the Fountain Gate, in front of them, they went up the stairs of the City of David, on the stairway of the wall, beyond the house of David, as far as the Water Gate eastward.

The other thanksgiving choir went the opposite *way*, and I *was* behind them with half of the people on the wall, going past the Tower of the Ovens as far as the Broad Wall, and above the Gate of Ephraim, above the Old Gate, above the Fish Gate, the Tower of Hananel, the Tower of the Hundred, as far as the Sheep Gate; and they stopped by the Gate of the Prison.

So the two thanksgiving choirs stood in the house of God, likewise I and the half of the rulers with me; and the priests, Eliakim, Maaseiah, Minjamin, Michaiah, Elioenai, Zechariah, *and* Hananiah, with trumpets; also Maaseiah, Shemaiah, Eleazar, Uzzi, Jehohanan, Malchijah, Elam, and Ezer. The singers sang loudly with Jezrahiah the director.

Also that day they offered great sacrifices, and rejoiced, for God had made them rejoice with great joy; the women and the children also rejoiced, so that the joy of Jerusalem was heard afar off.

a. **Appointed two large thanksgiving choirs**: The two large choirs were called **thanksgiving choirs** for a good reason. All praise and worship must have a strong element of thanksgiving to God for it to be genuine.

i. Notice that **the singers sang loudly**. They had to be heard, because as glorious as the instruments were, the people would follow the lead of the singers in worship.

b. **God had made them rejoice with great joy**: God's work caused the assembled choirs and all the people to rejoice. They were overwhelmed with joy and thanksgiving, considering all God had done.

c. **The women and the children also rejoiced**: This tremendous experience of worship was for all of Israel, including **women** and **children**.

d. **The joy of Jerusalem was heard afar off**: Their worship was a testimony to others, and what others heard was not so much the singing itself as the

joy. Believers often worry about others hearing them sing but what God wants to hear, and what others should hear, is not so much the singing of God's people, but the sound of their **joy**.

4. (44-47) Other aspects of this day of joy.

And at the same time some were appointed over the rooms of the storehouse for the offerings, the firstfruits, and the tithes, to gather into them from the fields of the cities the portions specified by the Law for the priests and Levites; for Judah rejoiced over the priests and Levites who ministered. Both the singers and the gatekeepers kept the charge of their God and the charge of the purification, according to the command of David *and* Solomon his son. For in the days of David and Asaph of old *there were* chiefs of the singers, and songs of praise and thanksgiving to God. In the days of Zerubbabel and in the days of Nehemiah all Israel gave the portions for the singers and the gatekeepers, a portion for each day. They also consecrated *holy things* for the Levites, and the Levites consecrated *them* for the children of Aaron.

a. **Some were appointed over the rooms of the storehouse for the offerings**: This was a day of *giving*. People brought their **offerings, the firstfruits, and the tithes** to the storehouse of the Levites, and they did it with joy because they enjoyed supporting the priests and Levites ministering on their behalf.

b. **Both the singers and the gatekeepers kept the charge of their God and the charge of the purification**: This was a day of *purity*. It was an ongoing concern, not a one-time ceremony.

c. **They also consecrated holy things for the Levites**: It was a day of *consecration*. Holy things were set apart for the Levites, speaking of the separation to God.

Nehemiah 13 – Nehemiah's Reforms

A. True worship leads to the nation's obedience.

1. (1-2) Hearing the Law brings a call to obedience.

On that day they read from the Book of Moses in the hearing of the people, and in it was found written that no Ammonite or Moabite should ever come into the assembly of God, because they had not met the children of Israel with bread and water, but hired Balaam against them to curse them. However, our God turned the curse into a blessing.

a. **No Ammonite or Moabite should ever come into the assembly of God**: As the people drew near to God in worship (as seen in Nehemiah 11 and 12), they became aware of God's standards. In this case, the standard they followed was stated in Deuteronomy 23:3-4, where it says that the Ammonites and Moabites were not to be regarded as part of Israel (unless they converted to the worship of Israel's God).

b. **Should ever come into the assembly of God**: Coming into God's assembly meant being regarded as a member of Israel and of the people of God. It meant one could fully participate in the spiritual life of Israel.

i. An Israelite was part of God's covenant by birth, but an Ammonite or Moabite was not. They had to become a part of the covenant by choice – by joining with God's covenant people and leaving the gods of their people. They had to choose to reject those gods and embrace Yahweh.

ii. This command was a powerful message. It said to these Ammonites and Moabites, "You were not a part of the people of God by birth. You must choose this and leave the thinking and deeds of your anti-God culture, and truly join in the spiritual life of God's people. Unless you leave one and join the other, you will never really be a part of this spiritual life. Come join us."

c. **Because they had not met the children of Israel with bread and water**: The Ammonites and Moabites were singled out because of their devious schemes against Israel when Israel came into the Promised Land, at least a thousand years before this.

i. Long before the Ammonites and Moabites had schemed against Israel, God had made a promise to Abraham, the father of the Jewish people: *I will bless those who bless you, and I will curse him who curses you* (Genesis 12:3). This command was simply another fulfillment of God's promise to Abraham.

d. **However, our God turned the curse into a blessing**: This refers to the events of Numbers 22-24, where God blessed Israel, even though the prophet Balaam wanted to curse them. It also reminds us that God is able – more than able – to turn any curse into a blessing.

2. (3) After hearing God's command, Israel obeys and separates from the mixed multitude.

So it was, when they had heard the Law, that they separated all the mixed multitude from Israel.

a. **They separated all the mixed multitude from Israel**: They could have thought of 20 reasons to *not* do what the word of God plainly told them to do. Instead, they simply obeyed.

i. They might have made familiar excuses:

- "That command was made long ago and speaks to a different time."
- "Things are different now."
- "Let's not go too far."
- "Let's assign a committee to examine the issue."

b. **The mixed multitude**: This refers to those who wanted to associate with the people of Israel but did not make a full commitment and embrace the covenant.

i. Even today, there may be people of good will in churches – honorable people, who have some respect for God and His word – who are yet part of **the mixed multitude** because they have not received God's covenant of salvation in Jesus. Such people are welcome, but it should be understood where they stand.

B. Nehemiah's reforms.

1. (4-9) Temple reforms.

Now before this, Eliashib the priest, having authority over the storerooms of the house of our God, *was* allied with Tobiah. And he had prepared for him a large room, where previously they had stored the grain offerings, the frankincense, the articles, the tithes of grain, the new wine and oil, which were commanded *to be given* to the Levites and singers and gatekeepers, and the offerings for the priests. But during all this I was not in Jerusalem, for in the thirty-second year of Artaxerxes king of Babylon I had returned to the king. Then after certain days I obtained leave from the king, and I came to Jerusalem and discovered the evil that Eliashib had done for Tobiah, in preparing a room for him in the courts of the house of God. And it grieved me bitterly; therefore I threw all the household goods of Tobiah out of the room. Then I commanded them to cleanse the rooms; and I brought back into them the articles of the house of God, with the grain offering and the frankincense.

a. **But during all this I was not in Jerusalem**: This section indicates that Nehemiah left Jerusalem and went back to his duties in the Persian court. He was gone from Jerusalem for anywhere from 10 to 12 years.

i. Nehemiah left sometime after the remarkable spiritual revival noted in the recent chapters. But the real test of revival – the real test of God's work in our lives – is in the long term. It is seeing where we are with the Lord ten years after a season of great work.

ii. **In the thirty-second year of Artaxerxes king of Babylon I had returned to the king**: As Jesus would later do, Nehemiah returned to the splendor of the throne room from which he came.

b. **I came to Jerusalem and discovered the evil that Eliashib had done for Tobiah**: When Nehemiah came back, he saw that **Eliashib the priest** had entered into agreements with one of the enemies of Nehemiah's work of rebuilding the wall – the man named **Tobiah**.

i. Incidentally, **Tobiah** was an Ammonite (Nehemiah 2:10) – one of the very mixed multitude who had been put out of the assembly of God's people some 10 years before. At this point in the record of Nehemiah, **Tobiah** was not only *present* among the assembly, he actually rented rooms in the temple courts (**preparing a room for him in the courts**).

ii. Apparently, Tobiah had not changed over the years. He did not join the people of God in the terms of His covenant. The problem was evident to Nehemiah – but **Eliashib** was completely blind to it.

iii. **I came to Jerusalem**: Like Jesus, Nehemiah had two "comings" to Jerusalem. The second coming of Jesus still awaits its fulfillment.

c. **And it grieved me bitterly**: There were many reasons why this was so distressing to Nehemiah.

i. It **grieved** him because rooms in the courts of the temple of God were being occupied by a man who was not only a pagan but who also had a history of actively opposing God's work in the days of Nehemiah.

ii. It **grieved** him because it reflected so badly on Eliashib (a man who was a spiritual leader in Israel) and those around him. It showed that if Eliashib was blind to a problem area, there was no one around him who could confront him with the problem.

iii. It **grieved** him because it made Nehemiah question the lasting value of the spiritual revival he witnessed when last in Jerusalem.

iv. "The last page of many a reformer's history has been, like Nehemiah's, a sad account of efforts to stem the ebbing tide of enthusiasm and the flowing tide of worldliness." (Maclaren)

d. **Therefore I threw all the household goods of Tobiah out of the room**: Nehemiah wasn't one to only sit back and grieve. Nehemiah acted.

- He threw all of Tobiah's **household goods** out of the rooms he occupied in the temple courts.

- He ceremonially cleansed the rooms.

- He put the rooms back to their proper use – as storerooms for the sacred things of the temple.

i. Nehemiah was much like Jesus, who later cleansed the temple from those who profaned it. Both Jesus and Nehemiah had the wisdom to not confuse love with being "nice" – and they both had the wisdom to know when to take bold action.

ii. Like Jesus, the "second coming" of Nehemiah was marked by judgment.

2. (10-14) Financial reforms.

I also realized that the portions for the Levites had not been given *them;* for each of the Levites and the singers who did the work had gone back to his field. So I contended with the rulers, and said, "Why is the house of God forsaken?" And I gathered them together and set them in their place. Then all Judah brought the tithe of the grain and the new wine and the oil to the storehouse. And I appointed as treasurers over the storehouse Shelemiah the priest and Zadok the scribe, and of the Levites, Pedaiah; and next to them *was* Hanan the son of Zaccur, the son of Mattaniah; for they were considered faithful, and their task *was* to distribute to their brethren.

Remember me, O my God, concerning this, and do not wipe out my good deeds that I have done for the house of my God, and for its services!

a. **I also realized that the portions for the Levites had not been given them**: The people did not obey God's word regarding giving. Because of the lack of support, those who should have given their time to the service of God and His people (**the Levites and the singers**) could not – and they had to leave that service (**had gone back to his field**).

b. **Why is the house of God forsaken?** The lack of giving was a way of forsaking the house of God. It wasn't just unhelpful to the **Levites and the singers**; it was a way of turning their back on God.

c. **I gathered them together and set them in their place**: Nehemiah set the situation right by expecting the Levites and the singers to recommit to the work of serving God and His people as they should. He also reorganized the collection, accounting, and distribution of the people's tithes and gifts.

3. (15-22) Priority reform.

In those days I saw *people* in Judah treading wine presses on the Sabbath, and bringing in sheaves, and loading donkeys with wine, grapes, figs, and all *kinds of* burdens, which they brought into Jerusalem on the Sabbath day. And I warned *them* about the day on which they were selling provisions. Men of Tyre dwelt there also, who brought in fish and all kinds of goods, and sold *them* on the Sabbath to the children of Judah, and in Jerusalem.

Then I contended with the nobles of Judah, and said to them, "What evil thing *is* this that you do, by which you profane the Sabbath day? Did not your fathers do thus, and did not our God bring all this disaster on us and on this city? Yet you bring added wrath on Israel by profaning the Sabbath."

So it was, at the gates of Jerusalem, as it began to be dark before the Sabbath, that I commanded the gates to be shut, and charged that they must not be opened till after the Sabbath. Then I posted *some* of my servants at the gates, *so that* no burdens would be brought in on the Sabbath day. Now the merchants and sellers of all kinds of wares lodged outside Jerusalem once or twice.

Then I warned them, and said to them, "Why do you spend the night around the wall? If you do *so* again, I will lay hands on you!" From that time on they came no *more* on the Sabbath. And I commanded the Levites that they should cleanse themselves, and that they should go and guard the gates, to sanctify the Sabbath day.

Remember me, O my God, *concerning* this also, and spare me according to the greatness of Your mercy!

a. **In those days I saw people in Judah treading wine presses on the Sabbath**: The Sabbath was being ignored in disobedience to God's clear command under the Old Covenant. On the Sabbath day when they were supposed to rest and trust God, foreigners sold and the people of Israel bought.

> i. At the root, this was a problem of priorities. There was nothing inherently wrong with buying or selling, but it became wrong when the desire to buy and sell or to make or spend money became more important than honoring God. This was a clear way in which the people of Israel put making and spending money before glorifying God.

> ii. The New Testament makes it clear that believers are not under the law of the Sabbath in the same sense Israel was under the Old Covenant (Colossians 2:16-17), but they are certainly under the same obligation to prioritizing honoring God over making or spending money.

b. **You bring added wrath on Israel by profaning the Sabbath**: Nehemiah knew that sin was not only a personal issue. When such open sin is winked at and left uncorrected among God's people, it invites the correcting hand of God.

> i. Nehemiah wasn't going to sit still for this; he threatened **If you do so again, I will lay hands on you!** He did not mean the gentle laying on of hands for prayer, but the rough laying on of hands for correction.

c. **Spare me according to the greatness of Your mercy!** Nehemiah confronted and dealt forcefully with the sin of God's people in his day. Yet he never did this with the idea that he had none of his own sin to deal with. Nehemiah understood that he too needed God to **spare** him, and he needed the **greatness** of God's **mercy**.

> i. "Nehemiah had no false notion of his own goodness; for, while he asked for recompense for these good deeds of his, he could not but add, 'Spare me according to the greatness of Thy mercy.' He who asks to be 'spared' must know himself in peril of destruction; and he who invokes 'mercy' must think that, if he were dealt with according to justice, he would be in evil case." (Maclaren)

4. (23-31a) Relationship reform.

In those days I also saw Jews *who* had married women of Ashdod, Ammon, *and* Moab. And half of their children spoke the language of Ashdod, and could not speak the language of Judah, but spoke according to the language of one or the other people.

So I contended with them and cursed them, struck some of them and

pulled out their hair, and made them swear by God, *saying,* "You shall not give your daughters as wives to their sons, nor take their daughters for your sons or yourselves. Did not Solomon king of Israel sin by these things? Yet among many nations there was no king like him, who was beloved of his God; and God made him king over all Israel. Nevertheless pagan women caused even him to sin. Should we then hear of your doing all this great evil, transgressing against our God by marrying pagan women?"

And *one* of the sons of Joiada, the son of Eliashib the high priest, *was* a son-in-law of Sanballat the Horonite; therefore I drove him from me.

Remember them, O my God, because they have defiled the priesthood and the covenant of the priesthood and the Levites.

Thus I cleansed them of everything pagan. I also assigned duties to the priests and the Levites, each to his service, and *to bringing* the wood offering and the firstfruits at appointed times.

> a. **In those days I also saw Jews who had married women of Ashdod, Ammon, and Moab**: In the years Nehemiah was away, the Israelites had resumed their practice of intermarrying with the pagan nations surrounding them. This was in dramatic disobedience to God's command.

> b. **So I contended with them and cursed them, struck some of them and pulled out their hair, and made them swear**: From this strong reaction of Nehemiah, it seems he considered this to be the most dangerous of their sins – pursuing ungodly liaisons, and getting involved in romantic relationships God had said "no" to.

> > i. His example of Solomon is well taken (**Did not Solomon king of Israel sin by these things…. pagan women caused even him to sin**). If Solomon, one of the wisest and most blessed men who ever lived, sinned with unwise and ungodly relationships, then no one else should consider themselves invulnerable.

5. (31b) Conclusion: Nehemiah's clear conscience.

Remember me, O my God, for good!

> a. **Remember me**: At the end of it all, Nehemiah knew he did his best to make the people of God strong, safe, and secure. Beyond that, he also led them to be pure, worshipful, and obedient.

> b. **Remember me, O my God, for good**: Nehemiah certainly carried a sense of failure. In Nehemiah 10 the people made a solemn covenant to God that they would *not* do three things.

- Have ungodly sexual liaisons (Nehemiah 10:30).

- Buy and sell on the Sabbath (Nehemiah 10:31).

- Fail to support the work of God with money as He commanded (Nehemiah 10:32-39).

  i. Nevertheless, in Nehemiah 13, some 10 to 12 years later, Israel was again steeped in the exact sins they had vowed to stop. Nehemiah had to address the problems of ungodly liaisons (Nehemiah 13:23-31), buying and selling on the Sabbath (Nehemiah 13:15-22), and failing to support the work of God as He commanded (Nehemiah 13:10-14).

  ii. In Nehemiah 10:39 the people promised: *We will not neglect the house of our God.* But later in Nehemiah 13:11, Nehemiah had to ask: *Why is the house of God forsaken?* It was forsaken because Israel did not keep its promises before God.

  iii. This makes a point vividly clear: the law – that is, rules, vows, promises, covenants, and all such – are all ultimately powerless to stop sin. Only the grace of God, alive and flowing in our lives, can give us the power to truly overcome sin.

  iv. Paul expressed this in Romans 8:3, among other places: *For what the law could not do in that it was weak through the flesh, God did by sending His own Son in the likeness of sinful flesh.* Too many Christians look for victory in the making of rules, of vows, of promises, and fail to find it, because all those things tend to make us look to ourselves, instead of looking to Jesus.

  v. The Old Testament history of Israel, from beginning to end, illustrates this principle. When the nation was first born at the Exodus, despite the most spectacular miracles, displays of God's glory, and revelation of the law, the people sinned by giving the credit for their deliverance from Egypt to a gold calf. And now here, at the end of the Old Testament history of God's people in the Promised Land, Nehemiah was pulling hair out – his own and those of sinners – because they couldn't keep their promises to God.

  vi. If we could be saved by our own promises or commitment to Jesus, then His death would have been noble, but unnecessary. We aren't saved by some vow we make, or some leaf we turn over, but by trusting in who Jesus is, and what He has done to save us.

Esther 1 – A Queen Is Deposed

"Esther is the last of the historical books of the Bible, so its main character is named Esther – that is, Venus, the morning star, which sheds its light after all the other stars have ceased to shine, and while the sun still delays rising. Thus, the deeds of Queen Esther cast a ray of light forward into Israel's history from a dark time." (Louis Ginzberg)

A. King Ahasuerus (Xerxes) holds a grand feast.

1. (1-2) King Ahasuerus and his domain.

Now it came to pass in the days of Ahasuerus (this *was* the Ahasuerus who reigned over one hundred and twenty-seven provinces, from India to Ethiopia), in those days when King Ahasuerus sat on the throne of his kingdom, which *was* in Shushan the citadel,

a. **It came to pass in the days of Ahasuerus**: This King **Ahasuerus** is well known to history, though more commonly under the name *Xerxes*. He inherited the vast Persian Empire from his father, Darius I (who is mentioned in passages such as Ezra 4:24, 5:5-7, 6:1-15; Daniel 6:1 and 6:25; Haggai 1:15 and 2:10).

i. The fact of the existence of this king and these circumstances is extremely well attested; archaeologists have discovered the ruins of the very palace where these events happened.

b. **In those days when King Ahasuerus sat on the throne of his kingdom**: At this time (approximately 483 B.C.), Ahasuerus was planning for a doomed invasion of Greece, which would take place several years later. At this time, the city of Athens was in its classical glory and in Greece they were celebrating the 79th Olympic games.

i. In its day, the Persian Empire was the largest the world had ever seen. It covered modern-day Turkey, Iraq, Iran, Pakistan, Jordan, Lebanon, and Israel, and parts of modern-day Egypt, Sudan, Libya, and Arabia.

ii. **In those days**, Ezra had returned to Jerusalem after it had been conquered by the Babylonians. The temple had been rebuilt some 30 years before, although more simply and without the glory of Solomon's temple.

iii. Forty years after these events, under the successor of Ahasuerus (Artaxerxes I), Nehemiah would return to Jerusalem to rebuild the walls of the previously conquered city.

2. (3-9) Three royal feasts.

That **in the third year of his reign he made a feast for all his officials and servants—the powers of Persia and Media, the nobles, and the princes of the provinces** *being* **before him—when he showed the riches of his glorious kingdom and the splendor of his excellent majesty for many days, one hundred and eighty days** *in all.*

And when these days were completed, the king made a feast lasting seven days for all the people who were present in Shushan the citadel, from great to small, in the court of the garden of the king's palace. *There were* **white and blue linen** *curtains* **fastened with cords of fine linen and purple on silver rods and marble pillars;** *and the* **couches** *were* **of gold and silver on a** *mosaic* **pavement of alabaster, turquoise, and white and black marble. And they served drinks in golden vessels, each vessel being different from the other, with royal wine in abundance, according to the generosity of the king. In accordance with the law, the drinking was not compulsory; for so the king had ordered all the officers of his household, that they should do according to each man's pleasure.**

Queen Vashti also made a feast for the women *in* **the royal palace which** *belonged* **to King Ahasuerus.**

a. **He made a feast for all his officials and servants**: The first feast was for all the government officials, where Ahasuerus showed off the glory and splendor of the riches of his kingdom. This feast lasted for 180 days.

b. **The king made a feast lasting seven days for all the people who were present in Shushan the citadel**: The second feast was for the citizens of the capital city, Shushan, and it lasted for seven days.

i. The basic reason for these feasts was, of course, pride. The king wanted to impress his subjects with a great display of his own wealth, power, majesty, and generosity. This is typical of the way that *the rulers of the Gentiles lord it over them, and those who are great exercise authority over them* (Matthew 20:25). There is little doubt that Ahasuerus paid for this feast out of the public treasury.

c. **There were white and blue linen curtains**: In the ancient Hebrew, the white material is literally described as "white stuff." This may be evidence that Esther was written with a man's eye for decorating detail, not a woman's.

d. **In accordance with the law, the drinking was not compulsory**: Among some of the ancients, each guest was obliged to have a drink with the current round, or else leave the party. At this second feast, the king commanded that each man could drink as he pleased.

e. **Queen Vashti also made a feast for the women**: The third feast was for the women in the royal palace, and was conducted by the wife of King Ahasuerus, **Queen Vashti**.

B. Queen Vashti is deposed.

1. (10-11) King Ahasuerus demands that Vashti display her beauty before the guests at the feast.

On the seventh day, when the heart of the king was merry with wine, he commanded Mehuman, Biztha, Harbona, Bigtha, Abagtha, Zethar, and Carcas, seven eunuchs who served in the presence of King Ahasuerus, to bring Queen Vashti before the king, *wearing* **her royal crown, in order to show her beauty to the people and the officials, for she** *was* **beautiful to behold.**

a. **When the heart of the king was merry with wine**: The clear implication is that Ahasuerus was drunk.

b. **To bring Queen Vashti before the king, wearing her royal crown**: According to Jewish tradition, this request came from an argument among the men at the feast as to which country had the most beautiful women. Ahasuerus decided to settle the issue by putting his wife, the queen, on public display.

c. **For she was beautiful to behold**: It is not specifically said, but the implication is that Vashti was expected to display herself in an immodest way.

2. (12) Queen Vashti refuses to appear before the drunken guests of the feast.

But Queen Vashti refused to come at the king's command *brought* **by** *his* **eunuchs; therefore the king was furious, and his anger burned within him.**

a. **But Queen Vashti refused to come**: Though Vashti was by no means a follower of the true God, she had enough wisdom and modesty to know that this was something she should not do.

i. The Bible says that wives have a special responsibility to submit to their husbands (*wives, submit to your own husbands, as to the Lord*; Ephesians 5:22). Yet it does not mean that a wife must obey her husband if he commands her to sin. Every command to submit on a human level is conditioned by the higher obligation to obey God before man.

ii. However, it is important for a Christian in such a situation to maintain a submissive and respectful attitude towards the one in authority. It is possible to disobey the command of another but do so in a submissive manner. It is impossible to say whether Queen Vashti had this attitude in this situation.

iii. Jewish traditions say that her refusal had nothing to do with modesty. These stories say that she was ready to appear before the banqueters completely unclothed, except that God smote her with leprosy just as she received the request (an obviously fanciful tradition).

b. **Therefore the king was furious, and his anger burned**: Queen Vashti was in a very dangerous situation. It does not seem that she put herself in this situation, because it appears that she was not even at this banquet.

i. Sadly, many women today put themselves in dangerous places, especially where alcohol is involved, showing a severe lack of wisdom. Nevertheless, it certainly gives no justification to the sin of men against an unwise woman in such a situation.

ii. "What woman, possessing even a common share of prudence and modesty, could consent to expose herself to the view of such a group of drunken Bacchanalians? Her courage was equal to her modesty: she would resist the royal mandate, rather than violate the rules of chaste decorum.... Hail, noble woman! Be thou a pattern to all thy sex on every similar occasion!" (Clarke)

3. (13-22) The banishment of Vashti.

Then the king said to the wise men who understood the times (for this *was* the king's manner toward all who knew law and justice, those closest to him *being* Carshena, Shethar, Admatha, Tarshish, Meres, Marsena, and Memucan, the seven princes of Persia and Media, who had access to the king's presence, *and* who ranked highest in the kingdom): "What *shall we* do to Queen Vashti, according to law, because she did not obey the command of King Ahasuerus *brought to her* by the eunuchs?"

And Memucan answered before the king and the princes: "Queen Vashti has not only wronged the king, but also all the princes, and all the people who *are* in all the provinces of King Ahasuerus. For the

queen's behavior will become known to all women, so that they will despise their husbands in their eyes, when they report, 'King Ahasuerus commanded Queen Vashti to be brought in before him, but she did not come.' This very day the *noble* ladies of Persia and Media will say to all the king's officials that they have heard of the behavior of the queen. Thus *there will be* excessive contempt and wrath. If it pleases the king, let a royal decree go out from him, and let it be recorded in the laws of the Persians and the Medes, so that it will not be altered, that Vashti shall come no more before King Ahasuerus; and let the king give her royal position to another who is better than she. When the king's decree which he will make is proclaimed throughout all his empire (for it is great), all wives will honor their husbands, both great and small."

And the reply pleased the king and the princes, and the king did according to the word of Memucan. Then he sent letters to all the king's provinces, to each province in its own script, and to every people in their own language, that each man should be master in his own house, and speak in the language of his own people.

a. **That Vashti shall come no more before King Ahasuerus; and let the king give her royal position to another who is better than she**: When King Ahasuerus heeded this advice from Memucan, he showed himself to be unreasonable and wrong. He should have honored the dignity of his queen. Yet, history's profile of Ahasuerus shows him to be an unreasonable and foolish man in many cases.

i. On one occasion, Ahasuerus executed the builders of a bridge because an ocean storm destroyed it; then he commanded that the water and waves be whipped and chained to punish the *sea*.

b. **That each man should be master in his own house**: The purpose of the harsh treatment of Vashti was so that she would not set a bad example for the other women of Persia. Ahasuerus wanted to reinforce the idea of a man's leadership in the home.

i. They were afraid that, because of Queen Vashti's example, wives would **despise their husbands**; that there would **be excessive contempt and wrath**; therefore, they wanted to ensure that **each man should be master in his own house**.

ii. The *goal* presented here was admirable and speaks to the need within every man to sense respect and honor from his wife. Paul's instruction to wives was summed up like this: *let the wife see that she respects her husband* (Ephesians 5:33). A wife's respect is the most precious gift she can give her husband.

iii. However, the *means* used here to gain and preserve this respect were foolish. A man cannot demand or coerce respect from his wife – if it isn't freely given, then it isn't worth anything.

Esther 2 – Esther Is Chosen Queen

A. The gathering together of a harem for King Ahasuerus.

1. (1-4) A search is made for a replacement for Queen Vashti.

After these things, when the wrath of King Ahasuerus subsided, he remembered Vashti, what she had done, and what had been decreed against her. Then the king's servants who attended him said: "Let beautiful young virgins be sought for the king; and let the king appoint officers in all the provinces of his kingdom, that they may gather all the beautiful young virgins to Shushan the citadel, into the women's quarters, under the custody of Hegai the king's eunuch, custodian of the women. And let beauty preparations be given *them*. Then let the young woman who pleases the king be queen instead of Vashti."

This thing pleased the king, and he did so.

> a. **After these things**: This is broader than just the events of the previous chapter. Esther 2:16 indicates that there was a four-year span between chapters one and two. During that time, King Ahasuerus made his massive, unsuccessful invasion of Greece and he came home a defeated man, wanting to cheer his heart through sensual diversions.

> b. **Let beautiful young virgins be sought for the king**: The plan was to assemble a harem from the most beautiful women of the land; to bring them into a harem for the king, and to choose the most favored woman to be his queen from that group. This was sort of a "Miss Persian Empire" contest, and the winner would **be queen instead of Vashti**.

> c. **This thing pleased the king, and he did so**: The ancient Jewish historian Josephus says that Ahasuerus had a total of 400 women selected.

2. (5-7) Esther and her family.

In Shushan the citadel there was a certain Jew whose name *was* Mordecai the son of Jair, the son of Shimei, the son of Kish, a Benjamite. *Kish* had been carried away from Jerusalem with the captives who had been

captured with Jeconiah king of Judah, whom Nebuchadnezzar the king of Babylon had carried away. And *Mordecai* had brought up Hadassah, that *is*, Esther, his uncle's daughter, for she had neither father nor mother. The young woman *was* lovely and beautiful. When her father and mother died, Mordecai took her as his own daughter.

a. **There was a certain Jew whose name was Mordecai**: Mordecai, the cousin of Esther, came to Persia in one of the waves of deportation that the Babylonians imposed on Judah when they conquered that land.

b. **And Mordecai had brought up Hadassah, that is, Esther, his uncle's daughter**: Esther (whose Jewish name **Hadassah** means "myrtle"; the Persian name **Esther** means "star") was raised by her cousin Mordecai after the death of her father and mother.

i. "In prophetic symbolism the myrtle would replace the briars and thorns of the desert, so depicting the Lord's forgiveness and acceptance of his people. (Isaiah 41:19; 55:13; cf. Zechariah 1:8)" (Baldwin)

ii. They were part of the large Jewish community that was forced to leave Judah but did not decide to return with Ezra. In the days of Mordecai and Esther, the land of Judah was regarded as a wild and backward place.

c. **The young woman was lovely and beautiful**: The Hebrew for **lovely and beautiful** is literally, "beautiful in form and lovely to look at." Or, as the NIV2011 has it, she *had a lovely figure and was beautiful*.

i. We regard that the Bible is generally given to understatement; when it says that Esther was **lovely and beautiful**, we know that it isn't an exaggeration.

3. (8) Esther is taken into the king's harem.

So it was, when the king's command and decree were heard, and when many young women were gathered at Shushan the citadel, *under* the custody of Hegai, that Esther also was taken to the king's palace, into the care of Hegai the custodian of the women.

a. **That Esther also was taken to the king's palace**: It seems that Esther didn't really have a choice about this.

b. **Into the care of Hegai the custodian of the women**: Hegai was the *king's eunuch* (Esther 2:3), a man entrusted with the oversight of the king's harem for obvious reasons.

i. According to Baldwin, Hegai is specifically mentioned by the Greek historian Herodotus as being an officer of King Ahasuerus.

B. Esther in the courts of the king.

1. (9) Esther's favored treatment in the palace.

Now the young woman pleased him, and she obtained his favor; so he readily gave beauty preparations to her, besides her allowance. Then seven choice maidservants were provided for her from the king's palace, and he moved her and her maidservants to the best *place* in the house of the women.

a. **Now the young woman pleased him, and she obtained his favor**: Esther *obtained favor* with Hegai, the man in authority over her. In this, her godliness ensured a fulfillment of Proverbs 3:3-4: *Let not mercy and truth forsake you; bind them around your neck, write them on the tablet of your heart, and so find favor and high esteem in the sight of God and man.*

b. **He readily gave beauty preparations to her, besides her allowance**: Because of this favor, Hegai gave Esther special beauty preparations, beyond **her allowance**. He also gave her **seven choice maidservants** to look after her beauty needs.

i. Esther was beautiful to begin with; now she looked like a model, and she looked that way all the time.

ii. The ancient Hebrew word for **beauty preparations** comes from the root "to scour, to polish." (Huey)

2. (10-11) Esther conceals her Jewish identity.

Esther had not revealed her people or family, for Mordecai had charged her not to reveal *it*. And every day Mordecai paced in front of the court of the women's quarters, to learn of Esther's welfare and what was happening to her.

a. **Esther had not revealed her people or family**: Normally, there is no good reason for hiding the fact that we are Christians. Far too many Christians act as if they are "secret agents" – and they always conceal who they are in the Lord.

i. We must take the warning Jesus gave in Matthew 10:32-33 seriously: *Therefore whoever confesses Me before men, him I will also confess before My Father who is in heaven. But whoever denies Me before men, him I will also deny before My Father who is in heaven.* We can't live a life of denial and expect God to recognize us.

b. **For Mordecai had charged her not to reveal it**: However, we do recognize that there are situations where God may direct us to be reticent about our Christian identity – not for the purposes of permanently concealing it, but waiting for the opportune moment to reveal it. Apparently, this is what

Mordecai sensed was right to do in this circumstance, and Esther agreed.

> i. For example, in some situations you might initially act as if you know nothing when approached by a Jehovah's Witness or a Mormon, and do it not to deny Jesus, but to seize a strategic opportunity.

c. **Every day Mordecai paced in front of the court of the women's quarters, to learn of Esther's welfare**: Mordecai's great interest in Esther's state shows his love and concern for her in such a potentially dangerous place.

3. (12-14) The method of preparing and presenting the women before the king is established.

Each young woman's turn came to go in to King Ahasuerus after she had completed twelve months' preparation, according to the regulations for the women, for thus were the days of their preparation apportioned: six months with oil of myrrh, and six months with perfumes and preparations for beautifying women. Thus *prepared, each* young woman went to the king, and she was given whatever she desired to take with her from the women's quarters to the king's palace. In the evening she went, and in the morning she returned to the second house of the women, to the custody of Shaashgaz, the king's eunuch who kept the concubines. She would not go in to the king again unless the king delighted in her and called for her by name.

a. **After she had completed twelve months' preparation**: Persia was one of many countries famous for its aromatic perfumes and ancient customs for the preparation of brides, including ritualistic baths, plucking of the eyebrows, the painting of hands and feet with henna, facial make-up, and applications of a beautifying paste all over the body, meant to lighten the color of the skin and to remove spots and blemishes.

> i. One reason for the lengthy time of preparation was to tell if the women had been pregnant upon coming into the harem, so that the king would not be charged with fathering a child that was not his.

> ii. Matthew Poole said that the oils and perfumes were necessary because, "The bodies of men and women in those hot countries did of themselves yield very ill scents, if not corrected and qualified by art."

b. **Thus prepared, each young woman went to the king**: It sounds wonderful – a year of constant spa treatments. Yet the destiny of these women should also be considered: one evening with the king. If he chose them from the 400 others to be his queen, then she would be his companion (until she displeased him). As for the 399 who lost, they were banished to the harem where they stayed the wife or the concubine of the king, but rarely, if ever, saw him afterwards. And they were never free to marry other men, essentially living as perpetual widows.

4. (15-18) Esther is selected as queen.

Now when the turn came for Esther the daughter of Abihail the uncle of Mordecai, who had taken her as his daughter, to go in to the king, she requested nothing but what Hegai the king's eunuch, the custodian of the women, advised. And Esther obtained favor in the sight of all who saw her. So Esther was taken to King Ahasuerus, into his royal palace, in the tenth month, which *is* the month of Tebeth, in the seventh year of his reign. The king loved Esther more than all the *other* women, and she obtained grace and favor in his sight more than all the virgins; so he set the royal crown upon her head and made her queen instead of Vashti. Then the king made a great feast, the Feast of Esther, for all his officials and servants; and he proclaimed a holiday in the provinces and gave gifts according to the generosity of a king.

a. **She requested nothing but what Hegai the king's eunuch, the custodian of the women, advised**: Esther's humble wisdom was shown in the way that she allowed the **custodian of the women** to assist her preparations.

b. **Esther obtained favor in the sight of all who saw her**: This was because of *both* Esther's godliness and beauty.

i. Beauty often gains people (especially women) favor with others. This is a fact that Christians must accept, wisely teaching their children what really matters, and refusing to rely too much on beauty for their judgment of people.

c. **She obtained grace and favor in his sight more than all the virgins**: Because of the great favor that she obtained with the king, Esther was selected to be the queen of King Ahasuerus.

i. Esther's life so far had been remarkable. She was the child of Jewish exiles, who both died; she was raised by her cousin in a foreign and often hostile land; she was taken by compulsion into the king's harem; she found favor with all whom she met; she was finally selected to be the queen of the realm.

ii. This remarkable course of events wasn't an accident; it wasn't just because of luck or fortune or Esther's good looks or sparkling personality. God had a plan, and Esther was part of it. As Psalm 75:6-7 says: *For exaltation comes neither from the east nor from the west nor from the south. But God is the Judge: He puts down one, and exalts another.*

iii. In the same way, we have a place in God's plan. Whatever your situation, God has a purpose for it – maybe a short purpose, or a long one; perhaps a large purpose or a small purpose, but God has a reason (Ephesians 2:10).

iv. To this point, the story of Esther also shows us that in the outworking of His plan, God can use the evil of man. God did not make Ahasuerus drunk or make him demand that his queen present herself in an immodest way before the lords of the kingdom. Yet God allowed this wicked action of man to fulfill a purpose in His greater plan. We find assurance in the truth that no other person, no matter how evil they are, can defeat God's plan for our lives, no matter what they have done to us or will do to us.

C. Mordecai saves the king's life.

1. (19-20) Mordecai's rises in prominence and Esther continues to conceal her Jewish identity.

When virgins were gathered together a second time, Mordecai sat within the king's gate. *Now* Esther had not revealed her family and her people, just as Mordecai had charged her, for Esther obeyed the command of Mordecai as when she was brought up by him.

a. **Mordecai sat within the king's gate**: This position indicates that Mordecai was associated with the decision-makers and men of influence in the kingdom.

b. **Now Esther had not revealed her family and her people, just as Mordecai had charged her**: Some have thought that the book of Esther carries this idea of concealment too far. This book has been criticized because it does not mention the name of God (neither does the Song of Solomon).

i. Some people say that the name of God was left out of the book of Esther because of its use in the festivities surrounding Purim, where people commonly became drunk. According to Huey, one rabbi taught: "A man is obligated to drink on Purim until he is unable to distinguish between 'Blessed be Mordecai' and 'Cursed be Haman.'" Some have wondered if, in that atmosphere, it would be too easy to profane the name of God if it were to be read at such a festival.

ii. Others see the name YHWH hidden in acrostics, based on the initial and final letters of successive words in Esther 1:20, 5:4, 5:13, and 7:7. In some manuscripts, the letters in these words are written a bit larger to give them prominence.

iii. Perhaps also the book of Esther does not contain the name of God because it was written under Persian rule and for distribution in the Persian Empire.

iv. Most likely, the book of Esther doesn't include the name of God because it shows how God works *behind* the scenes; God is always active in the book of Esther, even though it is in the background.

2. (21-23) Mordecai hears of an assassination conspiracy and informs the king, saving the king's life.

In those days, while Mordecai sat within the king's gate, two of the king's eunuchs, Bigthan and Teresh, doorkeepers, became furious and sought to lay hands on King Ahasuerus. So the matter became known to Mordecai, who told Queen Esther, and Esther informed the king in Mordecai's name. And when an inquiry was made into the matter, it was confirmed, and both were hanged on a gallows; and it was written in the book of the chronicles in the presence of the king.

a. **The matter became known to Mordecai, who told Queen Esther, and Esther informed the king**: Mordecai's attitude wasn't, "I'm a Jewish man in exile under a pagan king, so I do not care if he is killed." Instead, he anticipates Peter's thought in 1 Peter 2:17, before Peter ever wrote it: *Fear God. Honor the king.*

i. This threat of assassination was real. Ahasuerus was eventually murdered by his prime minister, who placed Artaxerxes I on the throne.

b. **Both were hanged on a gallows**: The word **gallows** is literally *tree*; the idea that they were *hanged on a tree* probably refers not to hanging with a noose around the neck, but to impalement on a stake, much like crucifixion.

i. "A pointed stake is set upright in the ground, and the culprit is taken, placed on the sharp point, and then pulled down by his legs till the stake that went in at the fundament passes up through the body and comes out through the neck. A most dreadful species of punishment, in which revenge and cruelty may glut the utmost of their malice. The culprit lives a considerable time in excruciating agonies." (Clarke)

Esther 3 – Haman's Conspiracy

A. Haman determines to destroy the Jews.

1. (1) Haman's promotion.

After these things King Ahasuerus promoted Haman, the son of Hammedatha the Agagite, and advanced him and set his seat above all the princes who *were* with him.

a. **King Ahasuerus promoted Haman**: Haman was an ungodly man, but God had a purpose in allowing him to be promoted.

b. **Haman, the son of Hammedatha the Agagite**: Haman was a descendant of Agag, the king of the Amalekites, the people who were Israel's sworn enemy for generations (Exodus 17:14-16).

2. (2-3) Mordecai's refusal to bow before Haman or to pay him homage.

And all the king's servants who *were* within the king's gate bowed and paid homage to Haman, for so the king had commanded concerning him. But Mordecai would not bow or pay homage. Then the king's servants who *were* within the king's gate said to Mordecai, "Why do you transgress the king's command?"

a. **Mordecai would not bow or pay homage**: There does not seem to be a Biblical command against bowing or paying homage to a political leader as a sign of respect (Genesis 18:2; 23:7; 43:26; Exodus 18:7; 2 Samuel 16:4). Rather, Mordecai must have known something about this man Haman, which persuaded him that Haman was unworthy of such honor.

i. "No self-respecting Benjaminite would bow before a descendant of the ancient Amalekite enemy of the Jews." (Huey)

ii. "'The reverence' which the king had commanded his servants to show to Haman was not simply a sign of respect, but an act of worship.... Mordecai stood erect while the crowd of servants lay flat on their faces, as the great man passed through the gate, because he would have no share in an act of worship to any but Jehovah." (Maclaren)

b. **Why do you transgress the king's command?** We do not read of a specific command from King Ahasuerus that everyone had to bow before Haman. Perhaps the command was implied in the promotion that he received (Esther 3:1).

3. (4-6) The wounded pride of Haman drives him to seek retribution against Mordecai and all his people – the Jews.

Now it happened, when they spoke to him daily and he would not listen to them, that they told *it* to Haman, to see whether Mordecai's words would stand; for *Mordecai* had told them that he *was* a Jew. When Haman saw that Mordecai did not bow or pay him homage, Haman was filled with wrath. But he disdained to lay hands on Mordecai alone, for they had told him of the people of Mordecai. Instead, Haman sought to destroy all the Jews who *were* throughout the whole kingdom of Ahasuerus; the people of Mordecai.

a. **It happened, when they spoke to him daily and he would not listen to them, that they told it to Haman**: Apparently, Haman did not at first notice Mordecai's stubborn resistance. It had to be pointed out to him by his aides.

b. **Haman was filled with wrath**: Haman was an extremely proud and insecure man; he could only consider himself a success if *everyone* else thought he was a success.

c. **Haman sought to destroy all the Jews who were throughout the whole kingdom**: Haman's anger led him to take out his wrath upon **all the Jews** in the kingdom. Haman's problem had exposed his basic hatred for all Jewish people.

4. (7) Haman determines the exact date that he will strike out against the Jews.

In the first month, which is the month of Nisan, in the twelfth year of King Ahasuerus, they cast Pur (that *is,* the lot), before Haman to determine the day and the month, until *it fell on the* twelfth *month,* which *is* the month of Adar.

a. **They cast Pur**: This was the Persian word for **the lot**, something like dice, which was used to leave a decision to chance – or to the God who guides what appears to be chance.

b. **Until it fell on the twelfth month**: Since this took place **in the first month**, the casting of the lot determined that the Jews would not be attacked and massacred for at least 11 months.

i. This proves the truth of Proverbs 16:33: *The lot is cast into the lap, but its every decision is from the LORD.* The long delay between the first month and the month of the massacre of the Jewish people was ordained by God.

B. Haman tells his plot to the king.

1. (8-9) Haman's proposal to King Ahasuerus.

Then Haman said to King Ahasuerus, "There is a certain people scattered and dispersed among the people in all the provinces of your kingdom; their laws *are* different from all *other* people's, and they do not keep the king's laws. Therefore it *is* not fitting for the king to let them remain. If it pleases the king, let *a decree* be written that they be destroyed, and I will pay ten thousand talents of silver into the hands of those who do the work, to bring *it* into the king's treasuries."

a. **Then Haman said to King Ahasuerus**: Haman's charge was the most dangerous possible; it was a half-truth. Yes, the Jews were a **certain people scattered and dispersed**; and yes, they had their own **laws**. Their own laws did not prevent them from keeping the king's laws as loyal subjects.

i. In fact, Mordecai's refusal to bow before Haman was *not* based on the law of God, but on the principle of personal integrity. It seems that Haman was almost completely unfamiliar with this principle.

b. **Let a decree be written that they be destroyed**: Haman suggested organizing the mass murder of the Jewish people. Haman also neglected to tell King Ahasuerus how many of these **certain people** there were in his kingdom; Ahasuerus probably considered this a relatively small number.

c. **I will pay ten thousand talents of silver**: This was essentially the promise of a bribe. This money would not come from Haman's own pocket; it would be obtained from the property of slaughtered Jews.

i. "The great bribe which Haman offered to the king is variously estimated as equal to from three to four millions sterling [$544 to $725 million USD in 2024]. He, no doubt, reckoned on making more than that out of the confiscation of Jewish property." (Maclaren)

2. (10-11) The king agrees to the plan.

So the king took his signet ring from his hand and gave it to Haman, the son of Hammedatha the Agagite, the enemy of the Jews. And the king said to Haman, "The money and the people *are* given to you, to do with them as seems good to you."

a. **Haman, the son of Hammedatha the Agagite, the enemy of the Jews**: As Haman is revealed to be more and more of a villain and **enemy**, his **Agagite** heritage is again mentioned. Haman was a descendant of the Amalekites, who were Israel's sworn enemy for generations (Exodus 17:14-16).

b. **The money and the people are given to you, to do with them as seems good to you**: Again, King Ahasuerus probably had no idea what he had agreed to; he probably believed that he had merely approved the execution of a handful of dangerous revolutionaries in his kingdom.

3. (12-15) The decree is published.

Then the king's scribes were called on the thirteenth day of the first month, and *a decree* was written according to all that Haman commanded—to the king's satraps, to the governors who *were* over each province, to the officials of all people, to every province according to its script, and to every people in their language. In the name of King Ahasuerus it was written, and sealed with the king's signet ring. And the letters were sent by couriers into all the king's provinces, to destroy, to kill, and to annihilate all the Jews, both young and old, little children and women, in one day, on the thirteenth *day* of the twelfth *month*, which *is* the month of Adar, and to plunder their possessions. A copy of the document was to be issued as law in every province, being published for all people, that they should be ready for that day. The couriers went out, hastened by the king's command; and the decree was proclaimed in Shushan the citadel. So the king and Haman sat down to drink, but the city of Shushan was perplexed.

a. **To destroy, to kill, and to annihilate all the Jews, both young and old, little children and women, in one day**: With this, an empire-wide death sentence on the Jews was announced by the king. This was like other attacks against the Jewish people in history, except that it was announced well in advance.

b. **So the king and Haman sat down to drink**: When the king **sat down to drink**, he thought he had done well – but he did not really understand what he had done. Haman also **sat down to drink** and thought he had done well – and he knew exactly what he intended to do. Despite this, **the city of Shushan was perplexed**.

i. The citizens of the empire knew Jewish people who lived among them, and that they were good citizens who caused no trouble. Therefore, they were confused that such a decree was published, one that treated the Jewish people were dangerous enemies.

ii. Again, all this came to pass because of the insecurity and wounded pride of one wicked man – Haman.

Esther 4 – Esther's Decision

A. Mordecai's mourning.

1. (1-3) He and the rest of the Jews lament their fate.

When Mordecai learned all that had happened, he tore his clothes and put on sackcloth and ashes, and went out into the midst of the city. He cried out with a loud and bitter cry. He went as far as the front of the king's gate, for no one *might* enter the king's gate clothed with sackcloth. And in every province where the king's command and decree arrived, *there was* great mourning among the Jews, with fasting, weeping, and wailing; and many lay in sackcloth and ashes.

a. **He tore his clothes and put on sackcloth and ashes**: Though Mordecai was anguished at all this, we remember also that his integrity was the cause of it. He **cried out with a loud and bitter cry**, but he would not change his mind and grovel at the feet of Haman to save himself or his people.

i. This was not only because of the personal integrity of Mordecai but also because he knew that the laws of the Persians could not be changed once decreed (Esther 1:19).

b. **There was great mourning among the Jews**: Mordecai's reaction was imitated all over the Persian Empire in public expressions of grief and horror.

2. (4-7) Mordecai explains the problem to Esther.

So Esther's maids and eunuchs came and told her, and the queen was deeply distressed. Then she sent garments to clothe Mordecai and take his sackcloth away from him, but he would not accept *them*. Then Esther called Hathach, *one* of the king's eunuchs whom he had appointed to attend her, and she gave him a command concerning Mordecai, to learn what and why this *was*. So Hathach went out to Mordecai in the city square that *was* in front of the king's gate. And Mordecai told him all that had happened to him, and the sum of money that Haman had promised to pay into the king's treasuries to destroy the Jews.

a. **Esther's maids and eunuchs came and told her**: Esther, living in the isolation of the palace, had not yet been made aware of this decree. Before she understood the decree, she could not understand why her cousin Mordecai made such a spectacle of himself.

b. **And the sum of money that Haman had promised to pay into the king's treasuries to destroy the Jews**: Mordecai knew well that this plot was in part motivated by the greedy desire to seize the money and the property of the Jewish people.

B. Mordecai's request.

1. (8-12) His first request and Esther's appeal to him in response.

He also gave him a copy of the written decree for their destruction, which was given at Shushan, that he might show it to Esther and explain it to her, and that he might command her to go in to the king to make supplication to him and plead before him for her people. So Hathach returned and told Esther the words of Mordecai.

Then Esther spoke to Hathach, and gave him a command for Mordecai: "All the king's servants and the people of the king's provinces know that any man or woman who goes into the inner court to the king, who has not been called, *he has* but one law: put *all* to death, except the one to whom the king holds out the golden scepter, that he may live. Yet I myself have not been called to go in to the king these thirty days." So they told Mordecai Esther's words.

a. **That he might show it to Esther and explain it to her**: After giving a copy of the decree to Esther through a courier, Mordecai challenged her to intercede on behalf of her people before the king.

b. **Any man or woman who goes into the inner court to the king, who has not been called, he has but one law: put all to death**: Esther explained the difficulty behind this – she was only allowed to go to the king when called, and if she came on her own, she could be executed for daring to approach the king without an invitation.

i. Apparently, the life of a queen of Persia was not one of great intimacy with the king. Esther said, "**I myself have not been called to go in to the king these thirty days**" – meaning she had not seen her husband for an entire month.

2. (13-14) Mordecai's second request.

And Mordecai told *them* to answer Esther: "Do not think in your heart that you will escape in the king's palace any more than all the other Jews. For if you remain completely silent at this time, relief and

deliverance will arise for the Jews from another place, but you and your father's house will perish. Yet who knows whether you have come to the kingdom for *such* **a time as this?"**

a. **Do not think in your heart that you will escape**: Mordecai reminded Esther that she could not remain insulated from this decree any more than anyone else.

b. **If you remain completely silent at this time, relief and deliverance will arise for the Jews from another place**: Mordecai's trust was in the faithfulness of God, not in the faithfulness of Esther. He knew that God would not fail in His faithfulness to His promise, even if His people fail to be faithful.

i. "Mordecai is sure that deliverance will come. He does not know whence, but come it will. How did he arrive at that serene confidence? Certainly because he trusted God's ancient promises, and believed in the indestructibility of the nation which a divine hand protected." (Maclaren)

ii. "He [Mordecai] is no fatalist; he believes in man's work, therefore he urges her to let herself be the instrument by which God's work shall be done. He is no atheist; he believes in God's sovereign power and unchangeable faithfulness, therefore he looks without dismay to the possibility of her failure." (Maclaren)

c. **But you and your father's house will perish**: Mordecai reminded Esther that though the fate of God's people rested on God and not on her, her *own fate* depended on her faithfulness to God.

d. **Yet who knows whether you have come to the kingdom for such a time as this?** Mordecai knew that God had promoted this orphan in exile for a reason – and Esther must have the courage and wisdom to see that reason and fulfill it.

i. This principle applies to us also. God promotes us or puts us in a place for a reason, and we need the courage and wisdom to see that reason and to walk in it. "Esther was made queen, not that she might live in luxury and be the plaything of a king, but that she might serve Israel. Power is duty. Responsibility is measured by capacity. Obligation attends advantages. Gifts are burdens." (Maclaren)

ii. "You have been wishing for another position where you could do something for Jesus: do not wish anything of the kind, but serve him where you are." (Spurgeon)

iii. "I believe that in dark times God is making lamps with which to remove the gloom. Martin Luther is sitting by his father's hearth in the forest when the Pope is selling his wicked indulgences: he will come out soon, and stop the crowing of the cock of the Romish Christ-denying Peter. John Calvin is quietly studying when false doctrine is most rife, and he will be heard of at Geneva. A young man is here this morning – I do not know whereabouts he is, but I pray the Lord to make this to be an ordination sermon to him, starting him on his life-work. I feel as if I were Samuel at Bethlehem, seeking for David, to anoint him with a horn of oil in the name of the Lord." (Spurgeon)

3. (15-17) Esther's decision.

Then Esther told *them* to reply to Mordecai: "Go, gather all the Jews who are present in Shushan, and fast for me; neither eat nor drink for three days, night or day. My maids and I will fast likewise. And so I will go to the king, which *is* against the law; and if I perish, I perish!"

So Mordecai went his way and did according to all that Esther commanded him.

a. **Go, gather all the Jews who are present in Shushan, and fast for me:** Taking the determination of the Lord, Esther decided that she would go and make a bold appearance before the king, but only if she was supported by prayer and fasting.

i. Jesus reminded us that special spiritual battles sometimes require special preparation with prayer and fasting. Regarding a stubborn case of demonic possession, He said, *this kind does not go out except by prayer and fasting* (Matthew 17:21).

b. **And so I will go to the king, which is against the law; and if I perish, I perish!** Esther carried a bold attitude towards her mission. She was determined to be obedient, no matter what the cost.

i. "This womanly soul was of the same stock as a Miriam, a Deborah, Jephthah's daughter; and the same fire burned in her, – utter devotion to Israel because [of her] entire consecration to Israel's God." (Maclaren)

ii. Jesus exhorted us to have the same attitude: *Do not fear those who kill the body but cannot kill the soul* (Matthew 10:28). Paul was also an example of this attitude: *To live is Christ, and to die is gain* (Philippians 1:21).

Esther 5 – Esther's Bold Request

A. The first banquet.

1. (1-5) Esther invites both King Ahasuerus and Haman to a banquet.

Now it happened on the third day that Esther put on *her* royal *robes* and stood in the inner court of the king's palace, across from the king's house, while the king sat on his royal throne in the royal house, facing the entrance of the house. So it was, when the king saw Queen Esther standing in the court, *that* she found favor in his sight, and the king held out to Esther the golden scepter that *was* in his hand. Then Esther went near and touched the top of the scepter.

And the king said to her, "What do you wish, Queen Esther? What *is* your request? It shall be given to you—up to half the kingdom!"

So Esther answered, "If it pleases the king, let the king and Haman come today to the banquet that I have prepared for him."

Then the king said, "Bring Haman quickly, that he may do as Esther has said." So the king and Haman went to the banquet that Esther had prepared.

a. **Esther put on her royal robes and stood in the inner court of the king's palace**: Esther showed courage in her willingness to appear before the king without being summoned by him. This took special courage because King Ahasuerus did not have a good reputation for treating his queens well.

b. **If it pleases the king, let the king and Haman come today to the banquet that I have prepared for him**: Esther also showed tact by not blurting out her ultimate request right away. She wanted to first win the king's confidence in her – and she wanted Haman at the banquet to ultimately expose his wickedness.

2. (6-8) Esther's request at the first banquet.

At the banquet of wine the king said to Esther, "What *is* your petition? It shall be granted you. What *is* your request, up to half the kingdom? It shall be done!"

Then Esther answered and said, "My petition and request *is this*: If I have found favor in the sight of the king, and if it pleases the king to grant my petition and fulfill my request, then let the king and Haman come to the banquet which I will prepare for them, and tomorrow I will do as the king has said."

> a. **What is your petition? It shall be granted you. What is your request, up to half the kingdom? It shall be done**: King Ahasuerus repeated this offer to Queen Esther. It was more of a proverbial expression than a literal offer for anything up to **half of the kingdom**.

> b. **Let the king and Haman come to the banquet which I will prepare for them, and tomorrow I will do as the king has said**: Esther put off the request for one more day, promising to reveal her petition at a second banquet on the next day.

>> i. It may be that Esther could not find the courage to present her request and used the successive banquets as a delaying tactic. "Some of us are very unaccountable, but on that woman's unaccountable silence far more was hanging than appears at first sight. Doubtless she longed to bring out her secret, but the words came not. God was in it; it was not the right time to speak, and therefore she was led to put off her disclosure. I dare say she regretted it, and wondered when she should be able to come to the point, but the Lord knew best." (Spurgeon)

B. Haman's plot against Mordecai.

1. (9-13) Haman's frustration with Mordecai.

So Haman went out that day joyful and with a glad heart; but when Haman saw Mordecai in the king's gate, and that he did not stand or tremble before him, he was filled with indignation against Mordecai. Nevertheless Haman restrained himself and went home, and he sent and called for his friends and his wife Zeresh. Then Haman told them of his great riches, the multitude of his children, everything in which the king had promoted him, and how he had advanced him above the officials and servants of the king.

Moreover Haman said, "Besides, Queen Esther invited no one but me to come in with the king to the banquet that she prepared; and tomorrow I am again invited by her, along with the king. Yet all this avails me nothing, so long as I see Mordecai the Jew sitting at the king's gate."

a. **He was filled with indignation against Mordecai**: Miserable Haman! Honored by both the king and queen of Persia, yet the disapproval of one man makes him feel worthless. This is an accurate description of how empty the rewards of this world are.

> i. Haman's deep-seated insecurities and need to be honored by *everybody* means that he could never be happy; God meant this hunger for acceptance in each of us to be ultimately fulfilled in Jesus Christ – because we are *accepted in the Beloved* (Ephesians 1:6), accepted before God because of who we are in Jesus.

b. **Nevertheless Haman restrained himself**: This is remarkable evidence of the hand of God. God would not allow the fury of Haman to be acted upon until all the proper pieces were set in place to ultimately defeat his plan.

c. **Yet all this avails me nothing, so long as I see Mordecai the Jew sitting at the king's gate**: Haman's problem wasn't Mordecai, it was the emptiness in his own heart. Even if he solved the "Mordecai problem," it would not fill the void in his heart.

> i. "The soul was made for God, and nothing but God can fill it and make it happy." (Clarke)

2. (14) Haman happily receives counsel to ask for Mordecai's execution the next day at the second feast.

Then his wife Zeresh and all his friends said to him, "Let a gallows be made, fifty cubits high, and in the morning suggest to the king that Mordecai be hanged on it; then go merrily with the king to the banquet."

And the thing pleased Haman; so he had the gallows made.

a. **Let a gallows be made, fifty cubits high, and in the morning suggest to the king that Mordecai be hanged on it**: For these friends of Haman, it wasn't enough to just punish Mordecai's people (remember the genocide against the Jews was already set in motion), or merely to kill Mordecai. They wanted Haman to ask for a public, humiliating execution of Mordecai on gallows 75 feet (25 meters) high.

> i. The **gallows** mentioned here was probably not for *hanging* a victim, but for violently killing and displaying the victim. "A pointed stake is set upright in the ground, and the culprit is taken, placed on the sharp point, and then pulled down by his legs till the stake that went in at the fundament passes up through the body and comes out through the neck. A most dreadful species of punishment, in which revenge and cruelty may glut the utmost of their malice. The culprit lives a considerable time in excruciating agonies." (Clarke)

b. **And the thing pleased Haman; so he had the gallows made**: We should never underestimate the destructive and distorting power of hatred. The irrational, violent hatred that made Haman want to see Mordecai hang to his death is the same irrational, violent hatred that made man want to hang Jesus on a cross.

Esther 6 – Honor for Mordecai

A. The king's question.

1. (1-3) A sleepless night.

That night the king could not sleep. So one was commanded to bring the book of the records of the chronicles; and they were read before the king. And it was found written that Mordecai had told of Bigthana and Teresh, two of the king's eunuchs, the doorkeepers who had sought to lay hands on King Ahasuerus. Then the king said, "What honor or dignity has been bestowed on Mordecai for this?"

And the king's servants who attended him said, "Nothing has been done for him."

a. **The king could not sleep. So one was commanded to bring the book of the records of the chronicles**: King Ahasuerus did what many people do when they cannot sleep. He brought out a book and used it to fill the sleepless night, hoping that the reading would make him sleepy again.

i. "Ahasuerus is master of one hundred and twenty and seven provinces, but not master of ten minutes' sleep." (Spurgeon)

b. **And it was found written**: This was a remarkable example of providence in action. King Ahasuerus cannot sleep, and he can choose 20 different diversions to fill his sleepless night – but he commands that a book be brought to him and read. The one commanded to bring the book could have brought any one book of the **records of the chronicles**, but he brought one particular book. The book could be opened to any page, but it was opened to the exact page telling the story of Mordecai and how he saved the king from assassination. God guided every step along the way.

i. Even as King Ahasuerus had a **book of the records of the chronicles** (literally a *book of remembrance*), so God also has a book of remembrance: *Then those who feared the LORD spoke to one another, and the LORD listened and heard them; so a book of remembrance was written*

221

before Him for those who fear the LORD and who meditate on His name. (Malachi 3:16)

c. **What honor or dignity has been bestowed on Mordecai for this?** Showing rare concern for a common subject, King Ahasuerus considered a reward for Mordecai.

2. (4-5) Haman in the courts of the king.

So the king said, "Who *is* in the court?" Now Haman had *just* entered the outer court of the king's palace to suggest that the king hang Mordecai on the gallows that he had prepared for him.

The king's servants said to him, "Haman is there, standing in the court."

And the king said, "Let him come in."

a. **Now Haman had just entered the outer court**: It was no *coincidence* that Haman entered the king's court at just that moment; it was no *coincidence* that Haman came at that moment to ask for the execution of Mordecai; it was no *coincidence* that King Ahasuerus wanted to honor Mordecai at just that moment.

b. **Haman is there, standing in the court**: If this book of Esther shows us anything, it shows us that God manages the affairs of men, even without their knowledge. God knows what He is doing and in the courts of heaven there are no coincidences or surprises.

i. Esther wasn't *lucky* to be queen; Mordecai wasn't *lucky* to have heard of the assassination plot; it wasn't *luck* or *chance* that made Haman enter the royal courts at this time with this heart. All of these events were orchestrated by God and not by luck.

ii. This becomes difficult, of course, when *bad* things happen to us. It is easy to see God's management of all things when we see good things happen. But what about the bad? Even then, we must trust God's total plan, realizing that *all things work together for good to those who love God, to those who are the called according to His purpose* (Romans 8:28). We understand that Paul says *all* things work *together*; any one event, taken in isolation may seem to make no sense, but when we see all things working together, we recognized the ultimate wisdom of God's plan.

3. (6) King Ahasuerus asks a question of Haman.

So Haman came in, and the king asked him, "What shall be done for the man whom the king delights to honor?"

Now Haman thought in his heart, "Whom would the king delight to honor more than me?"

a. **What shall be done for the man whom the king delights to honor?** God arranged all things: not only would all the Jews be ultimately protected, but Mordecai and Haman would each receive what they deserved.

b. **Whom would the king delight to honor more than me?** God often allows a proud man to fall into his own trap (Proverbs 26:27). Here God arranged that Haman's pride and arrogance would be the cause of his ultimate humiliation.

4. (7-9) Haman's answer regarding the honor due to them man who pleases the king.

And Haman answered the king, *"For* the man whom the king delights to honor, let a royal robe be brought which the king has worn, and a horse on which the king has ridden, which has a royal crest placed on its head. Then let this robe and horse be delivered to the hand of one of the king's most noble princes, that he may array the man whom the king delights to honor. Then parade him on horseback through the city square, and proclaim before him: 'Thus shall it be done to the man whom the king delights to honor!'"

a. **For the man whom the king delights to honor, let a royal robe be brought which the king has worn**: Haman, in his childish desire to be praised and honored by all, asked for things that really mattered very little except to puff himself up with pride.

b. **Thus shall it be done to the man whom the king delights to honor**: Haman was a tragic man who could only believe he had done well when he heard applause. It is a good and sometimes appropriate thing to have applause here on earth, but it is tragic to live your life seeking for it. We should instead seek and be satisfied with the applause from heaven.

B. The king's command.

1. (10-11) Haman must lead the chorus of praise for Mordecai.

Then the king said to Haman, "Hurry, take the robe and the horse, as you have suggested, and do so for Mordecai the Jew who sits within the king's gate! Leave nothing undone of all that you have spoken."

So Haman took the robe and the horse, arrayed Mordecai and led him on horseback through the city square, and proclaimed before him, "Thus shall it be done to the man whom the king delights to honor!"

a. **Hurry, take the robe and the horse, as you have suggested, and do so for Mordecai the Jew**: It would have been something to see the face of Haman at that moment; to see that the king took his advice completely, but gave the honor to his arch-enemy – the man whose execution Haman sought.

b. **So Haman took the robe and the horse, arrayed Mordecai and led him on horseback through the city square**: The ultimate humiliation was for Haman to honor Mordecai in such a public way; humiliation is only really humiliation when it is *public*.

2. (12-14) Mourning, warning, and a hasty departure to Esther's banquet.

Afterward Mordecai went back to the king's gate. But Haman hurried to his house, mourning and with his head covered. When Haman told his wife Zeresh and all his friends everything that had happened to him, his wise men and his wife Zeresh said to him, "If Mordecai, before whom you have begun to fall, is of Jewish descent, you will not prevail against him but will surely fall before him."

While they *were* still talking with him, the king's eunuchs came, and hastened to bring Haman to the banquet which Esther had prepared.

a. **Mourning, and with his head covered**: This means that Haman acted as if someone dear to him had died. In fact, his pride had been dealt a deathblow.

b. **You will not prevail against him but will surely fall before him**: Haman's wife and advisors could see the future well enough. Haman would not prevail against Mordecai, but Mordecai would prevail over Haman.

Esther 7 – Haman's End

A. The second banquet.

1. (1-4) Esther finally makes her request: please spare my life!

So the king and Haman went to dine with Queen Esther. And on the second day, at the banquet of wine, the king again said to Esther, "What *is* your petition, Queen Esther? It shall be granted you. And what *is* your request, up to half the kingdom? It shall be done!"

Then Queen Esther answered and said, "If I have found favor in your sight, O king, and if it pleases the king, let my life be given me at my petition, and my people at my request. For we have been sold, my people and I, to be destroyed, to be killed, and to be annihilated. Had we been sold as male and female slaves, I would have held my tongue, although the enemy could never compensate for the king's loss."

a. **Let my life be given me at my petition, and my people at my request**: Esther showed great tact when she finally made her request. She did not immediately identify herself as a Jew, targeted for massacre – even as Haman also hid the identity of the group he targeted when he made his request (Esther 3:8).

b. **Let my life be given me at my petition**: Esther also showed wisdom in how she framed her request. She appealed on a *personal* basis, knowing that she had never done anything but please the king.

2. (5) The king's reaction: who is this wicked man?

So King Ahasuerus answered and said to Queen Esther, "Who is he, and where is he, who would dare presume in his heart to do such a thing?"

a. **Who is he, and where is he, who would dare presume in his heart to do such a thing?** Perhaps Ahasuerus should have known that it was actually he himself who authorized such a plan. He was the one who gave authorization to Haman to carry out this plot (Esther 3:10-11), though he did it in ignorance.

3. (6) Esther identifies the guilty party.

And Esther said, "The adversary and enemy *is* this wicked Haman!"

So Haman was terrified before the king and queen.

a. **The adversary and enemy is this wicked Haman!** Esther exposed the truth about Haman – that he was not a faithful servant of the king, and was instead an **adversary and enemy**, more interested in his own fame and status than the benefit of the king.

b. **So Haman was terrified before the king and queen**: Haman never imagined that **Esther** was a Jew; now he stood before the king being rightly accused of plotting the murder of the king's wife.

i. The wisdom of Esther's strange request to invite Haman to these banquets could now be seen; it maximized the impact upon both the king and upon Haman himself.

B. Haman's wretched end.

1. (7-8) Haman's doom is sealed.

Then the king arose in his wrath from the banquet of wine *and went* into the palace garden; but Haman stood before Queen Esther, pleading for his life, for he saw that evil was determined against him by the king. When the king returned from the palace garden to the place of the banquet of wine, Haman had fallen across the couch where Esther *was*. Then the king said, "Will he also assault the queen while I *am* in the house?"

As the word left the king's mouth, they covered Haman's face.

a. **Then the king arose in his wrath**: The king was filled with **wrath**; probably because he now realized that Haman had deceived him as if he were a fool in getting this decree to kill the Jews into effect.

b. **Will he also assault the queen while I am in the house?** For all of Haman's pleading, he only got himself into deeper trouble – now he was accused of personally assaulting Esther!

i. A Jewish writing says that the angel Gabriel pushed Haman, so he fell on Esther's couch just as King Ahasuerus was coming back into the room.

c. **They covered Haman's face**: Haman's head was covered as a preparation for execution.

2. (9-10) The execution of Haman.

Now Harbonah, one of the eunuchs, said to the king, "Look! The gallows, fifty cubits high, which Haman made for Mordecai, who spoke

good on the king's behalf, is standing at the house of Haman."

Then the king said, "Hang him on it!"

So they hanged Haman on the gallows that he had prepared for Mordecai. Then the king's wrath subsided.

a. **Look! The gallows, fifty cubits high**: As in the case of the people executed in Esther 2:23, Haman was probably not hanged with a rope around his neck; he was impaled on a huge stake in an ancient precursor of crucifixion.

b. **Which Haman made for Mordecai**: Haman found his end on the same instrument he had intended for the death of Mordecai; he was caught in his own trap against Mordecai.

i. God often works this way. We should pray as the psalmist did: *Behold, the wicked brings forth iniquity; Yes, he conceives trouble and brings forth falsehood. He made a pit and dug it out, and has fallen into the ditch which he made. His trouble shall return upon his own head, and his violent dealing shall come down on his own crown.* (Psalms 7:14-16)

ii. Perhaps the greatest example of this was when Satan thought that he had won by getting the crowd to crucify Jesus, but the cross turned out to be the instrument of Satan's defeat.

c. **So they hanged Haman on the gallows that he had prepared for Mordecai. Then the king's wrath subsided**: The death of a substitute satisfied the **wrath** of the king. In the case of Mordecai and Haman, it was the guilty dying in the place of the innocent; in the case of Jesus and ourselves, it is a matter of the innocent dying in the place of the guilty.

Esther 8 – A Proclamation to Help the Jews

A. The appeal to the king.

1. (1-2) Haman's home is given to Esther; his position is given to Mordecai.

On that day King Ahasuerus gave Queen Esther the house of Haman, the enemy of the Jews. And Mordecai came before the king, for Esther had told how he *was related* to her. So the king took off his signet ring, which he had taken from Haman, and gave it to Mordecai; and Esther appointed Mordecai over the house of Haman.

a. **On that day King Ahasuerus gave Queen Esther the house of Haman**: Haman, the disturbed man who had seemingly achieved everything, ended with nothing – nothing even to pass on to his family. One might say that he had climbed the ladder of success, but it was leaning against the wrong building.

b. **So the king took off his signet ring, which he had taken from Haman, and gave it to Mordecai**: Think of how hard Haman worked to achieve all he did. Yet it was all for nothing; it was all a waste.

i. He should have lived his life after the conclusion of Solomon, who carefully considered these things: *Let us hear the conclusion of the whole matter: Fear God and keep His commandments, for this is man's all. For God will bring every work into judgment, including every secret thing, whether good or evil.* (Ecclesiastes 12:13-14)

2. (3-6) Esther's request for the salvation of her people.

Now Esther spoke again to the king, fell down at his feet, and implored him with tears to counteract the evil of Haman the Agagite, and the scheme which he had devised against the Jews. And the king held out the golden scepter toward Esther. So Esther arose and stood before the king, and said, "If it pleases the king, and if I have found favor in his sight and the thing *seems* right to the king and I am pleasing in his eyes, let it be written to revoke the letters devised by Haman, the son of

Hammedatha the Agagite, which he wrote to annihilate the Jews who *are* in all the king's provinces. For how can I endure to see the evil that will come to my people? Or how can I endure to see the destruction of my countrymen?"

a. **Implored him with tears to counteract the evil of Haman the Agagite, and the scheme which he had devised against the Jews**: With an impassioned appeal, Esther asked that the previous decree requiring the extermination of the Jews be revoked.

i. "One may say that it was a low motive to appeal to, to ask the despot to save a people in order to keep one woman from sorrow; and so it was…. She used the weapons that she had, and that she knew would be efficacious. The purpose for which she used them is her justification." (Maclaren)

b. **Let it be written to revoke the letters devised by Haman**: This was the request we might have expected to read in Esther 5:4, where Esther was first invited to make her request to King Ahasuerus. Yet God's wisdom operating in her life gave her the tact and ability to approach this great request in stages.

i. Even though Haman was defeated, the decree of the king still stood against the Jews. How could God's people be preserved when a decree of the king cannot be revoked (as we know from Esther 1:19)?

ii. Maclaren thought little of King Ahasuerus, even when he made a right decision: "He yielded to Esther's prayer as lightly as to Haman's plot. Whether the Jews were wiped out or not mattered nothing to him, so long as he had no trouble in the affair."

3. (7-14) King Ahasuerus makes a counter-decree, allowing the Jews to protect themselves on the day they were scheduled for annihilation.

Then King Ahasuerus said to Queen Esther and Mordecai the Jew, "Indeed, I have given Esther the house of Haman, and they have hanged him on the gallows because he *tried to* lay his hand on the Jews. You yourselves write *a decree* concerning the Jews, as you please, in the king's name, and seal *it* with the king's signet ring; for whatever is written in the king's name and sealed with the king's signet ring no one can revoke."

So the king's scribes were called at that time, in the third month, which *is* the month of Sivan, on the twenty-third *day;* and it was written, according to all that Mordecai commanded, to the Jews, the satraps, the governors, and the princes of the provinces from India to Ethiopia, one hundred and twenty-seven provinces *in all,* to every province in

its own script, to every people in their own language, and to the Jews in their own script and language. **And he wrote in the name of King Ahasuerus, sealed** *it* **with the king's signet ring, and sent letters by couriers on horseback, riding on royal horses bred from swift steeds.**

By these letters the king permitted the Jews who *were* **in every city to gather together and protect their lives—to destroy, kill, and annihilate all the forces of any people or province that would assault them,** *both* **little children and women, and to plunder their possessions, on one day in all the provinces of King Ahasuerus, on the thirteenth** *day* **of the twelfth month, which** *is* **the month of Adar. A copy of the document was to be issued as a decree in every province and published for all people, so that the Jews would be ready on that day to avenge themselves on their enemies. The couriers who rode on royal horses went out, hastened and pressed on by the king's command. And the decree was issued in Shushan the citadel.**

a. **You yourselves write a decree concerning the Jews, as you please**: The king could not revoke the previous decree, so he simply made another decree giving support to the Jews against their attackers.

i. We might think of our enemy Satan like Haman, and joyfully await the day God puts him away. But we still must deal with the righteous decree of God that demands our death: *The soul who sins shall die* (Ezekiel 18:4). In our sins, we not only have an enemy (Satan), but we also have a legal decree from a righteous God against us.

ii. God solves the problem, not by compromising His decree for eternal justice but by fulfilling justice in taking the punishment we deserved – His counter-decree saves those who believe: *that He might be just and the justifier of the one who has faith in Jesus* (Romans 3:26).

b. **The couriers who rode on royal horses went out, hastened and pressed on by the king's command**: There was an urgency to get the word out about this important decree of the king. Christians should show a similar urgency in being heralds of the decree that the justice of God has been satisfied for us in Jesus Christ.

B. Mordecai's advancement.

1. (15) Mordecai's promotion.

So Mordecai went out from the presence of the king in royal apparel of blue and white, with a great crown of gold and a garment of fine linen and purple; and the city of Shushan rejoiced and was glad.

a. **So Mordecai went out from the presence of the king in royal apparel**: God's purpose in all these matters goes farther than the sparing of the Jews from destruction; He also purposed to raise up Mordecai as the prime minister – as a replacement for Haman.

b. **With a great crown of gold**: Mordecai's previous humility and later exaltation (in contrast to Haman) was an outworking of the principle that God resists the proud, but gives grace to the humble (James 4:6, 1 Peter 5:5).

> i. "Mordecai is a kind of duplicate of Joseph, and embodies valuable lessons. Contented acceptance of obscurity and neglect of his services, faithfulness to his people and his God in the foul atmosphere of such a court, wise reticence, patient discharge of small duties, undoubting hope when things looked blackest fed by steadfast faith in God, unchangedness of character and purpose when lifted to supreme dignity, the use of influence and place, not for himself, but for his people." (Maclaren)

2. (16) Joy for the people of God.

The Jews had light and gladness, joy and honor.

a. **The Jews had light and gladness**: This joy came *before* the actual day appointed when the Jews would be attacked yet able to defend themselves. Nevertheless, because of the decree of the king, they could be assured of victory and rejoice in it ahead of time.

b. **Light and gladness, joy and honor**: In the same way, although our course is not yet run and our salvation is not yet complete, we can rejoice, because of our confidence in our king – *being confident of this very thing, that He who has begun a good work in you will complete it until the day of Jesus Christ.* (Philippians 1:6)

3. (17) Salvation for the Gentiles.

And in every province and city, wherever the king's command and decree came, the Jews had joy and gladness, a feast and a holiday. Then many of the people of the land became Jews, because fear of the Jews fell upon them.

a. **Then many of the people of the land became Jews**: As they saw God working on behalf of His people, they wanted the same relationship with God.

Esther 9 – Victory for the Jews

A. They defeat their enemies.

1. (1-5) Victory with the help of the king.

Now in the twelfth month, that *is,* the month of Adar, on the thirteenth day, *the time* came for the king's command and his decree to be executed. On the day that the enemies of the Jews had hoped to overpower them, the opposite occurred, in that the Jews themselves overpowered those who hated them. The Jews gathered together in their cities throughout all the provinces of King Ahasuerus to lay hands on those who sought their harm. And no one could withstand them, because fear of them fell upon all people. And all the officials of the provinces, the satraps, the governors, and all those doing the king's work, helped the Jews, because the fear of Mordecai fell upon them. For Mordecai *was* great in the king's palace, and his fame spread throughout all the provinces; for this man Mordecai became increasingly prominent. Thus the Jews defeated all their enemies with the stroke of the sword, with slaughter and destruction, and did what they pleased with those who hated them.

> a. **On the day that the enemies of the Jews had hoped to overpower them, the opposite occurred**: The Jews definitely had their enemies, those who wished to destroy them. Yet they had someone great on their side: the king, with all his resources. With the king for them, it didn't matter who was against them.

> b. **Thus the Jews defeated all their enemies**: We have our own enemies to face, but with the King of Kings on our side, we have no reason to fear – *What then shall we say to these things? If God is for us, who can be against us?* (Romans 8:31)

2. (6-10) Cities where they fought their enemies.

And in Shushan the citadel the Jews killed and destroyed five hundred men. Also Parshandatha, Dalphon, Aspatha, Poratha, Adalia, Aridatha, Parmashta, Arisai, Aridai, and Vajezatha—the ten sons of Haman the

son of Hammedatha, the enemy of the Jews—they killed; but they did not lay a hand on the plunder.

3. (11-17) At the king's invitation, Esther asks for the complete defeat of all the enemies of the Jews.

On that day the number of those who were killed in Shushan the citadel was brought to the king. And the king said to Queen Esther, "The Jews have killed and destroyed five hundred men in Shushan the citadel, and the ten sons of Haman. What have they done in the rest of the king's provinces? Now what *is* your petition? It shall be granted to you. Or what *is* your further request? It shall be done."

Then Esther said, "If it pleases the king, let it be granted to the Jews who *are* in Shushan to do again tomorrow according to today's decree, and let Haman's ten sons be hanged on the gallows."

So the king commanded this to be done; the decree was issued in Shushan, and they hanged Haman's ten sons.

And the Jews who *were* in Shushan gathered together again on the fourteenth day of the month of Adar and killed three hundred men at Shushan; but they did not lay a hand on the plunder.

The remainder of the Jews in the king's provinces gathered together and protected their lives, had rest from their enemies, and killed seventy-five thousand of their enemies; but they did not lay a hand on the plunder. *This was* on the thirteenth day of the month of Adar. And on the fourteenth day of *the month* they rested and made it a day of feasting and gladness.

a. **If it pleases the king, let it be granted to the Jews who are in Shushan to do again tomorrow according to today's decree, and let Haman's ten sons be hanged on the gallows**: Many have criticized Esther for this, saying it showed a lack of love towards her enemies. Yet she displayed the same principle found so often in Joshua – she would not settle for less than total victory.

b. **And they hanged Haman's ten sons**: Haman and his sons were descendants of the ancient Amalekites (comparing Esther 3:1 and 1 Samuel 15:8-33). God commanded Saul, the son of Kish, to execute the full extent of God's judgment against the Amalekites (1 Samuel 15:2-3). Saul failed, but two later descendants of the tribe of Benjamin through Kish (Esther and Mordecai, according to Esther 2:5-6) completed God's judgment against the Amalekites.

i. "Now it was God's intent that a last conflict should take place between Israel and Amalek: the conflict which began with Joshua in the desert was to be finished by Mordecai in the king's palace." (Spurgeon)

B. The feast of Purim established.

1. (18-19) A great celebration among the Jews of the Persian Empire.

But the Jews who *were* at Shushan assembled together on the thirteenth *day,* as well as on the fourteenth; and on the fifteenth of *the month* they rested, and made it a day of feasting and gladness. Therefore the Jews of the villages who dwelt in the unwalled towns celebrated the fourteenth day of the month of Adar *with* gladness and feasting, as a holiday, and for sending presents to one another.

2. (20-32) The institution of the feast of Purim.

And Mordecai wrote these things and sent letters to all the Jews, near and far, who *were* in all the provinces of King Ahasuerus, to establish among them that they should celebrate yearly the fourteenth and fifteenth days of the month of Adar, as the days on which the Jews had rest from their enemies, as the month which was turned from sorrow to joy for them, and from mourning to a holiday; that they should make them days of feasting and joy, of sending presents to one another and gifts to the poor. So the Jews accepted the custom which they had begun, as Mordecai had written to them, because Haman, the son of Hammedatha the Agagite, the enemy of all the Jews, had plotted against the Jews to annihilate them, and had cast Pur (that *is,* the lot), to consume them and destroy them; but when *Esther* came before the king, he commanded by letter that this wicked plot which *Haman* had devised against the Jews should return on his own head, and that he and his sons should be hanged on the gallows.

So they called these days Purim, after the name Pur. Therefore, because of all the words of this letter, what they had seen concerning this matter, and what had happened to them, the Jews established and imposed it upon themselves and their descendants and all who would join them, that without fail they should celebrate these two days every year, according to the written *instructions* and according to the *prescribed* time, *that* these days *should be* remembered and kept throughout every generation, every family, every province, and every city, that these days of Purim should not fail *to be observed* among the Jews, and *that* the memory of them should not perish among their descendants.

Then Queen Esther, the daughter of Abihail, with Mordecai the Jew, wrote with full authority to confirm this second letter about Purim. And *Mordecai* sent letters to all the Jews, to the one hundred and twenty-seven provinces of the kingdom of Ahasuerus, *with* words of peace and truth, to confirm these days of Purim at their *appointed* time, as Mordecai the Jew and Queen Esther had prescribed for them, and as they had decreed for themselves and their descendants concerning matters of their fasting and lamenting. So the decree of Esther confirmed these matters of Purim, and it was written in the book.

a. **Mordecai wrote these things and sent letters to all the Jews, near and far, who were in all the provinces of King Ahasuerus, to establish among them that they should celebrate yearly**: The principle of remembering God's great deliverance is good; we too often forget His great works.

b. **So the decree of Esther confirmed these matters of Purim**: Today, Purim is one of the more popular Jewish feasts, with costumes, games, and plenty of fun noise.

Esther 10 – Mordecai's Promotion

A. Epilogue.

1. (1-2) The glory of the reign of King Ahasuerus.

And King Ahasuerus imposed tribute on the land and *on* the islands of the sea. Now all the acts of his power and his might, and the account of the greatness of Mordecai, to which the king advanced him, *are* they not written in the book of the chronicles of the kings of Media and Persia?

2. (3) Mordecai is promoted to the position of second in the kingdom.

For Mordecai the Jew *was* second to King Ahasuerus, and was great among the Jews and well received by the multitude of his brethren, seeking the good of his people and speaking peace to all his countrymen.

B. Observations on the Book of Esther.

1. Esther shows how the hand of God can move in a supernaturally natural way.

a. "It has been well said that the Book of Esther is a record of wonders without a miracle, and therefore, though equally revealing the glory of the Lord, it sets it forth in another fashion from that which is displayed in the overthrow of Pharaoh by miraculous power." (Spurgeon)

b. "This book of Esther does not say much about God, but His presence broods over it all, and is the real spring that moves the movers that are seen. It is all a lesson of how God works out His purposes through men that seem to themselves to be working out theirs.... Ahasuerus, Haman, Esther, Mordecai, are His instruments, and yet each of them is the doer of his or her deed, and has to answer to Him for it." (Maclaren)

c. Think of all that God arranged in the story of Esther:

- God arranged for the noble Queen Vashti to lose her place.
- God arranged for a competition to replace Queen Vashti.
- God arranged for Esther to enter the competition.

- God arranged special favor for Esther among the other women.

- God arranged Mordecai's access to Esther and the affairs of the kingdom.

- God arranged the lot that was cast to give 11 months warning before the planned massacre (Esther 3:12-13).

- God arranged that the decree command that the Jews be killed by private hands, instead of by the army of Persia – which would have been much more difficult to stop.

- God arranged that Haman restrain his anger and not kill Mordecai immediately (Esther 5:10).

- God arranged for Esther to delay her request; first asking for a banquet with the king and then *another* banquet.

- God arranged for Haman's anger to come to a peak on one particular day.

- God arranged for Ahasuerus to have a sleepless night.

- God arranged for Ahasuerus to send for a certain book during his sleepless night.

- God arranged for Ahasuerus to hear the passage about Mordecai.

2. God's hand in history never rules out our actions. The actions of Esther and Mordecai were critical to the preservation of the people of God.

a. In Esther, God's will is accomplished, and yet men are perfectly free agents; Haman did as he pleased, Ahasuerus did what he wanted, so did Mordecai and Esther. We see no interference, no coercion – they all do their will, and bear full responsibility, yet God works out His eternal plan for the ages through it all.

i. "The king's criminal abandonment to lust and luxury, Haman's meanly personal pique, Esther's beauty, the fall of the favourite, the long past services of Mordecai, even the king's sleepless night, are all threads in the web, and God is the weaver." (Maclaren)

b. "There it is; man is a free agent in what he does, responsible for his actions, and verily guilty when he does wrong, and he will be justly punished too, and if he be lost the blame will rest with himself alone: but yet there is One who ruleth over all, who, without complicity in their sin, makes even the actions of wicked men to subserve his holy and righteous purposes. Believe these two truths and you will see them in practical agreement in daily life, though you will not be able to devise a theory for harmonising them on paper." (Spurgeon)

3. God, in His wise and providential plan, allows His people to be tested – sometimes severely so. We must not suppose that the servants of God will be protected from every trial, because the trials are part of God's design.

- It was a great trial for Mordecai; he refused to bow to Haman and *others* would suffer for his refusal to pay homage to Haman.

- It was a great trial for Esther; she heard the news of the coming slaughter of her people and had to boldly approach the king to make an appeal.

4. "Last of all, let each child of God rejoice that *we have a guardian so near the throne*. Every Jew in Shushan must have felt hope when he remembered that the queen was a Jewess. To-day let us be glad that Jesus is exalted." (Spurgeon)

Bibliography

Ezra

Adeney, Walter F. *Ezra, Nehemiah and Esther* (New York: Hodder & Stoughton, 1893)

Clarke, Adam *The Holy Bible, Containing the Old and New Testaments, with A Commentary and Critical Notes, Volume II – Joshua to Esther* (New York: Eaton and Mains, 1827?)

The Living Bible (Wheaton, Illinois: Tyndale House Publishers, 1971)

Kidner, Derek *Ezra and Nehemiah, an Introduction and Commentary* (Nottingham, England: Inter-Varsity Press, 1979)

Maclaren, Alexander *Expositions of Holy Scripture, Volume 3* (Grand Rapids, Michigan: Baker Book House, 1984)

Meyer, F.B. *Our Daily Homily* (Westwood, New Jersey: Revell, 1966)

Morgan, G. Campbell *Searchlights from the Word* (New York: Revell, 1926)

Morgan, G. Campbell *An Exposition of the Whole Bible* (Old Tappan, New Jersey: Revell, 1959)

Orr, James Edwin *All Your Need* (London, Marshall, Morgan & Scott, 1936)

Orr, James Edwin *The Second Evangelical Awakening* (London, Marshall, Morgan & Scott, 1964)

Poole, Matthew *A Commentary on the Holy Bible, Volume 1* (London, Banner of Truth Trust, 1968)

Selman, Martin J. *2 Chronicles, An Introduction and Commentary* (Leicester, England: Inter-Varsity Press, 1994)

Spurgeon, Charles Haddon *The New Park Street Pulpit, Volumes 1-6* and *The Metropolitan Tabernacle Pulpit, Volumes 7-63* (Pasadena, Texas: Pilgrim Publications, 1990)

Trapp, John *A Commentary on the Old and New Testaments, Volume 1 – Genesis to Second Chronicles* (Eureka, California: Tanski Publications, 1997)

Yamauchi, Edwin "Ezra-Nehemiah," in *The Expositor's Bible Commentary: 1 & 2 Kings, 1 & 2 Chronicles, Ezra, Nehemiah, Esther, Job,* ed. Frank E. Gaebelein, vol. 4 (Grand Rapids, MI: Zondervan Publishing House, 1988)

Nehemiah

Clarke, Adam *The Holy Bible, Containing the Old and New Testaments, with A Commentary and Critical Notes, Volume II – Joshua to Esther* (New York: Eaton and Mains, 1827?)

Kidner, Derek *Ezra and Nehemiah, an Introduction and Commentary* (Nottingham, England: Inter-Varsity Press, 1979)

Maclaren, Alexander *Expositions of Holy Scripture, Volume 3* (Grand Rapids, Michigan: Baker Book House, 1984)

Meyer, F.B. *Our Daily Homily* (Westwood, New Jersey: Revell, 1966)

Redpath, Alan *Victorious Christian Service – Studies in the Book of Nehemiah* (Westwood, New Jersey: Revell, 1958)

Spurgeon, Charles Haddon *The New Park Street Pulpit, Volumes 1-6* and *The Metropolitan Tabernacle Pulpit, Volumes 7-63* (Pasadena, Texas: Pilgrim Publications, 1990)

Swindoll, Charles R. *Hand Me Another Brick* (Nashville, Tennessee: Thomas Nelson, 1978)

Yamauchi, Edwin "Ezra-Nehemiah," in *The Expositor's Bible Commentary: 1 & 2 Kings, 1 & 2 Chronicles, Ezra, Nehemiah, Esther, Job*, ed. Frank E. Gaebelein, vol. 4 (Grand Rapids, MI: Zondervan Publishing House, 1988)

Esther

Baldwin, Joyce G. *Esther – An Introduction and Commentary* (Nottingham, England: InterVarsity Press, 1984)

Clarke, Adam *The Holy Bible, Containing the Old and New Testaments, with A Commentary and Critical Notes, Volume II – Joshua to Esther* (New York: Eaton and Mains, 1827?)

Huey, F.B. Jr. "Esther," in *The Expositor's Bible Commentary: 1 & 2 Kings, 1 & 2 Chronicles, Ezra, Nehemiah, Esther, Job*, ed. Frank E. Gaebelein, vol. 4 (Grand Rapids, MI: Zondervan Publishing House, 1988)

Ginzberg, Louis *The Legends of the Jews, Volumes 1-7* (Philadelphia: The Jewish Publication Society of America, 1968)

Keil, Carl Friedrich and Delitzsch, Franz *Commentary on the Old Testament*, vol. 4 (Peabody, MA: Hendrickson, 1996)

Kidner, Derek *Ezra and Nehemiah, an Introduction and Commentary* (Nottingham, England: Inter-Varsity Press, 1979)

Maclaren, Alexander *Expositions of Holy Scripture, Volume 3* (Grand Rapids, Michigan: Baker Book House, 1984)

Morgan, G. Campbell *An Exposition of the Whole Bible* (Old Tappan, New Jersey: Revell, 1959)

Poole, Matthew *A Commentary on the Holy Bible, Volume 1* (London, Banner of Truth Trust, 1968)

Spurgeon, Charles Haddon *The New Park Street Pulpit, Volumes 1-6* and *The Metropolitan Tabernacle Pulpit, Volumes 7-63* (Pasadena, Texas: Pilgrim Publications, 1990)

Author's Remarks

As the years pass I love the work of studying, learning, and teaching the Bible more than ever. I'm so grateful that God is faithful to meet me in His Word.

For another time I am tremendously grateful to Alison Turner for her proofreading and editorial suggestions, especially with a challenging manuscript. Alison, thank you so much!

Thanks to Brian Procedo for the cover design and the graphics work.

Most especially, thanks to my wife Inga-Lill. She is my loved and valued partner in life and in service to God and His people.

David Guzik

David Guzik's Bible commentary is regularly used and trusted by many thousands who want to know the Bible better. Pastors, teachers, class leaders, and everyday Christians find his commentary helpful for their own understanding and explanation of the Bible. David and his wife Inga-Lill live in Santa Barbara, California.

You can email David at
david@enduringword.com

For more resources by David Guzik,
go to www.enduringword.com

www.ingramcontent.com/pod-product-compliance
Lightning Source LLC
Chambersburg PA
CBHW022121080426
42734CB00006B/210